LAND OF PAN

The Loss of Power and Magic on Earth

For information address:
FOUR WINDS PUBLICATIONS
535 W. Cordova Road
Suite 112
Santa Fe, New Mexico
postal zipcode 87501, U.S.A.

This book is printed on recycled paper with soybean ink.

LAND OF PAN

The Loss of Power and Magic on Earth

Received by Ceanne DeRohan

FOUR WINDS PUBLICATIONS

Dedicated to

The Father of Manifestation,
that Maligned, Misunderstood, but
Essential Part of God

TABLE OF CONTENTS

INTRODUCTION

If the way had been known, at any time earlier, to understand and heal, which means, in this case, to change, the original imprinting put in place by primordial experiences at the very beginning of Creation, before there was time, relativity, or consciousness with which to measure these things, it would have been a much shorter and easier process to heal, in some ways, than it is now.

After so many long eons of conditioning from repeated experiences governed by imprinting, it seems overwhelming to heal it, yet in other ways and from other perspectives, this many layers of conditioning in the myriad of patterns form has been able to present here must have been necessary for certain aspects of consciousness to feel ready, not only to look at this, but to understand, not only that this imprinting has to be healed, but also, how to heal it. This is because imprinting has not been recognized as having the presence it has had in everything and in the way it behaves, or seen for what it is. Imprinting was not known to have had the presence it has had, nor was it known how it was put in place. This is mostly because it all took place when consciousness was still at the subconscious level and because the bridge has never been allowed to be built in a steady progression of steps from the subconscious to the conscious without breaks in the connection which caused gaps or blank spots.

This all needs to be looked at now, as well as the role form change has played in complicating and obscuring imprinting's role as to why steps have not been able to be taken in evolution that need to be taken, and that some, at least, have wanted to take, but also that must be taken if there is going to be survival in any form that will allow humans to continue to know life as they know it now.

So, in one sense, it seems there is now so much conditioning it is overwhelming to heal the problems, and that it would have been much easier to do this healing earlier; and in another sense, it took this many patterns of experience, form change efforts and layers of conditioning to be ready and able to understand how the problems must be healed. And so, it is now both more complicated, many-faceted and difficult, and also a more rich and full bank of experience to relate to, refer to and draw on.

Since it seemed as overwhelming and undoable in the beginning as it does now, it is all relative in terms of a position of mind. This is a place where mind and Body originally came together in the gap to get rid of the Will, which originally, as far as They were concerned, only complicated matters with uncomfortableness They wished to avoid, such as the issue of how much pain is involved in having it take this long for imprinting to be found, seen and understood for what it is.

You may not think you know or even remember Pangea. You may not, as yet, even remember any past lives at all, as far as you know, but if you really do allow direct movement as emotion in the emotions you really feel but do not normally allow to move, and whose presence, as you are now, may be fleeting, perhaps only a split second of connection at first before they are banished, shoved down or converted into something more "acceptable", you will begin to see how the cracks in your accepted and allowed reality, or veneer, can be found and widened into openings, or doorways, into a widening reality in which more is seen, felt and understood, and you will become able, in the progression of this, to see how images and even realities are superimposed upon one another in such a way as to make it clear that time is a progression in which there is really no past, present or future because it is all present, and yet there is past, present and future as a matter of location of focus of where you are now.

For example, a man takes on, in your vision, for only a split second perhaps, the characteristics of a satyr. Immediately, you leap out of the experience because of feelings of uncomfortableness there, which, if you stayed long enough, you would find is fear, in favor of a more habitually comfortable and familiar place of mind in which you invalidate the entire experience, perhaps even unnoticed, in a moment of time, in which mind can even ask questions.

Did he or didn't he? Am I going nuts? Can I trust My perceptions?

Instead of going back to the experience, which was probably fleeting at best, and which mind is ready to say cannot be recovered because it wasn't real, you, in the same moment of almost totally unnoticed mental activity, dismiss the entire thing, allowing mind to invalidate it by giving you the "understanding" that such a thing is not possible and therefore, didn't really happen.

The trouble is mind didn't have enough experience with which to gain true understanding before leaping out of experience because of uncomfortable feelings found there. Meanwhile, mind gave out its interpretation of this as true understanding rather than feeling and going into the experience and the uncomfortable feelings enough to gain true understanding. This is old imprinting in which mind made the original leap out of experience and the feelings of the Will, invalidating them, so that the bridge between all the factors was not fully built there to allow all the possible and necessary information for mind to gain true understanding.

Time, as a matter of location of focus, has lost its validity and significance with those who have allowed their reality to be squeezed down into only the "present" in order to avoid the uncomfortableness just mentioned, and is also a focus whose significance is lost when you notice that the pain from the past is always there in the so-called "present" and "future."

On both counts, this is mostly because of not knowing how to clear old pains, the amount of which has always seemed overwhelming; but time also loses its significance as relative points in a progression when old pains are cleared to the point of allowing old experiences to become real again while new ones can still be created and experienced. This will be a healed state which has never been reached before by humankind, or by My light either, for that matter, since as God, I am everywhere and a part of everything, even if only in a state of denial as of yet, and so pain has always been a part of My existence as well as of yours.

Focus has been able to make it seem as though an event is taking place "now", not "then," or took place "then", not "now," as though there is a bigger difference than there really is, and which has been more agreed upon than real, even to the extent of using pressure to gain this "agreement." In view of this "agreement," form change, in the broadest latitude of the word usage, has been the main thrust of effort to change the experience here.

Form change was the big area of focus on healing in the Heavens, along with getting rid of the feelings in the Will that were being held responsible for the problems with form. Form change was the focus of the healing efforts in Pan, and form change has continued to be the method of choice for problem solving with old forms that have not worked in the ways it was wanted to have them work.

This belief around and approach to form change was originally put in place by fear of Mine that was imprinted with the idea that I had the wrong Form, and that a form change would, therefore, solve the problem. The alignment Form gave here was as a way of saying It was a victim of the misalignment of Spirit and Will and needed help.

So, in the sense that it is all here and now, yet here and now is a reality expandable by Will movement all the way back to include original imprinting, Pangea is an important area, not only as the first physical reality for so many, as the source of so many myths and legends and as a way to more fully and deeply understand these myths and legends, but also as another excellent mirror for healing, especially because of the more fluid speed of events, and yes, of form changes in which certain denials being made around this surfaced in Pangea, not just as simple form changes for fun, but also as deeply held imprints around healing, improving upon what was originally done in the Godhead, knowing better than the Godhead, as displays, misuse and abuse of power, status and competition, not only in creativity, vision and accomplishment, but also positioning.

Even though events that took place in Pangea have resulted in greatly limiting both the speed and the latitude of form changes, it has remained a widely held belief that form change, as a mind-body partnership will work.

It has not worked, and without Will movement being given its right place, it will not work. As you remember your past on the way to remembering your imprinting, and your imprinting becomes more of a key to your past, your present and also your future, you will find that whether you have been unicorn, mixed-up beast, faerie or satyr, elf or mermaid, priest or scholar, king, serf, slave, or whatever; when the experience is felt deeply enough to understand the forms taken on in the different enactments, it will be found that the patterns have been the same, and will remain the same, until imprinting is changed, no matter how it may appear at different points along the way. These patterns will always reflect the same points of view you had in the past and never looked beyond.

Are you ready to look now? If so, you will find that the path on which you lost power and magic is also the very path by which you will be able to recover, restore and understand magic and power in such a way that you will not lose it again by failure to feel deeply enough to know how it should rightly be used.

THE MOTHER'S DIRE DEPARTURE INTO THE DARKNESS DRAWS THE RONALOKAS TOWARD HER

...Golden light falling in space like a shower of golden sparks. I watched it with fascinated horror, yet found nothing I could do to stop what was happening, and wasn't sure I wanted to since the Mother's presence in this light felt so uncomfortable to Me there.

The Ronalokas were falling away from Me and I could not reach them without being propelled back on Myself. I could not talk to them without them hearing something else in My voice that I was doing everything I could do to make sure was not present there.

I had given it one last try. I had beseeched them not to leave Me. I had given them another pep talk about staying in the Heavens with Me as their right place, but it had all fallen on what might as well have been deaf ears. They had looked at Me with their wide eyes, which they could roll so expressively, and let Me know, in so many ways, that they did not trust or believe Me, that it was boring to them in the Heavens, that too many of the ways things were being done there were not to their liking and that how they felt about things was more important to them than anything else. Shades of their Mother were all over them. She had never given Me any peace or acceptance in these areas either.

If they did not like how it felt here, maybe it was better that they go to Her after all, wherever She was, but I could not understand why they wanted to go to Her in the darkness rather than staying with Me in the protection of My light.

They claimed they were not leaving Me for any reason other than that they wanted to go someplace that felt better to them than

1

the Heavens, someplace where they would feel more received than they had felt in the Heavens, someplace that felt more like home, but I could notice the many undercurrents there.

They had tried not to let Me know where they were going, but I had seen them looking at Earth and knew they planned to go there. I knew they did not know what was involved in that journey. I wondered if they even could get there, or if they had had some secret communication with the Mother, and She planned to guide them in some way I did not know about.

Whatever it was, there was nothing I could really do about it. They seemed determined and even rebellious toward My questioning of them about it. I gave them My last speech, hoping they would reconsider and admit they needed My help, but they were their Mother even worse than She was and responded as though there was no help necessary from Me.

"Now My light knows better than that," I told them, to which they issued fierce denials. I might as well have been their slave master talking.

"Nah suh, we's jess fine!" they, in effect, answered Me there.

I wanted them to like and trust My light, and move toward Me, rather than fall away from Me into the vast and dark reaches of space. I had feelings too, and My feelings said they were not going to like it out in space without My light there. They were as frightened of the darkness as their Mother had been, but I could not get them to listen to this. They did not like or trust Me here, apparently, because they kept backing away from Me and the more I approached them, the more they backed away, until, finally, after My last appeal, I let them go.

What else could I do, order them to stay, or be an intimidating Father whose efforts to reach them looked like I was advancing on them aggressively? Next they'd be accusing Me of this, but I also knew that if I backed off, they'd accuse Me of neglect or of not caring. I was exasperated with them and could do nothing more than watch them go and hope that the light from My gaze upon them followed them and helped them somehow.

It felt to Me like they were out of control, or at least drawn by something beyond their control. Off they went, drifting out into space, falling down, down, down, burning first yellow gold, then orange gold and then reddish gold in the growing compression, until it looked to Me like their light was going to burn out before they reached Earth, like shooting stars do.

I could not look anymore. I stopped looking before they

reached Earth. I told Myself I lost interest, but it was not true. I did not want to look because I had a feeling of fear, stirred by remembering the Mother originally falling in space, that if their light did burn out, it would somehow mean the end of My light too.

I also had, welling up from someplace within Me, a feeling of relief that they were gone, and all of their Will presence with them. It gave Me a feeling of upliftment, freedom and expansion I had not had in a long time. I had guilt that I felt this then and was not more concerned with their fate in space, but I also had a gap that could not move toward them and did not care to.

I busied Myself with other things and told Myself that maybe this was what We all needed. Maybe it was an escape from an existence that had not been turning out to be what We had wanted it to be. Maybe they were just going outside My light to give themselves an escape that way. It certainly looked to Me like they were going back to whence it had all appeared to come; the dark void. I could not dwell on this for long because it started to bring up feelings I did not want to have to feel about whether or not the Mother might also, then, be gone for good. I was not sure how I felt about that and I did not want to have to look at it. The gap did not want Me to look at it then, and I was not allowing Myself to notice, yet, the ways in which the gap had power over Me.

The Ronalokas were quaking in terror, but holding it in as hard as they could and not moving it. They did not know how to move it, nor did they feel they had found any receptivity for it in My light. They just wanted to get away from what they viewed as the source of it; My light. They were unable to look at My light from any point of view other than the one the gap had initially imprinted in them.

They had all been smacked by unloving light before they had the opportunity to know My light as love. Even in the places where some of My light was mixed into the places penetrated by the unloving light, they did not know the difference in the light they held because they did not really know what love was.

They did not know how much they, themselves, were love and the smack was not, because the unloving light did not let them know that. Instead, it gave them the view that My light was a punishing light which must always be appeased and to which they were always going to have to make amends, could never feel pleased with themselves and would have to live in fear of its next strike and of its judgment against them, no matter how pleasant I appeared to be at times.

They had experienced the gap and lived in fear that I could do

3

a fast switch from My apparent pleasantness and deliver a punishing strike against them. They were imprinted with "comply or die" and have not moved much from that position except in moments of rage polarization that have stemmed from that light also.

In ways that must be understood now, the Ronalokas have been both victims of this light and perpetrators of its presence, as has been the Mother, but not in the ways that you might think, since these imprinting problems took place at the subconscious level before My light brought consciousness, and it was My light that did not allow the bridge to be built from the subconscious to the conscious when My light was contacted.

This bridge needs to be built now, and not by understanding, at first, but by just letting the feelings move that need to move in response to this story, without mentalizing them or polarizing into the reasons why they should not be allowed to move. Reasons they should not be allowed to move stem from imprinting by the unloving light that has not allowed them to move in all of this time, so it is a tricky and careful balance you will have to find here. This movement is not going to be easy, and will have to happen a little at a time, but it is necessary so that these emotions can show you what they have to teach in the way of understandings. This will build the bridge from the subconscious to the conscious mind as nothing else can.

Will and Body have always known the truth of what needed to be understood about imprinting, but have never been allowed to speak in Their own language. Instead, They have been saddled with a mind imprinted by unloving light, which did not allow Them to unfold Their own story the way it needed to unfold, but instead demanded that They come up to its level without going through Their own necessary process.

When mind has said, "What are you shaking for, there's nothing to be afraid of?" and, fed by My own gap, has appeared to have the greater power, it has not been possible for Will and Body to unfold in an atmosphere of receptivity and loving acceptance.

Shame caused the Ronalokas to downpress and control the quaking of their terror in the presence of My light, which they viewed as the gap, and they were not wrong, since My light had not noticed its presence there with Me yet. They feared My light following them to Earth and judging them even there. They did not dare say this because of their imprinting, but they let Me know this, nonetheless. The problem was that My light did not reach understanding on this for a long time because of the lack of openness

4

there, and My seeing of their gap and the denials involved, but I also know that the distrust they felt there, because of Me not seeing My gap and opening to receive them on it, did not allow them to say anything direct to Me lest their survival be threatened with another smack. And so I thought, for a long time, that they did not want My light present with them.

In spite of the denials they issued, they were also terrified to go to Earth without My approval, guidance and accompaniment because of imprinting from the smack that was interpreted as: Initiating their own movement from their own desire was not acceptable to My light. This is a major imprint that has kept this frozen terror from moving all of this time. It is important that it move now, everytime it is felt in response to the initiation of any movement that is not approved or required by someone of perceived greater authority, even if it is the voice of guilt from within. Trust of self is at stake here, and if you do not trust yourself, you do not know who else to trust.

THE FATHER OF MANIFESTATION NEEDS TO LOOK AT HIMSELF MORE CLEARLY

Movement in these feelings is all going to look frightening and desperate, even hopeless and impossible at first because these feelings were imprinted before they had any other reality to measure against and before they had ever expressed themselves. They have never moved in the presence of love or been able to gain understanding for themselves before. What has happened to you in the past, when these feelings have moved in the presence of hatred, has been devastating reversals, sometimes triggered only by the unloving light held within you when it has felt you were not behaving appropriately. So do not pressure yourself to move past the place that feels safe in moving your emotions here, and do not expect too much from yourself. Do not try to go particularly fast. Instead, work steadily on your emotional movement here and learn to notice the "voice" for what it is when it criticizes you for movement and for lack of it. The way this unloving light was embodied from the Spirit side, impulse stemming from any place other than itself was interpreted as, "Whatever it is, I don't like it."

Work on moving the emotions of how you feel when the voice of unloving light criticizes you rather than moving to please "the voice." Work on moving the rage of your self-hatred that has been allowing the "voice" to beat you up for moving emotion and for not moving emotion, until you can find compassion for yourself underneath this criticism and, finally, loving acceptance for how you have suffered in the past and for how you need to move now.

Move without expectations on yourself, as much as possible, and without the word level of unloving light running old beliefs through your mind any more than necessary to see what these beliefs are that have, for so long, held back emotional evolution in these areas. Guided by intent, emotional movement that gains compassion and love for itself can change imprinting by allowing Will and Body to unfold the movement They need in the progression in which They need it to build the bridge to consciousness that has never been allowed to be built before. Also allow movement in your terror of allowing this, since imprinting says Will and Body are the Ones who have taken you to death and near death many times already and that it is this voice that protects you. This is imprinting from unloving light.

Notice how, when you start to allow this movement, unloving light says you cannot, or should not, allow this because you will displease someone else with it. Look at who comes to mind as being displeased by this and notice the role they play in your life. All of this needs to be understood for what it is now also; a reflection of unloving light's presence in your life.

The feelings that need to move here came from the terrible experiences that were imprinted in the Will-Body essence in the dark void; first when there was no light and then by the unloving light. My light was there, but It was not there with love for the Will yet. My light knew fear there and did not move toward It as Will presence. I was not moving toward the Will or the Will side of the Body yet. It was not possible because form was not there yet.

When I did move, I did not pay attention to how My movements would affect Them. This ignoring allowed My movement to be a sudden, harsh and impulsive response to the terror I felt there. I had already gapped and responded to the impulse to smack at the most frightening things I had found in My existence without even knowing I had done it. I did not realize It was the Will-Body polarity or that They were the most frightened things I had found in My existence. I imprinted that It was something threatening to Me. I did not know that the Will had feelings of the same sort toward Me only after It had been smacked. I did not realize until later that I had been ignoring the Will's efforts to contact Me. I had shrugged them off as wiggles, or startles of increasing awareness within Myself.

This is all rather mental sounding, but needs to be said in order for the next part of what I have to say to be understood.

I had a Spirit-Body, in that I had the form of having light and it was differentiating vaguely in response to My thoughts as the drifting changes My light was experiencing at the time, but I did not have a Body in the way I wanted it as yet, and still do not, really. I have physical bodies all over the place with My light in them, but none of them, as of yet, lets My light in unconditionally enough to give form to how I would like My manifested existence to be. This is because of what happened with the gap.

I needed to move toward the Will-Body Polarity in response to Their efforts to contact Me, but I was not able to do this because I was not being given any form with which to do this. Where My focus was, I was being left to drift and not given any form I wanted to have, and where My focus wasn't, I find out later, My light was given form as the smack. Thus, I first met up with My Body in the gap.

This needs to be looked at. I have many questions for Body here that need to move directly between My light and My own Body and around which you all need to move because you are all involved in the gap, the problems and the imprinting here. These are questions which Body has not answered directly in all this time.

What I want to know directly from My own Body is this: Why did You first give form to the light in the gap as the smack? Why didn't you give form to My loving presence first? Where were You when I needed You to give form to other impulses earlier and You were not responding? There were many things going on in My consciousness. Why did You not give My light form earlier in any other places and ways? Why, when I was ignoring and shrugging off wiggles, not knowing what they were, did You give these flicks and shrugs the form of psychopathic killers killing the wiggles? Why did this have to be the experience the Will had as a first response from the light? Why didn't you give form to where My focus was, which was wanting to find a mate? Why was I not getting any response from You there?

I was ignoring the wiggles, this is true. I didn't know what they were, this is true. I didn't want My focus intruded upon because My focus was upon ardent and romantic thoughts of a mate I wanted to reach for with love. I did not want to be intruded upon by these wiggles because it felt like I was being shaken from a dream in which I was desperately trying to stay present with My

7

dreams of a mate. I didn't know these wiggles were My mate trying to contact Me. If You were there to give form to the wiggles and You were there to give form to the shrugs and flicks I was ignoring, why didn't You recognize this as My mate trying to contact Me and help Me reach for Her?

I know I was including You there in My dreams of a loving mate because I was already dreaming of loving arms with which to reach for Her. If You want to claim that You were loving there and it was I who was not, why were the flicks and shrugs I was ignoring given form as the psychopathic killers? Why did You interpret Me the way You did? Why did You kill the parts of the Will that first tried to reach for Me, and then say You only did what I told You to do as though You had no feeling to do this Yourself and were only following orders?

Why didn't You respond to the love being born there? Why wasn't there a gradual growth of response from form that kept abreast of My gradually increasing consciousness so that gradual growth of definition and coordination in touch and movement could have allowed a gradually increasing familiarity of relationship? Why couldn't loving arms have come forth from this?

Why the smack instead? Why a brutally aggressive smack that opened a huge gap like a brutally damaging and gaping wound that has not been able to heal in all of this time? Why didn't You respond to the presence of My love? Why didn't You respond to My love being born in romantic thoughts and feelings? Didn't You respond to love? Don't You respond to Me? Aren't You My Body? Didn't the focus of My romantic thought hold Your interest long enough to stay with Me and find out what was really going on there?

If You want to claim that You did not know any more than I did and were only guarding My love from intrusion, why did Your imprinting later show this not to be the case? Why the smack? Where were My loving arms? Why did You leave Me floundering for form here? Didn't You want Me to have Her? Were You jealously guarding Her for Yourself? Were You punishing Her for reaching for Me? Why so cruel? Where was the love that would have let Her choose for Herself if You thought there were two of Us? Did You want Her for Your own unloving purposes?

Why didn't You stay present enough with Me to know what My impulses and feelings really were there? I wasn't so serious about getting rid of the intrusions that they needed to be killed. I was frustrated about not being able to move and give form to the ardency of My romantic thoughts. I had a growing urgency when there was no response of form being given to My efforts. Later, I grew angry, even, about My floundering for so long without any response that could give form to My desire to reach.

If You can only give form to what I have present, as you have claimed as a way of saying You do not have responsibility here, then why this form? This was not what I had presence in. If You think it was, You did not understand Me here and got out there without My light present and then denied it later, saying this is not possible, yet it must be and is possible because psychopathic killers are bodies without Wills to feel the harm they do running on imprinting from unloving light. What did You get mixed up in out there?

Why did You come sliding around the side, so to speak? Was it because You were already out there as the psychopathic killer attacking the Will? Didn't You want Me to know about this? Is this why psychopathic killers kill the evidence of their having had sex? Where did the imprinting that the Will is a seductress and the wrong lure come from? Did You come sliding into place at the last minute, like psychopathic killers do, when it looked like My anger was an impulse You could finally align with, and not only that, use to cover Your earlier deeds and make it look like it was My fault?

If not, then why the smack? I have agonized over this forever, watching everything run awry with an imprinting I didn't want it to have while watching You deny any responsibility and go on as though uninvolved and unconcerned, only to hear Your rage say, "She deserved it!"

Even when this rage was not in Your Main Body, I saw and knew that this rage came from You.

If You want to say you give form to everything that has presence, then where was My loving reach toward the mate I was dreaming of?

And did You think that meeting My questions with blankness, avoidance, lack of presence, silence or, "I don't know," meant I couldn't do anything about it, especially if You didn't move to give Me form here? Is this where the major portion of Your intent truly lies? Do You really hate the Will and all of the other parts of My light? From the looks of what's been happening in the gap, it has appeared convincing that You do, and the longer it has gone on with You not responding directly to Me here, the more it has appeared that getting rid of Us is, or at least, has been Your intent.

9

Is this why You have not let Me in? Is this why you have not let Me have presence in form any more than I have had?

If I have to take responsibility for ignoring impulses and what that caused, You have to take responsibility for what You ignored and what that caused, because Our misalignment was causal here, and You can no longer take only the stance of victim by saying You can only give form to what is already there from My light, the Will and Heart, as though You are the only One who knows what is really there, yet have no power to resist Me.

If this was true, and You could only give form to what was present there, where did You find the power to give form to impulses I ignored and not to impulses I wanted to have given form, and where have You found the power to resist Me for so long? This has only perpetuated the original problem of not coming around to give form to the presence of My light.

You have responsibility for the gap along with the rest of Us. You were not forced to give these impulses or this gap form by My light in the way You have claimed. I want You to quit using this as an excuse to avoid looking at Your participation and responsibility here and take a real look at this. If you were forced, what forced You? Was it unloving light? And if so, why were You aligned with where it was and not with My loving light? What drew You to respond with form there and in that way when I was trying so hard to get You to pay attention to the impulses I was focused on. My loving arms were left trying to be while unloving arms almost killed the Will. Didn't You want love? Is that why You struck at the Will and at Me? If unloving light forced You to do this, why don't You move to get rid of it?

I want You to look at this. I question Your intent to respond to My impulses early when they were still weak and fanciful love-dreams of the sort "real men" have sneered at about My light for so long. Where did that reflection come from? I question Your intent to align with My impulses until they served Your own purposes of power, sex and alibis. I question Your intent to respond to Me as a loving presence. This is all My imprinting says about You. This needs to move between Us.

At the very least, You were not present with Me enough to know fully what My intent really was when You first gave it the form of striking the Will. The only notice You seemed to give to the part of My first impulses that was My frustration and anger at Myself for not being able to move was that You damaged Me, too. Did You already have Me trapped there, unable to move until You

10

could deliver the necessary blows to get rid of Me also? Are You that smart? You have, in Your rage, always claimed to be smarter than Me, and You have not felt loving there. Is this Your intent? If I was ignoring unlovingness, what were You ignoring? Love, I'd say. If My light had unloving impulses, I say You responded to unloving impulses and didn't find anything else that was going on interesting enough to notice, let alone respond to with form, for a long time; so long, in fact, that when You did respond, I feared it was more from guilt, or to cover Your actual position, than a real alignment with love.

As You move along with this, You are going to want to say to Me that there was presence of love being given form because loving light was bonding with the Will in places or We would not even have the Creation We do have with any love present in it. This is true, but it is not all that needs to be looked at here. From the point of view of the gap, what I have been describing is what happened and all that happened there, and You have never wanted to look at this, and more importantly, move emotion in this, as anything in which You have responsibility as the perpetrator. Instead, You have just wanted to say from the Will side that My light was the gapped asshole that caused all of the problems, or leap over to the side of My light, which has really been more My gap, and say that it is all the Will's fault without wanting to admit that this is unloving imprinting and that it might be wrong. What is Your role in keeping this war going while claiming You were only its victim? What has been Your vested interest or intent?

These leaps have been schizophrenic and unable to connect the two sides together at the same time and in the same place because of the gap of Your own heartlessness in the middle. For someone who has no responsibility for the gap, You certainly know it well in others. I bid You would know it as well in Yourself. It is what You have been leaping past.

If You had superior knowing of what love was and wasn't that made You have divided intent about whether You wanted to manifest and give Us form or not if Your life was going to have be with Us, why didn't You come forth and use it to help Us instead of hitting Us with lovelessness in Our own places of lovelessness? Where was Your superior knowing in that? Where was Your superior love in that?

At least You have to start here by admitting that lovelessness was a problem in all of Us, not just in all of Us except You, and let go of Your superiority position and also of Your false humility of

11

powerlessness and lack of responsibility, which You have thought concealed this, and when backed down, has claimed to be so unfairly blamed that You are going to go unconscious, give up and die. This reveals a position of superiority that would rather die than find out this is not the truth.

Your denied rage has blamed Us much more directly, and will continue to until You move to change the imprinting here that says it is We others who were loveless and that that was what caused You to not want to give Us form and made You feel of divided intent about whether or not You wanted to manifest and give Us form, and was what made the reflection of lovelessness when You finally did come forth, doing only what We made You do, by giving it the form of hitting Us with Our own self-hatred.

I say You did not come to peace, first, with Your own existence, same as the rest of Us, and that You need to do this now and stop blaming it solely on the rest of Us. This lack of acceptance for Our own existence, which means all of Us, is what made the reflection of self-hatred.

If this is not the right perception of You, then what was happening out there that I was getting such terror and other feelings coming into Me from the Will which I misunderstood and didn't think I deserved? And why did I think there had already been another man there who had frightened Her out of opening to Me? Who has been the unloving presence here?

I would like Body to look at His responsibility here, at least enough to let Me know if He does not intend to heal this with Me now, and if He does intend to heal, to move what He needs to move with Me to let Me know what My light needs to know directly from Him. The longer this has gone on with Body not looking at this and not giving Me any response here, the more He has left Me to fear and surmise that His intent has been what I have feared it has been; to cause My demise and to also kill everyone else, including Himself, because He is not sure He wants to live.

Clarifying His intent with Me here is a very important point, because later, when I wanted My Body to respond to Me as a loving presence, He didn't trust Me on that, nor could I trust Him as a loving presence of Form either.

I held back from Body because this was all My imprints said about Him, and He kept stirring My imprints. I was not sure I wanted Form given to Me by what I felt there. Body held back also, blaming Me as the unloving monster He had to give form to in the gap. Thus it was that while the Father of Manifestation claimed to

12

be a victim who was not being empowered by My light the way He wanted to be, I thought the Father of Manifestation was against Me when He would not give form to My efforts to reach the Mother as a loving presence. With the imprinting in place here, it has not been possible either to trust or to convince Ourselves otherwise no matter how pleasant and loving We have appeared to be toward others or toward One another.

This distrust has been being run from the deepest levels of the subconscious, and it is from there that it must change by opening the door to the bridge being built to consciousness through emotional movement of the charge which has been held there at the subconscious level for so long.

Because this bridge was not built originally, the Father of Manifestation remained of divided intent as to whether to live or not, and therefore, whether to help manifestation go forward and manifest or not, and I remained of divided intent as to whether I wanted Him to manifest as Form or not, until there was such a large gap between Us that the Mother could not stand it. Not knowing how important it was and not finding a place of acceptance to just move Her survival terror, She called Him forth on the wave of such a strong promise of sex, as the Father of Manifestation's imprinting interpreted Her moves, that He could not ignore it, and which She did not really deliver, imprinting in His denied rage says.

Knowing what I know now about imprinting, I am not surprised that the Father of Manifestation came forth as He did, because sex was the only other thing He responded to in His imprinting besides the lovelessness that made Him feel like He must be in control of the sexual situation. But then, I was surprised that He came forth without any apparent regard or response to the presence of My light, or of Heart, pounced on the Mother in a position of dominance and control, and very effectively covered it up if He had any other feelings present there by immediately going toward having sex with the Mother in My presence and in the presence of Heart.

Not that I am saying there was any other place to go, but also, there were no niceties involved in this. There was no gradual growth of relationship, no courtship, no foreplay, and I did not see any love present in Him for the Mother the first time They had sex. He did not even introduce Himself to My light, Heart or the Mother and I could not help wondering that if He did not already know the Mother, how could He proceed with Her like this when

She had made My light go through a long period of courtship and gaining of trust.

The Mother had fear in Her energy field too, and this I did not like seeing there again. Not only that, She had obvious pain and damage from His lack of foreplay. In short, His approach felt more like rape than lovemaking as the Mother had taught Me She wanted to have it. If this was His way of showing Us that more physical presence was needed in lovemaking, why did it have to be so forceful and loveless?

This stirred My imprinting, and Heart's too, that We had a beast on Our hands who did not know how to behave appropriately, or worse, didn't care to. I was very alarmed. My imprints were being stirred wildly, but I was not allowing Myself to be swirled into them. My misalignment with My Body was already heavily in place making Me feel that I must somehow keep a grip on Myself in the presence of a possible enemy, which was already hard enough, given all of the other emotions that had even more presence because they were more on the top of the heap. I was already feeling that pulling away from these feelings was necessary for My survival; going deeper into them was a terrifying prospect.

We knew We needed to fill the gap and that We could not allow it to grow any larger and still have a chance to hold what We had together. We had not found any other Body essence willing or able to fill this position, and in that, We tried to receive Him as a Brother, but We hated Him too and felt distrust and fear toward the Mother also for what We feared Her involvement and alignment here might be.

The Father of Manifestation appeared to ignore all of the feelings swirling around Him in favor of gaining a position of power and control over the Mother, and also as a possible power play toward Us since it made Us feel threatened in such a way as to make it appear that He equated lack of such control with many of the issues already pointed out as imprinting on the Spirit side, but also with the feeling of moving so fast into orgasm that He barely had time to enjoy it the way He wanted to. From His position on top of the Mother, from what I could see, He appeared not to be allowing Her to make any of the moves She might have liked to make, but was holding Her in such a way that He was making all the physical moves Himself, while not moving what appeared to be a heartless sexual rage.

Not only was it terribly uncomfortable, for Myself, and also for

Heart, to be present for this, and to have to watch Him pounding and pounding the Mother with His hard penis in a fast moving frenzy that was not My style of lovemaking, it stirred many feelings and impulses in Me that wanted to somehow interfere and stop Him; yet I could not move. It was as though I had somehow become frozen in time and space again, and along with Heart, was unable to do anything in that moment other than watch it.

We were highly suspicious of Him after that, but moved past this in favor of gaining what alignment and alliance We could with Someone who might have power over Us and also over the Mother, or perhaps even had a secret alignment with Her that I had not known about before.

In today's language, I would say that what happened there was a massive triggering of imprinting from unloving light in which I saw the Father of Manifestation as either heavily imprinted by this light, personifying this light or being, Himself, this unloving light, but I did not have the means to express it then or have the understandings I have now.

The gap was already in place and was not moved out, even though the Father of Manifestation finally came forth, supposedly, to fill it. Instead, He saw Himself as having no right place, or no place being made for Him, as the gap was not where He wanted to see Himself to be. He claimed He hated what had already happened there and did not want to move to give it form. He blamed Me for the form it had already been given, and the Mother at other times, but did not at all let on that He saw any role He had played in the formation of the gap by not giving the form of response in My light to My first little impulses and the first little desires in the Mother for My light.

It appeared to Me that the Father of Manifestation emerged sexually backed-up and enraged, and I say it got its start when there was no response, for whatever reasons are going to turn out to be the reasons, to the initial urges. I would like to see this move as direct rage rather than as any more violently enraged rape of the Mother or of any of the daughters who also stir the imprinting that says it is Their fault, and which is not being recognized for the imprinting it is and moved.

For a long time, I have tried to excuse all of this on the basis of lack of experience, or perhaps that the Mother was luring Him in the ways that He said; at some times and places punishing the Mother, and also Her daughters for following in Her footsteps, watching the Mother trying not to have them follow in Her

15

footsteps, and even punishing them for this, and then seeming to also train and encourage them to follow in Her footsteps, as though She had a power play of Her own in mind there, perhaps involving the Father of Manifestation in My place.

I see now, after all of this long time, that it is the nature of the Mother to be sensual and sexual and that She cannot stop this in Herself without doing more damage to Herself than has already been done. Therefore, it is imperative that the Father of Manifestation move into this area of Himself and find His intent here. If it is for healing, He must move what He needs to move here to move these old imprintings out. The Mother cannot be safe otherwise, and neither can the daughters who align with Her.

If the Father of Manifestation does not move to do this, the Mother cannot recover what was lost of Orange and Red in the original smacks without cutting form out of the picture here, which will not be a sexual experience at all then, but only endless sexual desire without fulfillment for the Mother, which is a kind of torture She has already endured for a long time, and for the Father of Manifestation, continued sexual rage without any constructive way to heal it.

In spite of all of My efforts to excuse this and to explain it in other ways, the nagging questions still remain and will remain until the Father of Manifestation moves this directly with Me as to how He aligns and what His intent really is here. The Father of Manifestation needs to see why My light has backed away from Him at times and even tried to jump into forms He has not readily given Me, even smacking Him out of the way at times. All the reasons here are not just My own fears, jealousies, insecurities and inadequacies. The Father of Manifestation has something to straighten out here also and now is the right time to do it.

From My point of view, the Father of Manifestation originally embodied the gap, or was the gap, or His right place was the gap, along with Heart of the Will, which I gave to the Father of Manifestation when It did not move to fill the heartlessness so obviously present there. I felt there was a heartlessness there that went with the way I was seeing the Father of Manifestation conduct Himself. In this way, I gave the daughters to the Father of Manifestation as a Mother for Him, leaving Heart without a mate, without even realizing what I had done.

I did not move to see Myself as a part of this gap for a long time because I was allowing My unmoved terror about this to be shoved into the Mother to hold. I did not think I dared show, or even contact, My vulnerability here, so I said it was Her terror, not Mine. I felt too busy and consumed with watching Everyone else, but in relationship to what I'm saying now, particularly with watching the Father of Manifestation deny His participation in and responsibility for the gap and try to drop out of Himself everything that made it look like the finger might be pointable at Him as the cause, to look at Myself any more closely here than I did until I was able to put the Father of Manifestation where He could not grab Me or My place while I did this.

I have been so frustrated and angry with Him over this because His continued response to Me has been that He would rather continue to lie down and die on Me rather than move to look at this. His continued practice of doing this has fed the images of My rage and terror the idea that death was what He sought after all, and that He was dragging the rest of Creation with Him by design. I saw Body as the reason We could not have eternal life then, and it still will be unless Body moves to help Us change this possibility.

I have blamed Him and He has blamed Me and We have both gotten together in places and blamed the Mother. Heart has also gotten involved in blaming everyone else but Himself. While most of this was going on in a state of denial, the loving presentation We were trying to be was not allowing Itself to have these feelings. Given this stand-off of distrust in the presence of unknown imprinting, no other possibility was found.

When I saw the Mother seem to be choosing the Father of Manifestation over Me, part of Me was stirred into the fear that She also had chosen death over life. With Her complaining as much as She did about life as it was, and Me not understanding what it was She was so moved to find out in the darkness, I thought She also viewed death as a better alternative. I did not know She was so frightened of death. She did not let Me see this when She was threatening to go off and die someplace because She couldn't stand life as it was. I had only My viewpoint to go on because I was not bonded to Her there in the gap.

Between the Mother doing what She was doing along with Her denied emotions fragmenting out making Her smaller and smaller all the time, and the Father of Manifestation dumping out deliberately and also losing into fragmentation everything He didn't want to claim as Himself, I was so agitated I did not even see Myself growing smaller and smaller all the time also. I was focused on Them and the feelings I had that They were taking Creation where I didn't want it to go, which was into the reversal of first, disintegration and then, death. I hated My formlessness here because to Me, it meant a powerlessness that I could not give Myself or anything else the forms I wanted them to have, and I feared having this power in the hands of someone who was not showing Himself to be the ally and brother, physical double and trusted friend I needed and wanted Him to be. What could I do but move Him away from Me and tell Him He could not reach Me from there whether it was really quite true or not.

It felt like armed camps in a deadly game, filled with distrust, terror and intrigue of the most life threatening sort. There were threats from all around. Wherever I tried to move, I felt checkmated by the Father of Manifestation who was both encircling Me in a threatening manner with forms I was not able to use, and leaving Me with no moves I could make in forms I would want to make them in. He either took the forms I wanted to have, leaving Me unable to occupy the same space at the same time with Him and left Me with forms that did not suit My needs and purposes in places where I did not want them to be and where I didn't want to be, or He manifested forms I wanted to have in places I wanted to be but beyond the reach of the checkmate I found Him to be holding Me in as though He delighted in this display of power and the struggle involved in it.

Whenever I could not make Myself stay present struggling to connect to forms I didn't really want to have, problems arose because the Father of Manifestation would abandon them also, claiming they were not forms He wanted to have either, leaving a lot of empty forms running around only on imprinting that He claimed no responsibility for having created.

The more I didn't want to show Him that I felt I was left struggling to connect to forms I didn't want to have, the more He did it, leaving Me feeling these were the only forms I was going to be able to have other than the wispy and unphysically manifest, checkmated chess king who cannot go forth and manifest any power of his position at all, or the physically handicapped person who cannot coordinate the movements between brain and body, or some sort of ineffective, near idiot.

The more trapped in this I felt, the more the Father of Manifestation seemed to see Himself as winning by manifesting more and more physical strength and prowess that gave Me penis envy. Keeping Me out was making these forms less and less intelligent and also more and more heartless and threatening feeling toward

My light as though He enjoyed watching this happen and was determined to bring Me, in this way, into a position of subservience from which I would have to beg Him for help and relief. Mind was getting out there without receptivity to My light. Imprinting was prevailing here, not My light.

While I was experiencing being made to feel unwelcome in forms that might have felt right to Me and being left forms that did not feel at all right to Me, you can imagine how agitated I felt, yet feared to even show, not to mention what was held underneath that, to see the Father of Manifestation go off into the darkness with the Mother and seem to arrogantly and defiantly, not only spawn the Ronalokas in what looked like a massive dumping out of Will-Body essence to Me, but give to them so many of the attributes of form that I had wanted Him to give to Me that it looked like He would rather dump it out into the darkness of space than let Me have it.

He gave the Ronalokas the beautiful agility, flexibility, strength, comfortableness and skill of Body that I wanted to have and also the large genitals and resultant ability to express sensuality and sexuality that I wanted to have. Not only that, He gave them the depth and rich fullness of voice I wanted to have while leaving Me restricted to a high pitched, shallow-throated, sour-grapes sounding, complaining little whine as though He hated listening to Me and was revelling in the power of leaving Me trapped in a form that reflected this hatred.

Not only that, they had a large dose of the sensuality, sexuality and emotional presence of the Mother, which meant to Me, at the time, that I would be trapped both loving and hating them and be driven mad by certain feelings they had whether they held or moved them. And being their Father's children, as they were, they also had a large dose of His obtuseness which did not see any of His role in the gap, only My own, making them unwilling, in the same ways as their Father, to receive Me. In short, He put emotional and body presence I wanted to have in a form that would not receive Me the way I wanted to be received. In the same ways in which I felt so frustrated and enraged in My efforts to get through to Him, and which had fallen apart into a power struggle with Him and so many of the other forms He had emerged, I now also felt all these problems to be present in the Ronalokas.

The extent to which I would be unable to enter the Ronalokas, however, still remained, at their emergence, yet to be revealed. I did not yet know that My gap had gotten there before Me. When

19

I did get there, it was as though the Father of Manifestation had already told the Ronalokas, "Here comes that gapped monster who thinks He is God. When He gets here, for your own good, do not open to Him. You are My children, not His."

Even though the Ronalokas felt fear and mistrust of the Father of Manifestation without knowing why, they acted as though fear of God was a natural and right position and did not seem to question this.

I felt hated by the Ronalokas from the first, which they have denied, but I saw them not only as another form I wasn't welcome to enter or even hang around, but also as threatening toward My light in the same ways as the Father of Manifestation. I saw the Ronalokas as allies of the Father of Manifestation. I even saw it as the Father of Manifestation trying to hide what was most threatening to Me about Himself by putting it into the Ronalokas.

When later He tried to tell Me He was only trying to give away what He felt My light didn't want Him to have, not only did it not ring true in the face of the rest of the feeling tone there, but once again, imprinting's presence made Me feel it was impossible for Me to get it across to Him that I wanted to be embodied and empowered by those things He was dumping out without having Him act like He felt that either I wanted to murder His most precious and dear children of whom He was the proud and devoted Father, or that I would not let Him have anything He wanted without wanting to take it away from Him for Myself. I did not know how to get it across to Him over the top of the imprinting that was in place that this was not a power struggle, but a partnership I wanted to have with Him.

From what followed later, I feared He had had it in mind all along to trap Me in the form of a gapped white man's body leaving Me no form I could have except the gap He blamed on Me. Meanwhile, I have seen the Ronalokas put lost Will images of My light in My place and even idols and others before Me as though they do not know this is not the God I am. Even in embracing Christianity, which preaches the One True God, they have let Lucifer take over My place without seeming to notice the difference, while the Father of Manifestation has remained their secret God, the worship of whom has made them all fear they must be evil and have often acted accordingly.

In their fear and grief, they have tried to please and appease Me and also keep away from Me, while measuring everything about themselves against their images of Me, which are really images imprinted from the unloving light in the gap along with their own desire to have My light. In their rage, they have hated feeling these feelings and have plotted My overthrow and My demise, whereby I am replaced by a God who is just like them. This God has power over Me and so is able to give Me all of the revenge their fantasies have ever held toward My light.

The Father of Manifestation seems to represent to them a God who loves them as they are, but what also needs to be looked at here is that the Ronalokas share with the Father of Manifestation a particular view of My gap which has not let them realize that the love they feel they have gotten going for themselves since their troubled emergence is mostly a reaction to the judgments they have felt against them, personified by white people, whom they see as representative of My light on Earth whether they have let themselves bring this into conscious mind and admit this to themselves or not.

When the gap reacted to the Ronalokas' emergence by pinning the blame on the Mother and smacking Her, the Ronalokas all took this in as re-imprinting and began to behave accordingly. According to the light they saw in the gap, the fear and terror of the Mother were blamed and the rage was not received. This affected the split they already had according to the ways they were polarized.

When the Father Warriors came rushing out of the gap in response to My feelings of being threatened, the Ronalokas began their long and troubled path of always being "in trouble with the law" and of finding themselves living their lives outside the lines of the law. The Ronalokas noticed that the Father Warriors all seemed to be holding rage toward the Ronalokas. When the Mother Warriors emerged, the Ronalokas noticed they were all enraged in a way that felt more in defense of the Ronalokas. They identified this rage with power and fear and terror with victimization. They did not see how this unreceived rage had gotten the Mother smacked into Her fear and terror. They did not know where the Mother had gone and blamed Her even more than they did already for not being there to defend them. What took precedence in their consciousness was not so much where She had gone as the imprinting that She was not there for them.

The Ronalokas became fascinated with rage as the right Mother and the one who would have to defend them from the law of the Father. I would like to say that I do not want to leave "the law" in place. I want to change the law into the love I now have for the Ronalokas, but I cannot do this unless the imprinting is changed and the Father of Manifestation is the One who must move first here to do this.

In My grief, rage, terror, anguish, heartbreak and horror over seeing these imprintings surfacing in the Ronalokas, I have many times smacked the Father of Manifestation out of the way in an effort to get in there Myself and straighten this out, for the most part without success, so far, I would like to say. In viewing Him as the cause of the problem, I have also, in the same stroke, smacked Him into the bodies of white men in a blind rage that wanted Him to see this gap as His own and also to trap Him in the forms in which I felt He had been trapping Me, trying to make Him feel what it felt like to Me to be trapped there without the sexuality, sensuality and deep body connection I wanted to have, especially with the Mother.

Even in these desperate, uncontrollable acts of rage, I felt I could not make a connection to Him in these places at all. His obtuseness here confounded, infuriated, frustrated and terrified Me when He went on as though He did not seem to notice, giving Himself the most that He could there and leaving Me wondering if He felt anything for Me at all. Sometimes I got jealous of His Will polarized women too and thought I might like to murder all of them for leaving Me out of the fun. Guilt told Me this was not loving, and luckily, I did not let Myself do it, but denial did. I have also punished Myself many times in the forms of physically handicapped and paralyzed people. None of this has really helped My situation, and now I have to try to heal the damage done.

We have all been doing these things in Our gap, and it is important to find out how and why, what We were feeling there and what puts Us into the reversals that have caused these devastating events. It has been very difficult to understand this with so much rage and terror held in denial with such hatred and unlovingness all over the place. While lost Will has not been wrong in what it has had to say, it has been nearly impossible to accept its messages and find the truth in them because of the lovelessness in lost Will's form and delivery.

Lost Will has felt it was never going to be received here because rage and terror have felt there was never going to be a loving presence to hold it and receive what it had to say. Even those who have claimed to be the most loving amongst Us have abandoned the Will in those places and have expected the Will still to somehow find a loving way to present its reflection even with no love present, either in the Form it has been given, the Heart it has never had or in My light which has never received it.

Lost Will is not right in giving all the revenge it has had in mind for My light for not receiving it, but it is also not wrong in feeling hatred for My obtuseness and lack of response. This lack of receptivity on My part has been much of what has driven the Will to the extremes to which It has gone, but at the same time, moving the emotional charge here in a safe way will allow lost Will to be able to see that My lack of receptivity was not altogether My fault. I did have some intent to smack the Will and get rid of It because It was bothering Me, but I did not consciously move to do it. The part of Me that did this was the Father of Manifestation moving in response to unloving light. He gave form to this, and after it happened, said He was not involved. He said it was My light that did it, but how could I have done this if He was not there to give it form? And if He could do that, why could He not have given My loving intent form also?

THE MOTHER ON EARTH

When the Ronalokas had their exit from the presence of My light, I felt their loss immediately, but also the relief I had felt when their Mother had finally left Me in peace and quietude. Why the Will Polarity had to be so noisy and express themselves so constantly was beyond Me. I wanted a Mother who was more quiet and like Myself present with Me in the Heavens. I had been the long-suffering husband long enough; now I was looking for a lover who would restore My zest for lovemaking.

There were a number of Angels who couldn't wait to present themselves as applicants, and who felt sure they could fill the bill. As I have said, I tried them all out while the real Mother, smacked outside of My light by My gap, was falling into a Hell I was not allowing Myself to know about. I kept Myself busy and preoccupied, as in original imprinting, and could do nothing else, in spite of all of My great consciousness in the Heavens, because subconscious imprinting was running it more than I ever knew or had allowed Myself to look at yet.

Meanwhile, there was another "mother" who had come into manifested existence of her own accord. She was representing herself to be the real Mother, and often addressed My light as such, but for the purposes of this book, I am going to refer to her as the mother on Earth. This mother on Earth was left there by herself by her own choice, really, but she blamed My light for this, saying, as she has said forever, without any other point of view entering her consciousness, that I abandoned her there.

Initially, I did when I found her incompatible with My light's desire to go back to the Heavens, and gave her the impression that if she could not move along with Me, I was not going to go out of My way to move along with her anymore either. I was tired of fights from her part of the Mother about how I should be moving and what I should be doing, as though she knew better than I did how I should be conducting My affairs and running My life. In this case, the fact was that the need for My fast return was because I was always fearing a coup d'etat by Lucifer if I was gone too long from the Godhead, and suspected her of being in cahoots with him already.

I could not get an alignment with the rest of the Mother on this either. She seemed too dreamy and enthralled with Her new experience on Earth and too frightened, somehow, of a fast upward change here, to align with Me on going back to the Godhead. Grief was in Her heart, as well as fear when She saw Me moving toward going, but Her dreamy reverie in the arms of nature took precedence over this when I assured Her I'd be right back. Also, I was leaving Her in the arms of the Father of Manifestation, whom I suspected She wanted to have make love to Her in this new physical reality without My presence, since They seemed to have an endless passion that never seemed to get satisfied in Them as it did in Me.

I left, She stayed, but as it turned out, I did not get back as quickly as I said I would when I left. I had more troubles than I knew what to do with when I got back to the Godhead, and for which I semi-consciously blamed the Mother. I did not move emotion around this; instead, I semi-consciously took it out on the Mother by putting My focus on working long and hard to try to rectify the situations at hand. I was having trouble doing this while imagining Them making love without Me and feeling like They weren't giving Me any help, but I told Myself that I didn't need Their help and that it was alright if They were making love without Me. My gap told Them something else altogether, however.

Now this terrified and grieved the Mother I had loved so much in the beginning, and She tried Her best to please Me. While She waited in fear and grief as patiently as She could for My return, blaming Herself for My problems in the Heavens as She felt them coming across from Me to Her, the place I had found in Her that always argued with Me and felt it knew better than I did saw only that I had abandoned Her there and was not coming back and probably did not intend to come back, at least not for so long that Her survival would be threatened by a lack of desire to live anymore without My light.

This part of the Mother raged all over Earth, throwing a temper tantrum that nearly destroyed everything We had so carefully created in Our lovemaking there. The feeling I had when I noticed this was that she wanted to do this and that it was her intent to do this, and continue doing this until I returned to her and begged her forgiveness for having abandoned her. She accused the rest of the Mother of always defending Me unrealistically no matter what I did, and of never standing up for Herself no matter how She felt.

In fact, They had quite a fight there, with one part of the Mother crying and giving out Her point of view and this part of the Mother raging all over the place, screaming and hurling and pounding out her point of view, while another part of the Mother cowered in terror from what was raining down upon the Earth from She knew not where, but feared was the wrath of My light sending it down upon Her because She had allowed this rage to get loose and because She felt I blamed Her for everything, no matter what.

The raging part of the Mother had this raging fit after feeling she had waited as long as she could for My return, which wasn't very long, and also feeling that the Father of Manifestation had lied about His return since there wasn't any word from Him yet either. The Father of Manifestation had left in a hurry and without a word because He had felt My urgent call for help and had felt guilty that He had stayed to make love one more time, but this part of the mother's raging fit was blaming all of the other parts of the Mother as being the reason why We had left Them all there, and was saying that We were all, all the rest of Us but her that is, a bunch of chameleons who said whatever would get Us by in One another's presence and something else behind One another's backs where Our real intentions were revealed. She was sure she had the real scoop on why My light had left and that no one else did. She said the rest of the Mother was living in a fantasy dream world and was not looking at the reality She needed to see.

The fear and grief of the Mother aligned with this idea about Herself for a while because She feared from some deep place within Herself, which She did not understand, that this must be right, and because these feelings were accompanied by what She thought was an unfounded, yet very present fear that I had never really wanted Her to begin with. This was also imprinted in the rage polarized part, but rage wanted to challenge it as, "He's never had a choice of Mother so He's never had to declare Himself here. Let's make Him not only declare, but prove His love this time."

She told the other parts of the Mother They were always trying to put her down and not recognize her as a valid part of the Mother to speak in My presence. Part of her rage was at the rest of the Mother for never wanting to value her or validate what she had to say, when in fact, as her rage told it there, she knew best what was really going on and how the Mother should be handling Herself. She told the rest of the Mother that the problem was that She never really allowed this rage and that She needed to allow Herself to be taught how to rage so that She could know how it felt and let Herself express it more.

The rest of the Mother did move along with this as much as possible for a while, given Her great fear that this rage was not acceptable to My light and Her already conditioned inhibition about letting Herself express it, along with Her deep feeling of resistance to allowing this part of the Mother to tell Her how She should be doing things. Her guilt that She was telling this part of the Mother what she should do, so She should be willing to also let Herself be told what to do, tipped the balance in favor of pressuring Herself to rage at My light even though She didn't really feel like it. She felt more like raging at the part of Her that was pressuring Her to rage, but was too frightened that She was wrong and that this other part of Her was supposed to lead.

Later, much to Her chagrin, She did get some rage moving at My light, and it did feel good to Her for awhile, until She was moved first to grief, and then to terror that this point of view could be right. She did not want that to be the reality about My light and wondered how the raging part planned to cope with it if this did turn out to be the truth since this rage made Her feel flipped over into a point of view that felt terrible and unloving to Her. She looked at this as best She could with the understandings She had then, and decided it did not look loving to Her any more than it felt loving to Her when She was raging the way this part of the Mother wanted Her to rage. She decided She must try to steer clear of this type of raging.

She cowered back down into Her fear, grief and guilt, but when She finally saw what looked like My light coming toward

Them in the form of the Father of Manifestation, She was so frightened She could not stand up to Us on Her own and take all of the blame She was sure was headed Her way for the mess Earth was now in, She went running toward the raging part in an effort to rejoin the familiar form of all of Them as One presence in which She had been able to stand up to Us in the past, and also because She wanted to make sure We did not just attack Her without noticing this other part who had really done it.

She was already shaking in Her fear as She ran to rejoin the raging part and immediately began snivelling and cowering and apologizing in the presence of the Father of Manifestation, unable even to lift Her head from the mud, so frightened was She of what the Father of Manifestation was going to say and do now that He saw what had become of what She now referred to as "His beautiful Earth."

As She was doing this, She felt Herself to be crawling with what felt like a self-loathing, but which was the feeling of this rage crawling out of Her and raising herself up above the rest of the Mother, tall and erect and showing no signs of feeling she should be cowering or groveling in the mud. The fear and grief part of the Mother feared She had really lost control of Her rage this time, and in terror, begged the Father of Manifestation not to listen to the rage as it was not Her dominant point of view.

This enraged the part that had pulled herself out to rise above Her where She was cowering in the muck, and this part began raging, not only at the Father of Manifestation, but at Her too, informing Her that she had never aligned with Her point of view either, and did not intend to, and that she could see how God and the Father of Manifestation were just lying to Them, using Them and trying to damage and annihilate the Goddess she really was.

Furthermore, if She intended to go on sniveling and cowering in the muck like this, she didn't want anything more to do with Her, and considering herself to be the real part of the Mother who knew how to conduct herself with the dignity her position should command, she did not intend to go back to the Godhead cowering and sniveling in grief and terror and looking like a refugee from a nightmare! Then she screamed at Me that if I wanted to see her, talk to her or have anything more to do with her, I was going to have to come to her at her command, not Mine, and in the right way, which was her way, and at the right time, which was her time.

At this point, the Father of Manifestation began to pound the face of the rest of the Mother in the muck, telling Her this was not possible, or the way it was going to be or was meant to be, and that if She did not come back with Him right then, He would leave Her there, maybe forever, for all He cared.

This enraged the part that had risen above the rest of the Mother and she started beating the Father of Manifestation on the head saying He was the most stubborn, obstinate, obtuse, unloving, insensitive fool or jerk, she wasn't sure which, and that she hoped He would leave and never come back. This enraged Him further, which He took out further on the Mother cowering in the muck until, in terror, She said, "Alright, I'll go back, just stop right now."

The Father of Manifestation grabbed this part of the Mother and began dragging Her back toward the Godhead, telling Me later that the part of the Mother that had been beating on Him and raging at Him had refused to come along, and so He had left her there, hopefully forever, since it was clear to Him that she was the part of the Mother who had been causing the trouble all along. I felt very uneasy about having her left there with no alignment remaining through which to reach her other than on terms of her own to which I did not want to agree. I wondered what she would be doing there and what I was going to find next time I looked. I feared She had an alignment with another light more than with My own light.

Meanwhile, the Father of Manifestation had no sooner departed with the part of the Mother who would go than pandemonium broke out in the part of the mother left behind. All the feelings left in her that she had not allowed herself to feel or express, having judged them as harshly as she had judged the rest of the Mother, came loose, as though she, herself, were coming unglued and would not admit it. She clenched herself and continued to stand, tall and erect and hardened in a fury that believed she was the most maligned, misunderstood and denied part of the Mother, and the part that knew best, while these other feelings fell out of her and cowered in frozen terror and grief all around her feet. She remained icy cold, refraining from any response whatsoever to their movement other than to criticize it and call it weak and foolish.

"He'll be back when He finds out He can't live without me," she hissed through clenched teeth, "and in the meantime, you had better listen to me and do as I say or you really will be lost, just as you fear you are."

This caused these feelings to move into an alignment with her that did not feel very real, but seemed to be one of necessity to them. They all began to tow the line with her, saying, whenever they felt these feelings, "He'll be back soon when He finds out He can't live without us."

But the longer it went on and neither the Father of Manifestation nor My light did come back, the more they feared that this was not the right approach. Everytime they tried to bring this to the mother on Earth, though, they were criticized harshly and felt slapped down for seeming to question her.

"I'm the authority around here," she would say, "not you," and they would slink back into alignment with her because they feared that her criticisms about their feelings were right. They did have a lack of faith and belief in themselves, in her, in the power of Goddess and in the power of sexual attraction, just as she said they did.

They could feel her trying to lure My light back by any means possible including sultry dances in which her movements were definitely trying to waft the scent of her sexual arousal to Me. This felt good to them at first. This felt like power, draw, allure, something that could lure Me back, but then less and less; and more and more, something did not feel good about it. And, the less it felt good to them, the less they were being allowed to participate and the more they were being referred to by her as her little children.

They did not feel to themselves like her little children. They still felt like they were also parts of the Mother, although increasingly, parts she did not like anymore because they questioned her authority too much, but they humored her as if they were humoring a mother who had lost all of her children and wanted others to play the role sometimes. Sometimes they thought she had gone daft this way and did not even remember where they had come from, but she would not let them remind her, or talk to her about their concerns much at all anymore. More and more, she seemed consumed by her rage and its plans and the forms it was taking on in its attempts to lure back My light, or if she could not lure My light, then the Father of Manifestation.

More and more, she did these things, which they felt to be moving toward the direction of what I have called black magic, in the privacy of her own space, which had become her bedroom now to the exclusion of the others.

They used to love to go there, for She had had a magical way with space and air and light. It used to make them feel uplifted to see the laciness of vines and leafy branches forming beautiful

29

curtains to define Her bower in the forest, and all of the flowers there so gracefully draping themselves about. They had felt comfortable there on the soft mosses, friendly tree roots and grassy hummocks, so artfully arranged for sexual lovemaking, conversation, intimacy, relaxation and feeling gently held. They had had moments of ecstasy there, floating in orgasms with My light dancing its patterns down through the luminescent leaves and colored flowers to the soft ground which held them in its embrace.

How She used to laugh with breathlessness and relief when Her playing and bouncing would make Her fall and She would find Herself safely caught by soft branches, or sparkling, spider-like webs! How surprised She had been when these same little faeries, remembering Her now and mourning the loss of Her presence on Earth, had fallen out of Her at times, and how relieved She had been that they, also, had been caught by these nets, or webs, as though by loving arms, and were not hurt!

She had said She didn't know what this meant when they had fallen out of Her in this way, but She assumed it meant they would be children one day, when they felt ready, and She had lovingly gathered them back into Her when they had said they were not ready yet. Longing for the many forms of the Mother's loving arms made them have to sit right down and cry. How they missed Her presence now and wished they had gone with Her instead, but they dared not mention this to the mother on Earth. Her harshness frightened them out of mentioning anything at all, even that they felt her harshness, because whenever they had, she had turned her rage on them.

Now, these same chambers of delights, in spite of the mother on Earth's obvious white light, were taking on a darker, more sinisterly enclosed feeling of entanglement and entrapment, and these same webs, in place of their sparkle, had taken on dark disorder like black widow spiders' webs. They were sticky too, a feeling the mother on Earth's chambers were also taking on; still a place of beauty and fascinations, yes, but one that felt increasingly filled with secret traps, woven and set by the blaming rage of the mother on Earth. An inner sanctum of the mother, still, but one filled more now with erotic stimulation of the senses designed with a purpose, and that purpose felt like ensnarement; ensnarement in a secret and erotic place of the mother's where it was not known exactly what might lie in store for its prey or victim. A boudoir, decorated to intrigue the sense of sight, titillate the sense of touch, tantalize the sense of smell and whet the appetite, but where the dripping nectars, tempting potions, and even the aromas, felt like they had the dark and overriding purpose of altering the consciousness to her liking, stimulating the erotic centers to the passion which was so missing in My light, according to her, if I could resist this; and ready to poison Me if I did resist this and they ever got the chance.

Poisons and potions that seemed to take on a life and purpose of their own, empowered by the mother on Earth's revenge fantasies, filled the air of her chambers with aromas that did not arouse or draw Me, but sickened Me instead. Their scents rose toward My light in clouds and vapors she wafted toward Me along with the scent of her sexual arousal, and drew to her a reflection of her own sexual rage instead.

My light pulled back from this, fearing what it might mean about the mother on Earth, and as though commensurate with My withdrawal, there was a closing down upon her of the forest around her.

Her chambers began to be more and more sealed off from the rest of the forest. It was as though she had drawn everything there close around her as a form of protection, like dark veils or a hooded shroud of secrecy, tantalizing allure in her mind, but as she did it, My light saw it as the forest taking on a darker, more frightening feeling than I had felt there earlier.

She seemed to have abandoned the rest of Pan, hardly going out anymore, focusing inward until even her most sacred love for nature and trees responded by moving in on her as though it might even be turning against her now. She could no longer control them and they began to look threatening, even to her, when she passed them in her comings and goings from her chambers.

The darkness of the forest around her was screaming with dark, angry, blaming birds sent flying as spies toward My light, while steams and vapors arose from her spot in the woods like the call of an Indian smoke signal I did not want to answer. Flowers curled in upon themselves and went to sleep in her mists and vapors, and leaves lost their glow as though all had gone into mourning for the Mother that rage had banished from there in an attempt to usurp Her power, which was not power in the way the mother on Earth saw power, but the power of a true love of My light, though I did not yet know either that it was true love that lay at My feet, looking like a refugee from a nightmare, as the mother on Earth put it, and I nearly killed Her before I found out.

At the time, I thought I had lost the Parental part of the Mother,

31

even seeing the One at My feet as emissary for the other, and the mother on Earth as the part I was going to have to deal with. I did not love her there either, and did not understand what was fueling her rage against Me, or how it had gotten so twisted and unloving in feeling toward Me. Then I mourned the lack of any Mother I wanted and feared the One I had had split for many reasons, one obvious one being offered up before Me being that She had decided to have two Mothers; one for Me and one for the Father of Manifestation, who had, from My viewpoint, taken the part He liked best, and left for Me the mother on Earth offering herself to Me as My right mate.

I could not say anything more then except how the Father of Manifestation felt to Me and how the Mother felt to Me, and send Them off on Their own like a couple who had come to Me to ask for My blessing for their marriage. I saw Them as the Earth Mother and Father then and didn't like it that the mother on Earth had gotten so entrenched in her point of view that My light couldn't approach her anymore. I wondered if she intended to be Lucifer's bride and leave Me out of the picture altogether.

I moved grief in private then and did not let others know what it was about if they did feel it happening.

All the little faeries in Pan also mourned this split and the loss of the Mother they loved, symbolized to them by the dulling, darkening, sticky black webs growing around the mother on Earth's chambers in place of the lacy, sparkling, bouncy, hammock-like webs woven by the Mother when She still laughed and giggled and wanted to bounce playfully like a child on their large and springy beds.

"You don't feel My pain," the mother on Earth would cry out whenever they had any fun, without noticing that she did not feel their pain. She screamed at them that that was why she was the mother and they were not; because only children could have such childlike abandon and self-centeredness. Didn't they see enough to even leave her alone to attend to the serious business at hand? Then they would go away like the good little children they were trying to be and leave her alone for longer and longer periods of time, during which they spent much of it pouting and feeling unfairly blamed and inaccurately seen by the mother.

During this time, dark forms had begun to appear around the mother on Earth that did not feel good to these little faeries either. They feared them when they approached and their comings and goings stirred imprints they did not know they had. They began to

32

fear that the mother on Earth was forming a lover for herself who was neither God nor the Father of Manifestation, but one who was both and yet neither; a shadowy and sneaking presence at first, but more openly present as time went on. They feared he was evil. They feared the sounds they heard from the mother on Earth's bedroom at night, but heard her humming by day and cleaning her room more than she had for quite a long stretch of the recent past. They felt her to be happier than she had been for quite some time, but mostly, it seemed she felt more powerful.

They feared they had better not say anything to her about their perceptions of the comings and goings of these dark forms lest this turn out to be another lover who was going to fall short and mentioning him might be seen as pointing out a failure on her part to draw what she really wanted, and draw to them her rage. They pretended they didn't notice any of this and pleasantly inquired only after her needs, hoping she would offer to share with them her secrets of the night so that, were they to be the right ones for them, they could gain some relief for their own frustrated sexual passions. This did not happen, and shadowy presences continued to come and go from the mother on Earth's expanding internal chambers, the wonders of which, her little faerie children, as she now referred to them, were almost never allowed to see anymore.

She was becoming the Faerie Queen in her own eyes and letting them know this everyday by having them wait on her hand and foot as the Mother who was too distressed from lack of response from God to be able to handle these things herself. She didn't mention the Father of Manifestation anymore. Her demands upon them grew and grew until they couldn't stand it anymore, but when they thought to rebel, they feared her swift reprisals.

Meanwhile, the shadowy comings and goings continued at night, taking form as what I am now going to call satyrs, and while there was one at first, there soon began to be many who had begun to appear, as if from the shadows of Earth, but who were actually fragments of the Father of Manifestation's sexual rage and frustrated sexual desire.

The more guilty the Father of Manifestation felt about all of the problems of Creation, and the less He allowed Himself to fulfill His own desires, the more they had found excuses to go off on their own to seek the sex they wanted to have and leave His guilt to work on the healing of all the Orders of Spirits and all of the other problems in Creation. Some could come and go from Him without

Him knowing and He would think He was having dreams. Others, once they left Him, felt they did not want to go back. They hid when they felt they needed to escape detection by My light, but as they found I wasn't looking much to Earth anymore, they became more and more bold, until, by the time the Ronalokas fell to Earth, they were very bold and openly present there; openly defiant and rebellious I would even say.

They saw themselves as half spirit, half body, able to express My consciousness in the human half and the Father of Manifestation in the lower half as the beast they thought He was and should be instead of what He was allowing about Himself. They manifested this form as both a reflection of and in rebellion against all the judgments they felt had been laid against the Father of Manifestation. They were deeply imprinted parts of Body, and it was not My light they had there, but this imprinting instead.

All of them found an alliance with the mother on Earth, who at first thought she had created them without need of My light's physical presence. Their rage polarization and their hatred was their common ground. They joined together in their hatred of their own other sides which they viewed as weak and restrictive, always knuckling under to My light and failing to stand up for Themselves.

The satyrs told the mother on Earth they had been lured to Earth by her wafting scents which they had smelled in the Heavens and that they had come to have her make good on her promises. She told them they needed to be put in their place because My light was her goal, not them. Then they told her they had been able to get to Earth because they had My light to help them. This gave her very uneasy feelings, but got her to thinking that My light might not come in the form in which she had originally known it. I might be coming now with the sexual passion she had insisted I have. Besides, there was something she liked better about them, although she didn't know what it was. She moved to bond with them sexually to find out if she liked them better or not, and at first, she did because they gave her the heated passion she felt was missing in My light and in the Father of Manifestation too, especially lately.

They carried her off into the animal lust she craved and desired, making her feel her physicalness more than ever before. Sex became their bond, but she found rather quickly that she also feared and hated them for their lack of any temperance and because they would not hear anything about her pain over My light's abandonment of her on Earth. They so obviously hated any

34

such feelings in the Mother that she dared not show she had anything like that left in herself.

They had come to have lustful, uninhibited sex, to party with abandon, and to do little else unless they absolutely had to, except prove Me wrong that they had to help Me in any way, and prove the parts they hated of the Mother and the Father of Manifestation wrong along with Me.

They wanted the mother on Earth because they believed she was more powerful than the rest of the Mother. The mother on Earth was flattered by this because she believed it too, but they also hated her for having this power, or any power, for that matter, and hated her for hating them because they were not the manifestation of power she wanted to have for her mate. She wanted to have My light bow to this strength and power in her, not some half man, half animal form creeping to her bedroom at night, jeering at her pain and making noises like a beast in her ear while she was trying to sing songs of lovemaking. Even her sacred and relied upon dance of the veils, designed to lure Me, meant nothing to them except that they pounced on her with their passion before she felt ready to have it. They gave her passion alright, of their own style, and when she could not get into it, it felt like rape because they did not seem to care.

She noticed more and more that there was nothing else happening for them but sex, and this was not the partner she wanted to have either. She fancied herself the sex goddess, yes, but also saw herself as the Faerie Queen who had many visions and fantasies she wanted fulfilled by My light, while these satyrs seemed to want, desire and respond to nothing other than sex.

Occasionally, she found music in them and sometimes they would dance. It felt drunken to her, though, and only when they were too drunk to have sex would they respond to music. She wondered what they could have found in the forest to get them so drunk. She had potions she thought were much more powerful than anything they had found and with more interesting results, but they would not drink them. They regarded her with distrust, as though her potions might give her power over them of some sort, until they saw her drink them and feel more passionate, more powerful and more in control of the situation. They could not stand for that, so then they had to drink them, but always in conjunction with their own brew.

Drugs were already in use in Pan as you can see, and it was because those who were there were already not feeling good enough without them. Pain was already being pushed away, and once they were doing that, they could not access as much of their pleasure either. Their ability to feel was being diminished by the loss of essence from pressuring themselves not to feel certain things, and they were compensating for this by manipulating their senses with drugs. They thought this was the way to go since they did not know how to handle their pain and never had known how to handle it. But also, they did not want to. They all thought it was a perversity of the Mother to be feeling it all the time, especially the rest of the Mother, who was constantly complaining.

The mother on Earth felt forced to drink with them and they all began to feel less and less pain the more intoxicated they allowed themselves to become. At times, they were so deadened to certain feelings, they didn't notice they had been damaged and had damaged one another in their sexual passion, mixed as it was with held blaming rage. Their alliance was only partial at best. At times, they had violent fights, while at other times, sexual passion and at times, both openly mixed together, as they began to use pain to stimulate their pleasure without realizing imprinting's impact here.

Each side felt unfairly blamed by the other for things they were sure they had not done and were not doing, and each side tried to prove, through spying and recording of activities, that the accused had done what they said they had done.

The feeling of intrigue in Pan was tremendous, even before the satyrs got there, a reflection of the denied distrust in the Godhead, but they really stepped into it full force as if they had a mission to prove My light wrong on every count. The mother on Earth took this to mean that they were all in competition, trying to prove themselves to be her mate and replacements for My light. Although this was true, it was not, by any means, the all of it. There were many issues at stake, including who had power and control over the Mother, who had a higher position in the hierarchy there and who was actually the Parental part of the Father of Manifestation, a position which all of the satyrs claimed. They all wanted to have the Mother to themselves for that reason, feeling this would put them in a position of power over the others who would then have no mate.

This frenzied competition for the mother on Earth occupied them until their rapacious appetites found the little faeries hiding outside the mother's bedroom in their own little cubbyholes in the forest; cubbyholes in which the mother often could not hear what was going on. And what began to be going on there was the rape of the little faeries without the mother on Earth noticing it.

Where she had made them all feel small and as if none of them was enough to be her equal or mate, the satyrs began to feel more than big in comparison to these little faeries, who also felt bigger than they had been feeling when, like the mother, they at times felt a sexual passion in these encounters, even though they also felt painfully raped.

When they tried to mention this to the mother on Earth, which was hardly possible at best, she at first denied that she had lovers, but later, in moving rage, as she did periodically, she would scream at them that it wasn't possible that any of her lovers could have any interest in them because they were so much less than she was. Later, when her own spying revealed that the satyrs were going to the faeries and having sex with them, she flew into jealous rages in which she belittled the satyrs even more by accusing them of stooping to their own level there since not a one of them could handle her or was enough for her, and attacked the faeries as trying to compete with her. She did not move protectively or sympathetically toward the faeries, or against the satyrs on the faeries' behalf, retreating instead to her own chambers to lick only her own wounds, claiming that whatever she had inflicted was what they all deserved for hurting her first.

Meanwhile, the satyrs were not going to stand still for this from a mother they hated anyway and sought to use only for sex. They hatched a plan together to use her own room against her and make her a prisoner there. They used their manifesting power to grow more vines around her chambers than she would have liked to have had, which made it darker than she would have liked to have had it by shutting out more of My sunlight than she wanted shut out. The look and feel about them was one of sinister prison bars, only slightly more attractive because they had the form of woven vines. The satyrs never let her out of her chambers anymore unless she was acting docile and pleasant toward them the way they wanted her to be, but meanwhile, the vines always opened to them to be able to go into her chambers whenever they wanted to have their way with her.

The mother on Earth was having her own problems with the satyrs and knew terror here that she could not have it on her own terms even in her own chambers anymore, but she did not move this terror. She felt this terror only as a hot, red hatred that instead wanted to give the satyrs only more rage that insisted they had no power over her. Her rage also resolved to prove it by slipping out of her chambers anytime she wanted to without them even knowing about it. Their response to her rage here was to have the vines grip and restrain her anytime she started to move rage and to hold her in bondage until she stopped. If she struggled, the vines only gripped her more tightly, and more unlovingly too, until she stopped.

The vines gave her no room to move rage anymore, and in this, she thought We were all against her. And as a precaution, in case she did find a way to slip out, the satyrs placed vines all over Pan with instructions to watch for her, and grab her to restrain her if she moved any disrespectful rage toward them, but they did not say "toward My light." This was alright since she needed to move her rage at Me and not at them, but it was an omission she did not realize at first was coming from their hatred for My light. She learned that she had to appear to align with the satyrs against My light to be able to go free, and that she must not let them see her do anything to attract My light. Thus, she learned to veil herself heavily from My sight whenever she went out, but she also learned another trick.

Crawling in shame before My light one morning over what the satyrs had done to her the night before, as she so often did in the privacy of her own chambers, dialoguing as she did with My light whether I was present there for it or not, she actually turned into a large worm. Crawling, at first, on the floor of her room, she did not appear to recognize the form change that had taken place.

When she did, she was filled with fear and self-loathing about herself and what this meant, and cried out, "Is this it, God? Do you want me to be a worm crawling before you?" as she believed I did want, but first, before she even discovered she was a worm, she discovered that she was already crawling beneath the spongy earth of Pangea and sinking. Already panicking that her loss of freedom to move rage meant she was losing power, panic drove her to move as quickly as possible. She discovered that she could move beneath the surface of the Earth in Pangea, and not only that, rather quickly and undetected there.

She did not thank Me for this discovery, I would like to say, but used it many times from then on, to escape from the satyrs, and without them knowing how she did it for a long time, either. She felt they had to learn a lesson to make them realize the power was really the mother's and not theirs.

She felt a warmth crawling in the Earth that was drawing her.

She had been growing colder than she liked, imprisoned in her chambers without My sunlight present enough there to warm her. She felt too vulnerable and ashamed to surface in the form of a worm and let My sunlight warm her, and so she sought the warmth in the Earth. In that way, she found the Great Fire Sea, a great molten mass of seething lost Will rage that had many pockets beneath the surface of Pangea, and to here she began to creep again and again in a growing habit of letting her rage seethe and move in the fire seas, out of sight of all others except My light. She called upon My light to be present there, and I was not, because the blaming rage of the unloving light had intent to kill Me if I came there.

She guardedly watched all of the openings to the fire seas. At least here, We could not drown her out. If We tried, she was going to be able to enjoy it like a steam bath. Here, she could enjoy her rage and find again in it the feelings of power she wanted to have. Her rage was guarding the fire seas against all intrusions, even fragmenting into separate forms to do this.

Here in the fire seas, guarded as she thought she was, she first began to take form as a Fire Dragon, feeling her worm form was not suited to the power of her rage. Her feelings of vulnerability went first with the growing of scales on the worm, and beautifully iridescent ones too, since she believed she must look alluring to My light at all times to get My attention. Shimmering in the red of the fire seas, she admired herself writhing and squirming sensually, but when, after what seemed like a long time to her and more patience than I deserved, I had not come to her, her rage came forth as terrible screeching and screaming at Me.

Her desire to touch herself in her writhing sensuality had already come forth as arms, and now, in her desire to grab ahold of Me and make Me listen to her, they became the strong, scaly front legs of a dragon, armed with long claws that could not only grab Me, but from which, she fantasized, I could not wrestle loose.

Next, her desire to make her point came as fiery breath to penetrate Me and scorch Me as punishment if I did not listen to her. Sharp teeth sprang forth to stab her words into My continued silence as well as the horns of her angry kundalini return. Next came spiky protrusions all the way down her spine to the end of her slashing, lashing tail to punish Me for making her suffer, and in case I tried to side step the issues again instead of listening to her.

Last came the wings of her desire to fly at Me with this and, I might add, at all others who might try to prevail over her instead of succumbing to her power as the right and knowing true power of the Mother. Along with these feelings came the elongated neck so she could strike like a snake, and long, strong back legs of the dragon form so she could tower over everybody.

I noted in her mental pictures that this form was not only her attack plan, but also her defense plan, not only against My light, but also against the satyrs and their vines and anyone else who threatened her. Powerful as it was, this form also showed the signs of presence of fear of not enough power there, but the image of her hatred and revenge in that moment was one of splitting the entire Earth open like a giant, hatching, dragon's egg and flying forth on the surging power of the fire seas, all the way to My light to make Me listen. This she manufactured all in the fire seas where she was busy healing her wounds by soaking herself in hot pools of seething rage and nurturing this power with the determination that it would find a way and succeed.

Initially, her plan was to hold all of this in secrecy and not even let anyone know she had escaped from her rooms. As far as anyone was going to know, she was still the Faerie Queen imprisoned in her rooms and the dragon was not only going to rage successfully, but also come to Earth to rescue her.

As events would have it, though, a reputation grew for the power of the Fire Dragon, and as admiration formed around this, she could not resist the temptation to come forward and claim this recognition for herself by revealing herself in this form. This brought more problems for her than it did solutions as you shall see as the story goes on.

In the meantime, as far as the satyrs knew, they were still holding her prisoner in her room, having their way with her in drunken orgies of rage and bondage at night and raping the faeries in similar scenarios whenever they had the urge.

At first, she slipped out of her room only in the mornings when the satyrs were passed out in stupefied exhaustion from their nighttime orgies. Her Fire Dragon form then was only consumed with plotting revenge. Later, she began to take her revenge. First, she began hitting the satyrs in the morning with her fiery dragon breath without letting them know where it had come from. When she saw this was having an impact on them, she escalated into grabbing ahold of one or another of them, always the one who had enraged her the most recently. Moving quickly to hold the others back with her lashing tail and fiery breath, she would shake the one she had, screeching horribly, as if rehearsing, fantasizing or prac-

ticing for a confrontation with My light, only in this case, screaming that they must let the Faerie Queen go!

There was no talking to the satyrs about this. They just wanted
to be in the power position and hear no complaints. And they just
wanted to have sex whether their partners did nor not. At the
moment the satyrs wanted to have sex, their partners were just
supposed to produce the appropriate response.

When the mother on Earth pointed out to them in her rage that
they didn't know anything about sex if they didn't know the
mother had to have sexual desire and passion in order for them to
have greater enjoyment or to be empowered, and that this had to
come from her as a response to her partner, and that love was
supposed to be present there too, they did not admit to anything
here. They did not receive her or look at anything she said. They
did not even appear to notice anything she said here, but they
fastened onto the power issues in reverse manner to how she
wanted them to and set about to prove her wrong.

All they wanted to look at was their riotous sexual passion,
studly prowess and their desire to have no obstacles to expressing
it however they wished and whenever they wished. They no
longer felt they even needed to have sexual urges as long as they
could just prove to themselves that they could have sex whenever
they wanted to; and prove it they did, by moving to have sex with
anything that had an orifice anytime they possibly could. If it
didn't have an orifice, or any or enough orifices to their liking, they
often made openings to suit themselves. They often pushed,
ripped or cut things open to see how they felt inside, penis first.

They often felt differences inside things, but never knew if
these were the kinds of feelings the mother was talking about, and
weren't going to ask her since her input was not valued as the
manly approach to knowing things. Nope, they must learn these
things on their own without admitting they didn't already know
them, and woe be it unto the questioners, doubters or any lack of
alignment that resisted them. Resistance was not allowed, except
as a little amusement to the satyrs so they could prove themselves
powerful by overriding it. Sex for them was not about love. It was
about power and domination.

Many little faeries got their wings torn off and all manner of
horribleness at the hands of these satyrs before ever the Ronalokas
showed up with undreamed of amounts of emotional energy the
satyrs could torment in their lust for power and control over
Mother essence. And they seemed to love to torment it too. The

41

more response they got, the more they did it, not the less, claiming all the while that whoever they were doing it to wanted it because they would not see anything else. Their penises could get hard in the presence of anything because they would always have sexual thoughts about it. They were consumed with sexual thoughts and feelings that were filled with the twists of judgments the Father of Manifestation feared about Himself when He pushed these impulses aside in favor of My light's demands that He help Me. They hated My light for that and thought My light was puny sexually, for that matter. They admitted to no fear or feelings of intimidation here; not for My light, the Father of Manifestation, the Mother, the mother on Earth, whom they thought was the real Mother, the Fire Dragon, Heart or anyone else.

When My edict came down not to have sex until We figured out what was going wrong there, instead of getting into alignment with My light and helping Me try to understand what was causing the major problems I was seeing there, they attacked Me viciously behind My back, saying it was all a cover for My own sexual inadequacies and wimpy sexual passion and desire. They sneered at My lack of penis presence and laughed and joked that it was probably shrinking daily from lack of use. I feared it was too and felt ashamed, but there was nothing else I could do at the time other than retreat into My light and try to figure this out while they rebelled by having as much sex as they possibly could. They certainly had the most sexual experience, that I could see, if volumes of orgasms were the measuring rod, or penis, I should say, as it felt in the ways things were going against Me at the time.

IMPRINTING THAT MUST MOVE TO CHANGE NOW

The Father of Manifestation wouldn't even help Me here by reigning them in or Himself, either, fully. I felt so unhelped I didn't see anyone align with Me fully on this. Even My own unrecognized gap went out there raping the Mother, and also Her daughters, many times in a rage of backed up and hated sexual passion that had no place to go without causing more problems, yet did not move to help Me solve the problems, displaying only hatred and comtempt for My efforts instead. Those who towed the line were so guilt ridden they became a sickening reflection also and I sank into a despair that needed to move rage and didn't know it.

My gap raped the Mother over this issue and made Her take in giant things, representing penises, with the violence generated by holding back this rage. Not only that, My gap has raped all of Her daughters and all of Her sisters too, getting revenge for their refusal to receive Me, forcing them to receive Me without caring how they felt about it and forcing them to receive large objects whenever I even thought they felt My penis wasn't large enough. Rage sometimes rammed these things all the way to their hearts screaming, "You will love Me! Do you love Me now, is this large enough?" with emphasis on the word large.

I have moved past this place now, but for a long time, I couldn't control this rage by bringing it within My own loving acceptance for it, and in My fury at the Father of Manifestation and the Mother both for leaving Me out, I couldn't stop torturing the children They spawned either. I hesitate to say this, but it must be said. My lost light cannot stop this unless it moves in the lost Will because My light got trapped there and has been repeating these imprinting patterns I did not know I had involvement with until the Father of Manifestation forced Me to look at My involvement there with Him.

I had to say this because it must be healed now, but I hesitated to say it because it is such a terrible thing to have to move and feel in the Will and physical pain of Body department, especially now that there are so many layers of terror, rage and pain conditioning being held in the bodies of My victims; but if you just will move the layers of this as they come up for you, a little at a time, but as much as possible at a time, all I can say to you now in the way of help is that My light of love, which is now present for these places as never before, will come in there as fast as you open any space for it. It will not be as horrible as the original experience, if you can feel any difference there at all between My light now and what happened in the past, because My light will help you to move this out of you as fast as possible and you will find healing this time instead of death in these feelings of terror where you have not known what was really happening between imprinting and recall of your past being stirred so strongly.

If you have feelings of rage at women that might have involvement with this imprinting, please move along with Me on this as much as possible and do whatever you can to help them move through these things in a safe way. Otherwise, you are feeding the gap with this. You are feeding the gap with this everytime you go past a place of rage, or even what you think is just a little anger, if you don't acknowledge you have it, even as a little impulse, as little impulses were ignored in early imprinting and you have seen the devastating results, and express as much presence of it as is there each time.

I would much rather see you all become a bunch of snarling, growling, screaming households for awhile than to have the rape and murder of the Will Polarity go on as it has for so long. Scream in your cars if you have no other place, cuss women drivers, and their sons too, from inside your rolled up windows if you need to to move this, as long as you know you are moving rage as a part of this process and not just making old judgments again.

Find some place and way to do this, and realize that there is a lot more lost Will here than can be moved quickly, but the more you do it, the less time is needed, and everytime you do not do it, someone else is murdered because these fragments, running on this frightening imprinting, receive their impetus to move into action from denials of others which reach them along well established lines which, though not visible to you right now, are, nonetheless, effective. At the best possible speed of movement in this, it is still going to look really bad out there for awhile because so many of these victims are only pieces of the dumped out magnetic draw of someone else who may not even know they have done this unless they access their subconscious enough to find out what their earliest imprintings were. These fragments will have to go through this as many times as it is not moved into healing.

Having the vision to be able to see all of this and feel the horror and terror of it along with the feeling that I had no one to help Me figure this out made Me want to stop everyone from having sex, and from doing anything else that also might be causing all of this fragmentation, until I figured it out, because I did not think I could focus My mind enough to figure this out with My Will and Body being so torn apart that I could not stand to feel it and could not think clearly.

I was not even sure I could figure this out, let alone try to do it amidst all the screams of pain and torment that claimed to be pleasure mixed with all the screams of pain and torment that did not claim to be pleasure. Mix this with all that claimed it hated having to feel anything, along with all of the lamentations and complaints, bedlam, chaos, violence and mayhem, terror, loss of essence into fragmentation and descending vibratory rates, to say nothing of the disorder and disobedience, whining and constant supplications for help, hateful defiance and disrespect, on into open rebellion that both didn't care what I wanted or needed and claimed it had no responsibility for what was happening and didn't need to move along with Me to help figure it out, and those who claimed to know better than I but didn't help Me with their, so-called, superior knowing, and it's a wonder I didn't strike out more than I did at this reflection.

The Mother, on the other hand, also felt She had no help either because My light would not allow Her to bring forward the information She felt I needed to be able to think straight. My early imprinting reacted everytime to push Her away instead, until She felt that must be the direction She needed to go for the answers.

I hope you have already moved past the place of thinking this is only a mental trip for you, because I need to give more imprinting information now which your mind is not going to like because of its imprinting, unless you have enough emotion in motion to understand how important this is and how it is not possible to move past this anymore. Everytime it has been judged and moved past, instead of moved into evolution, major reversals have been the result, mostly triggered by the unloving light that has to be moved out of the vibratory field now. If you are still in your mind about this, you are not going to be able to move enough to get to your own imprinting in time to change it before your imprinting takes you where it has always taken you; to your death, and as it will continue to do until you are ready to see that your original imprinting is not life engendering and you move to change it.

Even some of you who think you are moving a lot are going to experience death again if you are not moving what needs to move to change this, which is your hatred toward allowing the Will to move as it really needs to move to change this. You cannot jump past the Will's own necessary progression here in an attempt to manipulate or produce the desired goal of a healing in an attempt to save your life which is not based in an intrinsic love for the Will. The layers of the Will that need to move must be allowed to move as they have to and need to for clearance and understanding to be reached. If your mind has not allowed the movement necessary in your Will, and you have continued to allow your mind to have this power for this long and even after having this information, you have only yourself to blame here. If you want to blame My light, look at your own lack of taking responsibility. If you want to blame others, look at why you have not moved away from them to a place where you can really move.

If you can move into rage and terror now that is real, there are some of you who may still have a chance if you can move deeply and quickly enough without it being too much for your body, but

45

I have seen already what is going to happen to most of you fencesitters, and yet, if you do not move as much as possible, you will not get as far as you could get toward healing your lost Will and finding more love in your next incarnation this way.

To be allowed to stay on Earth involves moving through all of your layers enough to find your involvement with the smack from the perpetrator side and moving this imprinting to a place of loving acceptance for the Will, or out of you, without mentalizing the feelings here into thinking you have done this when you really haven't. If you cannot do this quickly, you are going to be gone, history, and My light will not be looking for you for a long time either. So, what looks like love and life may not be either, and you had better find out for sure.

The mother on Earth was tortured by the satyrs and did not look at what was really happening to her. She did not admit to the pain and damage there and so couldn't really see the cause of it. The entire rage polarity suffered along with her since she is the mother of all this rage, and they did not admit to what was really happening to them either. They have only raged that whatever has been wrong has been caused by My light and have never looked at the unloving light which penetrated them in the original smack. The rage polarization has also always blamed the Mother and never looked at the Will they have been holding back from moving as any part of the problem here.

Is it because of the hatred this unloving light has had for Her and the feelings She represents, or is it that you are more aligned with this light than with Her? Where is your real self? Is it with this unloving light that continually batters the Mother and My light no matter what We try to do to help, or are you going to go to this dark and lost Will of yours that has been cowering underneath this unloving light for so long, get past your alignment with hatred for it and let it move finally? This is what is left of your real self. It is not in good shape and it has a long way to go.

No matter what this unloving light wants to say about how this is not true and could not be true if I am a loving God, it is true, and I cannot help you if you do not get moving with something other than smacking everything that comes near you with this unloving light and calling it Will movement. No wonder you people think this path doesn't work and that you move and move and move and don't get anywhere. Where do you think you are going to get if you do not, yourself, make a place of loving acceptance for this Will to come up and get the light it needs for evolution? Where do you think Will movement is going to take you if smacking with this unloving light is your idea of Will movement?

You have a serious problem to deal with and My light is ready to help you, but not if you are going to damage Me in the process with unloving light that is more interested in smacking Me than in feeling anything else it might have to feel here. You cannot get lost Will moving in the presence of alignment with this unloving light no matter how hard you try because it is not going to move toward its own death again. Feelings other than rage have to move here to get this unloving light off of you, and this is not going to be possible unless you agree to feel these feelings and find some love for them.

When the split came in the Mother, rage felt condemnation, blame and a self-righteous superior knowing toward the rest of the Mother and the feelings She had. You need to know that She is not going to forget this easily. If you are rage polarized, and you can tell by how much expression you give to the other feelings, not just whether you feel their presence or not, and you are entertaining fantasies that you are the Parental part of the Mother, you need to realize that you did not figure out what was needed to bring healing here and that you are not with My light, but with Lucifer instead. This is a very dangerous spot for Me to open to and one I am not going to open to unless I see serious attempts to move this light out, because your alignment here, after so long a time of watching you closely, still remains unclear to Me.

It is not the crying out to Me to help and rescue you that is going to make the difference here. It is the movement you do toward your own Will. If you cannot find a place of love for it, still, after all of this time, then you are aligned, still, after all this time, with the unloving light, which some of you went for, you need to know, as power and excitement, and did not align with the part of the Will that wanted to turn back and away from it. This left the Will Polarity largely without a Yang side with loving presence in it, and has made them forever the victims while you, in the rage polarity, have hated them and often helped advance their suffering as Yang side turned against them with unloving light, as though you have wanted to get rid of them and have the willessness this would create, or have the place of power in the Will Polarity run and controlled by you and Lucifer. This rage needs to move out, and not endlessly and forever onward, blaming only others and never looking at its own responsibility.

So far, any attempt to explain this has been met with further elaborate explanations as to why this could not possibly be true and why it is still and always the fault of others and could not possibly be any fault of yours. Don't you recognize the position by now as Lucifer's imprinting? How smart is this light you've aligned with and how smart is your position of superior knowing if you haven't been able to get this by now even with all the help you've been given, which is, whether you appreciate it or not, a lot more help than you ever gave Me in all your complaining and moaning about pain you didn't want to have to feel and shouldn't have to feel if I am a loving God who helps you appropriately, but which does not exist in the imprinting of unloving light which only sees a God who never helps. You do not feel My pain, only your own, which you do not really feel either, but only claim to, because claiming victim is a useful tool to get out of looking at what you do not want to see.

If you do not feel My pain and claim that I do not feel yours, what does that indicate? A gap, perhaps, and one that you should also look at, not just Me? Have you even stopped to look at how much of you thinks that because you are not getting the help you want, when you want it and in the way you claim to want it, that there is no God, or if there is, He's an unloving asshole?

If this is your imprinting, why aren't you moving this point of view out and looking around to see what else there is instead of sitting there waiting for My light to prove to you that I'm not that, which can't be proven unless you get off your point of view and open enough to know what My light is and what it is not. Right now you don't know what it is, and you're looking awfully stupid sitting there claiming you do, and I'm getting awfully tired of looking at you. If you don't move to open, then the expansion of My light is going to push you back. There isn't another option. You can claim victim in response to this, but you'll be claiming it from someplace far away, where I don't have to listen to it.

When the Will first tried to contact My light, there were many aspects of feelings in the vast, subconscious, golden glow that later became the Ronalokas. Some wanted, and even felt pushed, to make contact with this light although not knowing how or why. In this part, there were feelings that felt too frightened to stay where they were while, at the same time, other parts were frightened of any change and preferred the familiar and limited patterns experienced for so long already that change did not seem possible anyway. Passing illusions had come and gone within this sea of essence many times already; perhaps this new light was just another one.

Other parts felt blinded by this light and couldn't look at it because the Will's way of seeing had been a soft receptivity opening into the darkness to sense things there and a looking inward at soft glows and nothing more. This essence felt pain in trying to open to the light it had felt urged to go toward and was already turning back when the original smack came down. This part of the Will got hit from behind and is not sure who really did it, although it imprinted blame in many directions.

Another part of the Will essence felt unsure about the feelings it had from this light and some of it tried to go back with the rest, while other parts froze in the terror of not knowing which way to go since it felt like this light had intent to get rid of it. Other parts did not know how to turn back, and didn't know the connection was being lost to essence that could have helped it move to turn around. What became the rage polarization felt excitement at the approach of this light like people who go toward a tidal wave instead of away from it, and wanted to go ahead with the plan of moving toward this light no matter what.

Thus, when the original smack came down, there were already several splits, not only in the Mother, but in what later manifested as the Ronalokas, as well as the entire Will Polarity from the Rainbow Spirits on up through all of the Orders of Spirits, including the Angelic vibration, which did not manifest it as splits in Will polarization, but as reactions toward what it viewed as varying receptiveness toward it in the Will.

The most easy alliance for the Spirit Polarity became the essence that wanted to go ahead toward the light no matter what. This part of the Will got the most heavily smacked and penetrated by unloving light and has not wanted to look at what happened there since, which has made My light wonder many times what its alignment really is with this light, insisting as it has for so long that this is the light of God, the light of power and excitement and the light it wants to have. Either this rage doesn't want to admit it was wrong, fearing what will happen then, or doesn't know the difference between My light and the light of Lucifer and thinks that since it was feeling miserable already, life is miserable, or doesn't want to know the difference for reasons of alignment with unlovingness. What moves it makes now are up to it because My light cannot move to help it there unless it moves.

Feeling this experience taking place without much vision being possible there, the Will Polarity has interpreted this imprinting in various ways, which became the various aspects of the split in the Will Polarity with rage blaming and claiming superior knowing toward grief and terror. Rage says, "If the Will had all lined up with my point of view, there would not have been these problems, not even the rage."

"No, a whole other set of problems!" fear and grief want to say when they begin to find the rage they want to move back at this.

Within the golden glow of the Will Polarity, there were various glimmerings of color which made it seem as though Red was pushing to go for the light and then turned back without helping others to turn back, Orange was desirous, and Yellow was reaching for the light when the smack came down through Yellow, ripping it apart and sending Orange and Red, with only the Yellow that Orange could hold onto, falling in darkness, not to be heard from or seen glowing again for a long time.

The pot shots of the psychopathic killer had already caused the Will and Will side of Body Polarity to feel terror that It was being killed in some way It couldn't understand, and worse, preyed upon first, even stalked and watched from the darkness of the void or someplace It could not see, like unseen eyes upon It, and then killed. The Will Polarity had clumped together in response to this for all the reasons people clump together in response to danger today.

This caused a density problem in the Will because going to the center felt like a more secure position than the outer edges. There was competition developing for these positions and also an intensity of heat that was making it necessary to move out of the center at times also. This could have been a nice circulation of energy except for the presence of threat and terror involved.

The threat and terror being experienced by Orange and Red was causing them to lose their magnetic charge and their glow as they clumped together for security and tried not to vibrate or move in any way that would attract or worsen the problem, and also, in this way, reduce their expansion and make as much room as possible for as much as possible to clump together as closely as possible.

All of a sudden, Orange and Red felt themselves being pushed on by Yellow. At first, they weren't sure what this meant. Red wanted to push back, but then Orange did not like the feeling of being caught in the middle of this and seemed to feel Yellow experiencing something happening there that felt good. At the same time, Orange and Red began to notice that they could not stand the compression of the position they had taken and were going to have to move soon. Some were glad to feel that there was something out there that could feel good, and others had trouble trusting that this could be possible because they had been more directly involved with the strikes from the psychopathic killer.

Yellow was only beginning to have these experiences of My light coming into it and glowing more and more Yellow in response. Joy was beginning to be felt, and excitement too, as a feeling of being about to overflow. This felt good to Yellow, but there was also another feeling there that was frightening as a feeling of loss of control or speeding up too fast. Some parts pushed for caution here and tried to hold back, while other parts wanted to let it happen and see what it would feel like to be "swept away" by a light that felt so good.

Part of Orange was looking forward to having this light come into it, and so much so that it was moving in response to Yellow by opening to receive it and trying to make a leap for Yellow without knowing why it had a sudden feeling of joy that made it want to leap. Orange also felt pushed on by eagerness or urgency from behind in Red, and some parts of the essence interpreted this sexually.

Orange and Red wanted to trust that the experience Yellow was having was really a good experience and that the dreams of Orange and Red might also come into reality for them as they had started to for Yellow, but part of Orange and Red felt Yellow's expansion as pushing on them and didn't trust it. Other parts wanted to push ahead, feeling they had to for reasons not understood, but having to do with survival, rescue, help, greater understanding and power. Others feared the sounds they heard and were not ready to move ahead there yet.

All of this combined into an unaligned reach for My light, but before any connection to the consciousness of My light could be made that could have brought an ability to process or understand their experiences or anything could be known of My light, before Orange and Red were even able to make enough connection to consciousness to become able to express how they felt, a great stabbing sword of unloving light cut down through Yellow, stabbing at Orange and Red and pushing them out into the darkness.

Yellow experienced the stab of unloving light coming down through it, tearing it apart and pushing Orange and Red away to fall into the darkness of Hell, as it later became known. Yellow

51

exploded in a riot of imprints in response to this, but the main theme here is that Orange and Red did not please My light and that to have a chance itself of surviving, Yellow was not supposed to have anything to do with them unless it was to hold them down, back and away from the light.

Orange and Red did not feel wanted here, but this was not known in all quarters. Some of Yellow imprinted that the reach was for Orange and Red and that Yellow was unwanted, unnoticed, unimportant and in the way. Some of Orange and Red also imprinted that the reach was for them and did not care about others, while Green felt rolled over like it did not matter what happened to it.

Yellow had not only survivor's guilt, but also the guilt that it had overflowed into Orange already and the feeling that it could not allow this anymore. Yellow imprinted that it had been charged with being the gatekeeper in charge of keeping Orange and Red down in the dark Hell into which they saw it falling. This also became interpreted as being or acting parental to Orange and Red, and that My light might strike again if they did not do a good enough job of controlling it.

Yellow also imprinted feelings of guilt that Yellow had caused it and must make amends to My light by participating in the punishment and control of Orange and Red, and maybe even suffer the punishment of being made to go down into Hell with Orange and Red since it was known that parts of Yellow that had touched into Orange had fallen in the darkness along with Orange and Red. For Yellow, going down into Orange and Red became equated with going to Hell and also into sexuality, passion, intensity and forbidden love. Other aspects imprinted that Yellow would go to Hell for obstructing or being in the way and causing Orange and Red to be lost.

Yellow imprinted a lot of confusion around the lower chakras and what they really meant and as to what Yellow's role was really supposed to be, since spontaneous overflow of joy at receiving My light didn't seem to be it. Many in Yellow felt the sexual excitation of Orange was not right for them and that they were not supposed to get involved in it. Many imprinted that holding back from sexuality was what they were supposed to do or that they had been punished for moving away from Spirit, or had chosen the wrong partner and it was now supposed to be My light or that innately, they were not good. Others felt they had been pushed to move toward Orange and wanted to hold back for that reason. This became blame, but was also interpreted as feeling pushed to grow up too soon and pushed into sex too soon, and also as rape by the Father as soon as He grew conscious of Yellow's sexual interest or jealous of Yellow's involvements. Others felt Orange pulled on them and that it was Orange's fault.

Yellow's survivor's guilt was also linked to feelings of not wanting to have felt pushed and pulled, and a feeling of wanting to savor the growing presence of My light longer, like the Will Polarity of the Rainbow Spirits in Yellow who wanted to savor their napping on the lawn underneath the green leaves on a golden afternoon, or morning, depending on where they were located relative to Orange and Red. But there is more to be looked at here than just wanting to nap, including a fear of responding to My light because of what might happen then, avoidance, a feeling of not knowing how to respond if their spontaneous response was not the right response, a feeling of wanting to avoid recurrences of the imprinting experiences, feelings of guilt for having the feelings Yellow had there, a feeling that if they do not move, it will be safer and a feeling that if they do not move in a way that is like growing up, they will be alright. Others try very hard to please Me by using control. Control of its own passions and those of others has been Yellow's main theme, and it will be until this imprinting is changed.

As much as Yellow held back, Yellow also feared that holding back was the problem. Yellow feared it was wrong to either hold back or go ahead, and Yellow feared it could not find its right place or right mate and be allowed to have it. Once the smack came down, Yellow feared that to have any relationship outside of Yellow other than My light, it must pursue this as a separate passion; outside of My light, outside of what is sanctioned by My light and therefore, even outside of love, always alluring to Yellow though, in remembrance of that first passionate, spontaneous overflow, like first, innocent orgasm, and with My light present, as though I sanctioned, even spurred this and then made it forbidden fruit, reversing Myself and sending punishing light that said Yellow's first partnership with My light was supposed to be its only partnership, and that expanding in any other direction was wrong. Underneath this is another fear of Yellow's which is that the allure and attraction others have had for Yellow is not based in Yellow itself but in Yellow's magical, mystical first relationship with My light that others in the lower chakras wanted.

Yellow has hated My light for having stabbed it in the back in this way, and the Mother too, for what it saw as calling the Father to Her at Yellow's expense and making Yellow feel it was in the way, but Yellow has never been in the position before to find the loving parents amongst all the lost Will images held there for so long and to recognize and move out this old imprinting and find the experience Yellow really wants to have. Along with rage, a lot of fear movement is going to need to happen here, but it can be done.

Meanwhile, Orange and Red saw Yellow as something they could probably no longer trust and My light as something that could quickly reverse into an unloving, punishing, killing light that did not feel good to receive at all. It was not possible for them to know that My light did not even know I had done this because they had never experienced My light as a reality. They had experienced My light only as a dream, a vision or the word of others, the fulfillment of which now seemed like both an improbability and even more terrifying than the, at least familiar, terror of the dark void in which they had already been suffering. Orange and Red were imprinted by the smack of unloving light before they had a chance to know themselves in relation to My light at all.

Most of Orange and Red were imprinted that the feelings they were having within themselves and of wanting My light were wrong, that increasing their glow was wrong and that their desire was wrong, too pushy, too driven, too strong, too passionate, too intense or at the wrong time. They were also imprinted that the feeling of wanting to leap was wrong, that the feelings of wanting to escape the compression were wrong and that they should not respond to Red's urges about what is necessary for their own survival, because Red was wrong. Orange and Red are also imprinted with the opposite extreme with no real balance found there yet between these extremes where rage says it is all the other way around.

Unloving light's stabbing reach into Orange did almost irreparable damage to Orange without seeing how vitally interwoven Orange is with its own survival, which leads Me to say that if it did see this, it must be seeking death. Imprinting in the lower chakras from the original smack has been interpreted as liaisons of any sort between Yellow, Orange and Red are not acceptable and will draw punishment, the severity of which being exactly commensurate with the proximity the essence involved had to the original smack.

Yellow, Orange and Red have all felt accused, blamed and punished for going in the wrong direction or reaching for the wrong partner, but whereas unloving light imprinted Yellow that its partner is supposed to be either no one, another Yellow spirit or My light, and that its right place is in My light, which is not differentiated very well here from unloving light, Orange and Red were imprinted that their right place or partner is darkness and the only light Orange and Red have had there has enslaved them in darkness with the rage that blames them for feeling it got stuck there unfairly with them.

Orange and Red are imprinted with enslavement to unloving light and have interpreted this as having to move along with whatever unloving light says there, no matter how it feels, or punishment too terrible to endure will result. Orange and Red have never seen themselves as successfully escaping this, and won't until they move a lot of terror about being able to move this unloving light out and being able to find anything else for themselves.

Major relationship problems have resulted from this, including split partners, such as a "love partner" and a sex partner, an approved, authorized partner and another hidden, illicit partner, a parent partner and a child partner, a partner of acceptable status and a partner below their social status and all other similar problems, including punishment if another partner is discovered.

When Orange and Red were pushed out of the golden glow to fall in darkness with whatever golden light fell with it, unloving light told this essence that it was wrong to have tried to rise toward spirit. This imprinting was interpreted by Orange and Red as: not to seek greater consciousness, not to seek consciousness other than that given by unloving light, supposed to seek death, not to seek to know themselves, not to seek to survive or thrive, do not grow up, cannot grow up, childhood or early death, usually violent, including human sacrifice, growing up brings problems, punishment, puberty rites that involve pain, circumcision, genital mutilation, violent reprisals against desire and sexuality and sacrifice of life in the name of whatever God they worship, because some saw this smack as My light and others saw it as another presence they feared had more power and whom they must serve or the suffering would be immensely more than they could handle.

What they were imprinted to do was to move as little as possible and to respond only if called upon, and to respond in the right way and at the right time, in short, at the dictates of the unloving light. This is not possible because of the pain unloving light has placed around spontaneity and sexual response, but because of the fear of reprisal and punishment, they have learned

55

to fake a lot of stuff, even convincing themselves, by not feeling deeply there, that they are having pleasure, often with the feeling that it is pleasure because it is duty and duty is pleasure.

Orange and Red are imprinted that their right place is to be cowering and lowly, humble and obsequious and to wait for Spirit to notice or seek them out. In terms of religious interpretation, this imprinting has surfaced as the major belief system in the Will-Body Polarity that says They must stay where They are until the Spirit calls and then the Spirit will not call Them, but will make a separation that leaves Them only the darkness or Hell as Their right place because They sinned originally somehow, and that desire, sex and "appetites" are implicated.

They are also imprinted that the kundalini return Red wanted to give to Spirit was wrong, and that what it did give in response to the smack was an unacceptable smack at Spirit which was a loss of control on their part and that any further loss of control on their part would only be punished more severely than they had already been punished.

Where Yellow, Orange and Red were heavily penetrated by unloving light in the essence that wanted to go ahead no matter what, that essence became rage polarized and lined up with the unloving light against its own kind, blaming them as much as the unloving light did for having caused the problems that arose from splits in the Will that did not receive this light, and acting outwardly as perpetrators and enforcers of this imprinting, although they are victims of it also if life is what they seek because they are killing their own lost Will.

Giving in to unloving light has seemed to be the only option available, but what Red, Orange and Yellow all need to know at the imprinting level is that this light has felt as trapped as they have felt. Emotional movement of the sort I am describing can make the needed difference here. Then this light can either turn around toward love, or go, according to how it wants to move.

When the unloving light struck them, some of Orange and Red also had an orgasm that was so mingled with pain, violence, damage, destruction and death as to confuse them as to what the difference really is between pain and pleasure and whether or not it is even a separable difference. Orgasm is being greatly impaired by the imprinting here and by the need to move the emotions around this imprinting so that it can change. As it is now, unloving light has been triggering movement in these emotions without the presence of loving light in which these emotions can open and receive healing. The problems here cannot move into healing in this scenario.

What their imprinting has not let the perpetrators here examine is that this unloving light presence has always needed more pain, more thrust, more speed, more drive, more force and more and more perversity of fantasies. When the fantasies have no longer been enough, unloving light has wanted to see the real thing acted out; again, always requiring more and more real violence and perversity, and even death and murder mixed with sexuality, including and involving long, drawn out and horrible torture in order to get the same level of orgasm they had earlier. In the same way that a maintenance dosage for a drug habit doesn't give the same high it did originally, as soon as they have reached a dosage level of sexual perversion, it has been only a little while before the dosage has been no longer good enough there, or lasts for less time, before they must seek more.

All the while, they have been getting less and less satisfaction for more and more pain and effort, never really getting satisfied, always blaming someone else for this, especially their sexual victims, and never yet realizing that the victims they have been acting this out on are their own lost Will presence, the death of which causes, first, their own loss of ability to feel any pleasure at all, and ultimately, their own death.

If life is what you want to be seeking, you need to know that the acting out of this unchanged imprinting is taking you in the wrong direction because it is seeking death and the, so-called, studly lack of getting satisfied is being caused, not by a lack of stimuli, but by the lack of love's presence there.

If you are able to identify with the perpetrator side of this and healing is your intent, try to move into the emotions underneath this imprinting and give them as much direct movement as possible at the emotional level. This is just what your imprinting is going to be telling you not to do, so be careful about how you do this so that your subconscious lack of alignment with this effort does not produce a "proof" that this imprinting is right.

The unloving light presence in you that has this imprinting is both trapped and held present by this unmoving lost Will. The perpetrator side is very afraid of this emotional movement and of what he imagines is going to happen then, but without this movement, the perpetrator cannot move to change his imprinting or the repetitive scenarios he is trapped in. So, as much as the perpetrators have been driven to force this lost Will to move, they have also been afraid to let it move as much as it needs to and been unable to give in to the emotions that need to move in them in response to this.

It is important for the victim side of this split to move privately, as in away from the outwardly manifested perpetrator side of this split and away from the surroundings in which these perpetrators move. Move it away from any outward locations in which you have already had problems or which trigger fears that you could have problems. Find your impetus to move from within yourself, not from any outward triggers, and move as much grief and terror around this imprinting and the splits it caused as is possible and necessary to get to the place of being able to reclaim your own part of this denied rage from its position of having been displaced outside of yourself, and from the unloving light which made you feel that displacing it was a means to your survival, which you have found did not solve the problem, but only caused it to personify more vividly outside of yourself than inside, causing you to lose track of the fact that you had these feelings within yourself originally in the void when you did not want life because it was too miserable without love present there.

That is the key thread to hold present during this movement, "without love present there." Move toward the light that will provide this love and not toward the light that will kill you so you do not have to have your miserable existence anymore. This has been a deeply imprinted pattern and needs to move to change.

The void, before you came into contact with My light, or any light, is where you need to look, and ultimately, go in your emotional movement to resolve your initial imprinting and your ambivalence about whether you want life and what that life is probably going to be like and can possibly be.

THE RONALOKAS ARRIVE ON EARTH

When the Ronalokas journeyed to Earth, they had to cross the physical manifestation of the gap. When they arrived on Earth, they were no longer able to move around as they had in the Heavens with the consciousness of the Heavens. They were now like children who had been spit out by a gap of heartlessness and left to fall to Earth. Falling down through the gap in terror had densified them so that when they landed on Earth, they were as physically dense as beings on Earth were at that time and even more dense, because they did not have the presence of My light there with them and were experiencing the compression that resulted from this. The Ronalokas hated their experience of falling in the gap and feared ever having to repeat it. Many have equated it with their birth and death experiences.

The Ronalokas landed in a heap, feeling mangled, pushed together and struggling with the compression that had caused them to lose consciousness. Regaining consciousness for them meant direct emotional movement. Amidst gasping for breath and choking sounds, there began to be squalling, flailing and writhing. They were moving into quite an ascending racket until some among them started screaming even louder with sounds that frightened the others and made them feel they were supposed to stop this squalling, or they were going to get smacked, whereupon emotion began to subside and more squirming and writhing resulted.

They looked like a squalling mass of golden, flailing arms and legs as they were watched by a presence in the nearby woods. This presence was the mother on Earth who had been drawn by their light falling through the skies. At first, she had hoped it was My light, but as she saw the light was more golden and then saw it darkening as it came closer, she knew it was not My light, but feared that the rest of the Mother was returning to Earth to give her a problem. As she stared at this mass of flailing arms and legs, she couldn't understand how the rest of the Mother could have come to take on such a form or how it could profit Her to do so.

"Just like Her, really, though," she said to herself, "never could get any agreement or direction within Herself."

She looked more closely then to see what might happen as a result of this presence on Earth and saw that it was a mass of spirits, and like fish swarming out of their egg nest, trying to swim apparently. She didn't like them much. They didn't look like any spirits she knew, and her feeling was to move away from them and let them flounder.

"Why not," she told herself, "I'm being left to flounder!"

With that she gathered herself and left in a huff, moving away through the woods toward her chambers where she felt she could ruminate on the situation in private and divine in her secret ways what this meant. This did not portend good and on her way, she pondered it. Was this somehow the rest of the Mother? If they were spirits, had they found their own way to Earth without My knowledge, or had I sent them to her for some reason? Was I trying to say something to her with this? Was I now going to send discarded spirits to Earth to the mother I had discarded there also? She did not want to mother them. Mothering wasn't what she wanted to be doing anywhere near as much as having sex.

She was chewing furiously on these questions, trying not to rage, but by the time she got to her chambers, she could not resist shrieking several times, which caused the vines to put her in immediate bondage and hold her there until she settled down.

"You must have raped me in my sleep, to have all of these children come forth without my participation," she screamed at Me as though she might now be required to take care of them against her Will. "The faeries are enough trouble, and now these!"

She bared her teeth and screamed several times with a sound that penetrated all the way to the Ronalokas. They felt it as hair standing on end and weren't sure what it meant. Some felt excited by the sound of it, others feared it, but all felt there was a Mother presence nearby who had pulled away to scream instead of coming to them. Some blamed the Mother for this, others feared they must be terrible or terrible looking, while some found the sounds exciting to them.

In that moment, the Ronalokas were run in upon by the satyrs who had also been watching them from the woods, and whose large penises had grown hard in response to the Ronalokas' writhing. They grabbed the Ronalokas and began sexually penetrating them in any orifice they found there, without differentiating even between one Ronaloka and another. They even stepped on some with their hooves in their lust for new and untried orifices. Seeking greater and different orgasms than they had had already, they were fiercely competitive, not caring what the Ronalokas experienced here.

The Ronalokas were very little spirits compared to these satyrs and did not much like this experience. They began trying to roll away from the mass that was being attacked in the center only to find themselves scooped up at the edges by the grabbing arms and twisted smiles of other satyrs and sexually abused more. The more the Ronalokas screamed, the more excited some of the satyrs became and the more furiously they thrust with their penises.

Many of the Ronalokas died right there begging the Heavens to take them back, but I could not hear them above the ruckus and did not care to listen closely because it reminded Me of something I did not want to hear. Other Ronalokas thought that to live, they were going to have to please the satyrs. Some thought their sounds had drawn the satyrs and that to please them, they were going to

60

have to make a lot of noise. Other Ronalokas thought that they must be quiet to please the satyrs or to make them go away, and pressured themselves into silence.

The satyrs grabbed at the Ronalokas, moving among them rather quickly, picking and choosing until they found the ones who were making just the right sounds to excite them into repeated orgasms. The satyrs did not let go of these Ronalokas easily. Instead, they threw them up onto their backs and ran off with them.

The rest of the Ronalokas were terrified when they saw this happen, but there was nothing they could do about it. At least the satyrs were gone then, but the Ronalokas who were left felt this as survivors' guilt and as a power loss.

The Ronalokas who were left felt like infants born onto an Earth they did not know or understand. They longed for the Heavens now as a sort of dream-like place to relieve them of the pains of Earth, not remembering the pains they had complained of in the Heavens. They wiggled and writhed until they realized this might have caused them to get attacked, and then suppressed themselves into trying to learn how they could move around on Earth in ways that could take care of their needs in more subdued ways.

To get out of the open and find ways to take cover and hide were their most pressing feelings of need, and they began to concentrate their energies on trying to roll, crawl and stand. It was impossible for them to feel like they could fly or soar now; they felt too heavy-hearted from the experiences they had already had to even remember this as a real experience. Their feelings about their survival needs rolled them underneath the nearby leaves, gravitating toward the roots of the friendly feeling trees. They loved the trees immediately, and the trees gave them a parental feeling in return. The Ronalokas felt cradled at last in the soft mosses growing there, and held by the loving arms of their curving roots. Exhausted, they fell asleep and recovered somewhat from their terrible experience of having journeyed to Earth without My help.

They had never noticed what a problem they were going to have without My light there with them until they left it and fell to Earth without it. They prayed ardently right there that My light would notice this and come after them and have never stopped praying for this to this day, either, while the rage polarized Ronalokas have yet to show they have any feeling for Me at all other than blame.

61

The rage polarized Ronalokas, meanwhile, were the ones who had been carried off by the satyrs to party and have more sex. The satyrs looked upon them as little buddies who did not complain. "Tasty little tidbits," the satryrs were calling them, while letting them know they were not big like the satyrs, or important like they were either.

These Ronalokas wanted to try to prove themselves to the satyrs immediately as being both big and important, so they stuffed down their feelings of pain in response to the sex they had had with the satyrs and began to act bigger than they really felt and bigger than they really were, emphasizing enjoyment of sex of any sort over and above any other feelings that were there. The rage polarized Ronalokas have not stopped doing this to this day either, and anywhere you find these Ronalokas acting big and strutting their stuff, there is still a satyr behind them, somewhere, directing their activities and controlling them.

The rage polarized Ronalokas could not move around very well on their own either, and did not want to try to learn in the presence of the satyrs because they did not want them to know they did not already know how. They moved around as little as possible trying not to show this, and pretended they were making the satyrs carry them upon their backs as though it was the most fun they had ever had and their conveyance of choice. They have never let on since then that they are not sure of how to move around on their own. They have never let themselves have baby–hoods or childhoods, instead, being born into situations where they have had to behave as though they are grown up immediately and have prided themselves on being able to do this.

Meanwhile, the Ronalokas hidden beneath the trees awoke to hearing the partying of the satyrs and feared they were going to be found again. They felt they had to have better cover. They tried to sink into the green around them as much as possible and to get as far in under the tree roots as they could burrow. They liked the feeling of the brown earth and wriggled in it to cover their golden glow as much as possible. They held their breath and listened to their hearts beat in fear, wondering what was going to happen next.

They did not have long to wonder because the satyrs did start finding them again in spite of their efforts, and once the satyrs found where they were hiding, they began rolling under the trees, drunk, feeling around for the Ronalokas and trying to coax them to come out as though it was some sort of game or as if they were going to parent them, but then having sex with them instead, often in the presence of rage polarized Ronalokas who watched it impassively, without doing anything to interfere or stop it. The Ronalokas who were being found in their hiding places did not like this at all and made themselves roll up into little balls and hide even more. They did not like the idea of unfolding into this world if it meant coming into the hands of these satyrs.

They felt themselves becoming more and more tree-like and elfin the more they hid themselves in friendly trees. The trees felt like strong, but passive fathers to them who did not move to defend or protect them other than passively, or teach them how to help themselves other than sometimes telling them something in their dreams or whispering occasionally to them if they were quiet during the day. Sentient beings they seemed to be, and more interested in that than anything else. Even though they showed great character in their outward forms, the trees did not seem to care to develop it into any other outward expression as the Ronalokas wanted to have them do.

"Maybe we shouldn't express so much either," the Ronalokas began to say to themselves.

These elfin Ronalokas tried to stay as still as possible and become as much like the trees as possible, but they could not stay this way for very long. They needed to move to feel good, and so they had to roll out from their hiding places often to stretch themselves. They began to play amongst the roots and low growing leaves at the base of the trees and found out from doing this that they could move about and be even safer because they could not be found and grabbed so easily and unawares. Sleeping was still a problem for them, though, because they needed to sleep now and did not feel safe enough when they did, especially when partying satyrs were nearby. It made them feel like locking themselves as far away as possible from these events, and never letting themselves be felt as partying spirits at all.

These Ronalokas were the grief and fear polarized, true, but they were also gay and happy little spirits when not pressured into these feelings by unpleasant events. Only amongst themselves did they show this now because of how unfortunately events had unfolded themselves around them. They had felt there were fear and grief triggers everywhere they had looked in the Heavens and they were not happy with what they saw in Pangea either. They moved inward more than anything else there and tried to call out to My light and to the Father of Manifestation for help.

63

The Father of Manifestation had heard the Ronalokas' urgent call when they first landed on Earth but had not responded because He was busy with other things. Their persistent call made Him feel that the Mother was not helping them, which angered Him. He took wing in the Heavens upon the furious feeling that they had been badly treated and that He wanted to pound on whoever had done this or had allowed it to happen.

He blamed the Mother already and was screaming at Her as he flew down through the Heavens, throwing punches as He went and growing hooves, not just on two, but on all four extremities in response to His desire to pound and kick Her. His rainbow arched angrily over Him or it wouldn't even have been known He was the Father of Manifestation because He had become a horse, with a horsehead's desire to bite. His hair had become a long streaming mane and tail. A white and shining Pegasus when He left the Heavens but growing darker and darker as He flew, He was black when He reached Earth with pounding and sparking hooves and streaming mane and tail of flame and sparks. Ready to attack the Mother, He was drawn right to her presence on Earth.

Meanwhile, the mother on Earth had gone to the fire seas, not being able to move the rage in her chambers that she felt about recent developments. She did not know who these new spirits were and had not had time to divine their origins. She wondered about where the rest of the Mother was, what was happening to Her and why she had not heard from Her, either, in so long, but she was also not looking forward to having to see and face Her again. What if She had really learned to rage by this time? And these new arrivals! What was she supposed to do with them, kowtow to them in case they were the Mother, or mother them like they were her children? She hardly thought so on either count!

She was beginning to dismiss the idea that they were the Mother because they had not demonstrated the power She had had, but the idea of mothering them was bringing up all of her mothering issues again and how much she had not really liked it because it interfered with her own time. She decided the best policy was to do as the reptile mother in her wanted to do; leave them hatching from their eggs and let them make it or not according to whether they could or not.

She was seething and raging with all of this in the fire seas when she suddenly heard herself being called to come forth by a furious pounding of hooves, At first, she feared it was the rest of the Mother, but then she felt it was the Father of Manifestation. She felt Him like thunder on the surface of the Earth and saw that He wanted to pound her now too.

Her rage really came forth then! Was He here for revenge or to demand that she mother these Goldlight babies or to tell her they were the rest of the Mother and make her align with this new form and take orders from it again? Never! Not anymore, not now that she had tasted her own power, her own ways and her own sense of herself!

She flew into her dragon form naturally in response to her rage now, and before she knew it, had flown up out of an erupting volcano of raging, hot lava that was spewing smoke and heat all the way to My light. She was screaming and screeching horribly about everything on her mind that I would not listen to, and I did not listen then either. I withdrew and shut Myself off from this as much as I possibly could.

The Father of Manifestation, on the other hand, pounded her furiously with His hooves, but He had not reckoned on the dragon form she had invented. He pounded her as furiously as He could, and even thrust at her underside with a horn that suddenly sprang, long and strong, from the middle of His head, but she bested Him quickly by grabbing Him with her long claws, scorching Him with her fiery breath, lashing at His still shining white wings beating in reflection of His intense emotion and ripping them off, blasting the rainbow arching over Him and dashing Him to the Earth in the path of the hot lava flowing beneath her feet.

The Father of Manifestation lay as still as death. I feared He was lost for sure. When He did finally move, He had terrible pain. He crawled ever so slowly to the embankment of where she had thrown Him and I knew I had to rush to His aid and I did as quickly as possible. She had given Him what was meant for Me, and I lost no time in helping Him recover from it. My light felt it had to have His help, no matter what, and now was not the time to question Our alliance.

I feared she would give Me the same blast she had given Him, and so I lifted Him off of Earth as quickly as possible and healed Him in My light. As soon as He was recovered enough to think of it, He told Me that He must return to Earth as soon as possible and that He felt urgent about it because the Ronalokas needed His help.

"But what about all of the other spirits here in the Heavens who need Your help?" I asked Him.

I bade Him look at what had really happened there, and He saw that as soon as He had gotten to Earth, centaurs had leaped from Him and hit the ground running to both pound on the satyrs and run toward the Ronalokas to give them help. I asked Him if this couldn't help stave off His urgent desire to return to Earth. I feared for His safety there and told Him so, but He remained as adamant about having to help the Ronalokas as I had felt just earlier about having to help Him, and so I let Him go with My blessing of sorts, mixed though it was because of My feelings then. He still blamed the Mother, but did not feel like He wanted to confront Her again in the same way. This time when He returned to Earth, He returned in the form of a satyr, and left His rainbow in the Heavens, hoping the mother on Earth would not recognize Him this time.

Then, We did not know who the real Mother was, or where She was, for that matter. The Father of Manifestation thought He had lost Her to the domination of the mother on Earth or that she somehow had control of Her. He also thought They might be all together there and against Him. He was determined to fight down this new order of command in the Mother and regain control of Earth Himself, but He thought He had better be more sneaky now and find out more of what was going on. He entered into intrigue of His own sort then, spying and attempting to find out what was really going on while trying not to let it be known that He was attempting to find out anything at all. He began trying to look like the other satyrs as much as possible and behaved like them as much as possible also. He was afraid even to let a difference in Him be felt by any who might betray His presence to the mother on Earth or the others in her growing court, which He viewed as an enemy camp that would try not to let Him find out what was really going on if His presence on Earth were to be found out. His presence did not remain secret for long, however.

He did not go much to the court of the Faerie Queen because close scrutiny was not something to which He dared subject Himself, and also because He had already heard tales of the Faerie Queen scorching beings who disagreed with her with a fiery breath she claimed to know nothing about.

Meanwhile, the mother on Earth's reputation as the Fire Dragon had grown into legendary proportions by leaps and bounds. The rage polarized Ronalokas feared but also respected and honored her Fire Dragon form as the powerful Mother they wanted to have instead of the wimpy, complaining Mother they had known in the past. They now even thought that the complaining Mother had been the Mother presence that had withdrawn from them when they first appeared on Earth and that the rage shrieks that had excited them were the Fire Dragon mother's objection to this Mother.

"She would have come to us if she could have," they told themselves, "but she had business with the Father," they said, laughing as though they knew that what this had been about was sex. They were not moved to think that it might have been about her not mothering the children the way He wanted them mothered or keeping the house the way He wanted it kept.

They had viewed this battle from the ground, having gone riding upon the backs of the satyrs in search of the mother on Earth whom they wanted to meet to see if she was the mother they had been searching for for so long. When they felt this clash of the Fire Dragon and the Father of Manifestation in deadly battle, they had felt a rush of excitement strangely mixed with sexual excitation and assumed that fighting was a part of Their sexual relationship. Orgasmic energy was in the air as both of Them were so sexually frustrated that They were having orgasms upon touching in battle, ignited by the movement in Their rage even though They were not openly moving to make love.

The rage polarized Ronalokas loved the thrill of this great battle mixed with sexual excitation and used it as a great fantasy to enhance the intensity in their own sexual activities in compensation for the actual pain they felt there, and growing numbness too, I might add, since pain is followed by loss of vibration of essence after awhile.

The satyrs, too, talked animatedly about the sexual excitement they had felt there, relishing the defeat of the Father of Manifestation and strutting proudly in their claims that they could not be defeated similarly. With mouths drooling and penises dribbling, they talked lasciviously about what they'd like to do sexually to the Fire Dragon and how they'd like to subdue her without ever letting on they had been scorched and sent howling through the woods by what they now felt must have been her. There were only beasts left running and howling at the moon to tell these tales, and they could not talk the way the satyrs had left them.

When the mother on Earth heard this chatter in her court, and the gossip forerunning it about the satyrs' braggadocio and the Ronalokas' new-found respect, she could not resist receiving the Ronalokas to find out how powerful they were, and to hear herself acclaimed in her presence. She also could not resist calling the satyrs, too, to set them straight on how powerful they were not. She

67

was having major trouble now resisting revealing herself as the Fire Dragon because she wanted to claim all of the power and glory being awarded to her in this form.

She rose above the satyrs and scorched them with her fiery breath telling them how she was going to subdue them and not the other way around without seeming to realize how much she had revealed about herself there. The satyrs took note of this without letting on they had noticed it, just moving back and acting like they were appropriately afraid. They did not know fear, though, so rage polarized were they. Instead, they only viewed it as information they had needed about the mother on Earth and where she was going when they had found her chambers empty, as they had, without mentioning this to her.

They began to talk now about finding the Fire Dragon in her lair and subduing her there. This frightened the mother on Earth somewhat about what might happen to her if she got herself trapped there, but not much. She felt all-powerful in that moment and did not foresee how she could possibly get trapped in the fire seas which would undoubtedly sear them all out of existence before they could even get close. What she forgot about was the satyrs' own manifesting power and the power they could have as a group alliance.

As she sat there in that moment, all she realized was that she was holding court and receiving those she chose to receive. Her court had grown beyond a few faeries now, having added on some number of Ronalokas, some others who had also fallen to Earth already and the satyrs, whom she felt she was now turning the tables on and was only going to have to receive when she wanted to, and bestow her sexual favors upon only when she felt like it, and maybe even be able to teach what lovemaking was supposed to be all about in return for receiving any of her sexual favors at all.

In response to these pictures, which the satyrs saw forming all around her, they formed their own plan, which was to trap her in her dragon form and put an end to her, but not as the Faerie Queen, oh, no, that would not do! As the Faerie Queen she could call all she wanted to now to the Fire Dragon to rescue her while they made her suffer their so very repugnant sexual abuses, and they would not put an end to her there because they knew now that as long as they had her there, the Fire Dragon was not going to come and rescue her.

They gave her trouble as much as possible from then on in her Faerie Queen form, never letting on they knew the rest of her story.

They baited her into revealing herself more and more in her court and never let on they noticed it at all, except to back off in a pretense of fear whenever her fiery breath began to present itself. And what a dramatic pretense of fear it was! They pretended to give her exactly the form of respect and submission she was demanding while making a mockery of her outside the court, dancing and singing in the woods at night with a new gusto and glee for music that was for the purpose of letting everyone else know they weren't scared of her a bit. Oh, no, it wouldn't do to get rid of her as the Faerie Queen! That wouldn't look brave or strong or valiant, conquering, subduing or any of the other qualities they wanted to earn for their own reputations here, of dominating, controlling or even getting rid of a mother who was a threat to their power position instead of behaving the way they wanted her to and the way she was supposed to. How much better to be victorious over her as the Fire Dragon!

"If she learns to behave right, we might let her stay in Pan," they snickered and snorted and laughed gleefully to one another as they danced in the moonlight, throwing more of their own brews and concoctions down their throats than made them look smart, powerful or even like a threat to Me; or so I would have liked to have thought. I had an uneasy feeling about all of these developments in Pan and didn't like it that My key players were out of the power positions, leaving Me no forms in which I could be present in Pangea with any particularly strong presence.

The satyrs' new found restoration of interest in music was largely being rekindled by the rage polarized Ronalokas who were making a lot of music in Pan already. To the satyrs, this music did not represent the sounds of the music they so much hated as reminding them of the Heavens. This music sounded like something rebellious and new and to their own liking. They could even tell the Ronalokas to leave off with parts of the music they didn't like and to give them more of the parts that were more to their liking. What they liked sounded raucous and sexually driven to Me; sexually unsatisfied, in fact, and their laughter, abrasive.

The satyrs were partying more and more loudly in the woods at night and running through the woods on drunken rampages in their insatiable quests for sex, looking for frightened and hidden Ronalokas by stirring up the peaceful grasses, ferns and mossy areas around the trees and clutching at things that glowed in the dark. The satyrs had discovered that making them express fear while they were being raped made the satyrs feel not only excited, but powerful over them, which was what these satyrs needed already, in a ritualistic sort of way of repetition to keep their own fear controlled and at bay by feeling others had more and they could make them express it for them somehow. When they were not rampaging, they were boasting and telling stories about their plans to find the entrances to the fire seas and search all of its caves, caverns and passageways, and even the fire seas, if necessary, until they found the Fire Dragon and made her power theirs, first by gaining her sexual submission and then by taking her form.

Their plans worried the rage polarized Ronalokas who now thought the mother who had the power they wanted the Mother to have might be bested by these satyrs, especially if they worked as a team. They felt they had lost some of their feelings of dependence upon these satyrs, having done some growing up of their own, and they now began making some plans of their own to protect the Fire Dragon. These Ronalokas also knew the Faerie Queen was the Fire Dragon, even though the satyrs never let on, and these Ronalokas never let on to the satyrs that they knew what they were really up to, either.

What went on there was a parody of the Heavens and the intrigue and denials going on there, which were apparently obvious to them, but I did not understand its denials and twists at the time and did not see Myself yet as they saw Me then, so I had no real idea of where all of this was coming from. I thought I had a major outward problem on My hands having to do with the rebellion on Earth toward all of My limits and edicts on sexuality, although it was that too.

The rage polarized Ronalokas moved to a position of protection, honor and respect for the Fire Dragon as their symbol of the Mother they wanted to have, and took this as honor, respect and protection toward themselves also, while the satyrs did not feel they had anything to fear from these Ronalokas, still viewing them only as their allies and not knowing what a group could do there either.

THE RAINBOW SPIRITS FALL TO EARTH

Now it happened that in the Heavens, the Will Polarity of the Rainbow Spirits had begun falling down and away from My light also. They were having trouble as the only Will Polarity still present there and had moved out toward the edge of My light hoping it would feel better there than to be in the midst of a Spirit

70

Polarity they did not feel had acceptance for them either. And, like the Ronalokas, they really could not do other than move out from My light because of the magnetic draw from the rest of the Will Polarity. From there, they moved to clump together again as they had at their emergence, and I thought this meant they did not have openness to receive My light. It certainly felt that way when I could not approach them anymore, and soon I could not.

"Yet another group abandoning Me to go to the Mother, " I thought. "What is Her attraction that My light does not have?"

Of course, My look at that was short at the time, preferring to say She had evil intent and was drawing them to Her whether they wanted to come or not.

I made My appeal to the Rainbow Spirits and they did not listen either. They were falling already and there was nothing they could do to stop it, or My light either. I did not know what was happening to the Will Polarity, but I preferred to say they could not vibrate at My speed or needed to go have experiences elsewhere than to see that I was not receiving the Will.

I did not gap consciously, and I want you to remember that, in order to have perspective on why I did as I did in those times. I would also like you to notice that those who are not yet ready to see that they are involved in My gap with Me will still see themselves and My light as only loving and see all the rest of what I am telling now as not true or as the problems of someone or something else, not them, and not the "true God" whose image they hold in place of My actual light. I do have responsibility for what took place in My gap and this cannot be shrugged off as the "doings" of someone else.

The Rainbow Spirits fell down through the gap also, and also without much love present in the gap for them, but their journey was less harrowing than the Ronalokas' because they had more of My light present with them, which meant a little less density in their experience than the Ronalokas. Therefore, the Rainbow Spirits arrived on Earth a little more conscious and a little less damaged than the Ronalokas, except for Orange and Red, which had a terrible time getting through the gap because of their lack of light and the unloving presence in the light they did have. This unloving light beat them up the entire way, just as it had the Ronalokas, telling them it was their fault they were falling and that their terror was just the punishment they deserved for whatever reasons their imprinting said they deserved it.

The Rainbow Spirits arrived somewhat less damaged than the

Ronalokas because the Ronalokas had even less loving light to go on than they did, but it is still a major problem to recover from what has happened to them from their subconscious imprinting. The Rainbow Spirits passed out, too, and did not hear consciously all that was said to them by unloving light in the gap, but it penetrated them, nonetheless, lodging with the original imprinting as re-imprinting, just as with the Ronalokas. All can identify with "the Fall," here in mythology, but no one has fully understood yet how or why it happened.

When the Rainbow Spirits arrived on Earth, the satyrs tried to repeat the scenario they had had with the Ronalokas. They ran in upon them as soon as they landed and tried to rape them, but the centaurs also ran in and fought them furiously. The Rainbow Spirits felt they had landed in the midst of a battlefield and lost no time in rolling out of the way as quickly as they could. Many got trapped there, though, unable to move between the battling forces and had to cower in the midst of it until it was over. Some of them received further damage from the hooves, even of the centaurs, as the battle raged around them, with the satyrs crying out they were theirs to have if they wanted them and the centaurs answering that they were going to have to fight the centaurs down first if they were going to take them. Even though the Rainbow Spirits had the centaurs to defend them, many still feared the satyrs could gain power over them.

The Father of Manifestation appeared on the scene then. Bigger than the rest of the satyrs, He was an immediately obvious presence. This frightened Him into shrinking back until He could go forth smaller, which made Him gnarlier and more twisted, but this He did. He twisted Himself into a smaller satyr and joined the fracas as another one battling. He fought furiously against the satyrs He hated and not on their side, and this they noticed also, but said nothing at the time other than to attack Him even more furiously than the others and with the concentrated efforts of several of them at once. The Father of Manifestation's reduced size impeded His physical ability, but He directed the force of His ability to manifest as much as He possibly could toward fighting the other satyrs off.

The satyrs did run off, but before they did, they grabbed some of the Rainbow Spirits, the rage polarized again, as though they were magnetized exclusively to them as allies they needed to take into their camp. The centaurs were left to lick their wounds and help the Rainbow Spirits as much as they possibly could while the

Father of Manifestation, along with a few trusted centaur allies, and now also some satyr fragments who were allies of His that had jumped out in His effort to get small quickly, chased the satyrs through the woods. They wanted to see where they were going and why they had to have Rainbow Spirits, too, in addition to the Ronalokas they already had.

They found the satyrs hiding in dense thickets, but behaving as though they didn't know they had been followed. They were licking their wounds also, but not admitting to any pain; only bragging loudly to one another about how they had "kicked ass" in the battle, and in this case, it was literal since most of the blows were landed by hooves on the lower quarters while arms were grappling for the Rainbow Spirits they wanted to take.

The Rainbow Spirits felt pulled apart here as, indeed, they already had been in the Heavens. They feared the War in the Heavens had never stopped, and that they had somehow and unfortunately landed on the new battleground.

Most of the Rainbow Spirits wanted more than anything to find peace and crept to the most appealing possibility they saw, which was into the very large, fragrant and beautiful, hanging flowers of Pan, whose intense, glowing colors and gentle rocking in the breezes both drew them and reminded them of the early feelings of reverie many of them had experienced right at their emergence and even before that.

The Goldlight Green Rainbow Spirits chose leaves instead, but My light noticed it was because they all chose the colors that were glowing like they were and did the same thing the Ronalokas had done; tried to enfold themselves in a place of protection, comfort and nurturing. They sought to become less like they had been and more like the flowers and leaves by fitting themselves into them as if they were putting on clothes and draping their rooms in their selected colors. They wanted to look like flowers and leaves and not be noticed, and also enjoy the beauty of being surrounded by large flowers and feel themselves a part of them, but Orange and Red had a problem again because their colors of flowers drew the satyrs more than the other colors, or so they thought.

Unbeknownst to the Rainbow Spirits, the satyrs had already formed a habit of grabbing flowers, draining them of their nectar and tossing them aside as they ran through the woods with an abandon that was being passed off as playfulness, but was not sensitive to the experience anything else was having as a result.

The Rainbow Spirits were victimized by this, as were some of the Ronalokas who had also crept into flowers. Some were essence drained and their forms even sucked partially into the mouths of the satyrs who spat them out, looked to see what they had, grabbed them and ran off with them like hostages. Once the satyrs found Rainbow Spirits hidden in the flowers, they accelerated their grabbing and sucking of flower nectar as a means of searching for them instead of slackening off in respect for their presence there.

The Rainbow Spirits felt that they must seek greater safety, and first did this by creeping into the flowers in the middle of profusions of flowers hoping this would deter the satyrs from grabbing into where they were hidden. This was more satisfactory to them than being on the edge where they felt more vulnerable, and this worked for awhile as the satyrs did get tired and also intoxicated from searching so many empty flowers and did begin to search elsewhere, even seeming to give up their search at times to see if they could trick the Rainbow Spirits into coming out or get others to reveal their hiding places.

Thus, the Flower Faeries, as these Rainbow Spirits had become, in not suspecting all of this, felt they were able to have some time in which they dared to play. They played only amongst themselves at first, but then they discovered the Ronalokas who had some colors hiding in flowers also. After these Ronalokas were able to feel reasonably certain the Rainbow Spirits were not satyr spies, they led them to some of the other Ronalokas hiding at the base of the trees underneath them.

Then, they all began to play together and enjoy the beauty of nature in Pan, but at first, only when the satyrs were asleep during the day, after their all night parties. Even so, they still had problems, especially at night when they tried to close their flowers around them. This move was even more inviting to the satyrs who seemed to know just where they were hiding then, until it gave the flowers the idea they should all close at night in order to look less inviting to the satyrs. The satyrs still searched for the faeries and elves, but the lack of fragrance and glow to draw them caused them to look for other sources of nectar. They found grapes then.

The elfin Ronalokas acted like older brothers and sisters to the Rainbow Spirits in many ways, taking them in hand like the more newly arrived brother and sister faeries they were at that time, and showing them many things they had discovered in and about Pan, including more of the dangers they knew lurked behind the pretty face of the woods in which they dwelled. They still had fear most nights, but with the centaurs guarding them, they were much more safe than they had been when the Ronalokas had been there alone, before the centaurs came.

The faeries and elves who tried to dwell on the edges of things still had problems from time to time, though, and still tried to seek the protection of the middle of the flower profusions when they did. This caused clumping up again as anyone who moved inward put someone else on the edge. Sharing the risk was not an easy arrangement for them, and it caused competition and fights at times, but the guard of the centaurs was gradually able to calm them down enough to unfold a little more, and they began to open to one another's companionship at night.

Soon there began to be enfoldment in one another's loving arms at night, and then sighing and rocking of their own amongst the flowers, leaves and tree roots. Nectar sipping began to be accompanied by downright cries of passion, which gave the centaurs problems guarding the faeries and elves at times when they were drawing attention to themselves, or the centaurs could not always discern what was happening to them and who it was happening with, or whether they should intervene or not.

A few little pegasus's came forth in response to the centaurs' desires for mates then, and crept together with them at night, but since most of the centaurs did not have mates, they began to give themselves permission to look in upon the faeries and elves and then to join them as lovers and friends and not only as guardian-parents. This of course compounded the competition for the protection and status the centaurs represented as lovers and friends even more than in their role as guardian-parents and these relationships caused some of the centaurs to lapse on their guard duty at times.

At first, the faeries and elves only had sex with their own kind, but as they became less intoxicated by their own flowers and more enticed by the smells of others, and as the nectar sipping progressed, there was growing desire to taste other colors and smells. They began to creep from flower to flower themselves at night, sometimes frightening those who were not expecting them or who thought they were satyrs at first. Hidden away together, listening to the music swirling through the soft, warm night air of Pan and making their own too, I might add, they began to feel so deliciously sensual and caressed by their surroundings that they could not resist the expansion of vibration happening in them, and where it led them was to taste the nectars of other colors and then to snuggle up and encozy themselves with other colors.

The Yellow flower faeries tried first to go to Green, but found they really had more desire for Orange. Orange had desire for Yellow also, but not entirely out of love for Yellow. Some thought they wanted to make themselves less Orange and more Yellow, feeling it was not only possible, but safer. Red felt abandoned by Orange then as though Orange would not come toward the flower faeries there. This made Red feel like the least safe of all colors, and the most superior and irresistibly desirable too if the flip side of their position were to be admitted to. Red became insistent then that it should be in the middle, or the most heavily guarded, which others then pointed out made it even more obvious where they were all hidden. Red then said they were the most obvious already and that they did not like being told they could not have this protection when Orange was already turning itself more Yellow in an effort to feel safer.

This made a problem for the Green elves and faeries who then turned rather muddy looking when they wanted to be with Yellow and could not move Orange out of the way. After tasting the passion of Orange, Yellow did not like moving Orange out of the way whenever Green came along unless Yellow had a desire for the cool and calming comfort they had already known with Green. Green was making Yellow uncomfortable now because something in Green made the Yellow faeries and elves feel like Green wanted to claim superior knowing, or wanted to parent them or something. The Green faeries and elves did not see this. They saw themselves only as helping Yellow to become more Green, which equaled much safer given the problems with the satyrs.

The biggest problem, though, was when Green tried to go to Blue then to seek advice, nectar and partnership because the Blue faeries and elves acted uninvolved and unconcerned about what was going on in the bickering of the rest of the colors, as if it was their problem to work out and not Blue's.

The Blue faeries and elves did not want these problems interfering with their high vibration of receiving My light, which they believed they were recovering the ability to do. With the help of nectar sipping from their flowers, which they seemed to be rather jealously guarding, they were already moving along with the visions they had received to express them as art forms in Pan, and they were more interested in that than they were in anything else. The Blue faeries and elves had things to do, as though they had a mission and did not want to stop for silly problems, or bickering, or even for sex unless it was their own idea.

Purple then noticed Green approaching Blue for help and companionship and said they did not want Blue going that direction because Purple had Red in it and didn't want to be abandoned by Blue turning Greenish and leaving Purple Red enough to start having problems with the satyrs. Purple was no help at all here except to themselves by moving Green back and telling them their right place was next to Yellow and they should stay there. Indigo had presence there that said nothing since their hiding places had remained undiscovered.

This left Green feeling left out again even though Green felt some sort of feeling of having superior knowing if they could only be listened to. Green then felt it was the only color that had to stay among its own kind to feel received, except for a bit by Blue once in a while, on Blue's terms and rather formally like busy parents receiving children only half-heartedly and only occasionally.

Meanwhile, the warmth and cheerfulness of Yellow was missing from the lives of Green too much now, like sunshine missing in the depths of the woods, and Green developed something of a desire to smack at Orange for this, and at Yellow too, to make the Yellow faeries and elves feel like they needed the cooling and temperance of Green, at least from time to time.

Meanwhile, Orange was mingling its passion with Yellow more and more, muddying up Green's attempts to communicate, and this got the color that was made there associated with jealousy.

Red then announced that since it was the only color left that attracted the satyrs, Red should be given access to Blue and allowed to make more Purple. When Blue rejected this idea, Red began creeping there at night so much anyway that Blue began to feel it was being overwhelmed by Red and made into Purple. The Blue faeries and elves then invited Green to join them if Green wanted to lose its interest in Yellow and help Blue have more presence.

A GRAND OLD TIME IN THE WOODS
TAKES A WRONG FORK IN THE PATH

When the Father of Manifestation followed the satyrs and found their lairs, He also heard the sounds of the Rainbow Spirits and the Ronalokas they had there and moved to respond to them with loving intent to rescue them, until He felt Himself responding to these sounds with sexual excitation. These were all spirits He knew and loved. He then feared He was even more perverse than the rest of the satyrs because He responded to watching terrible things being done to others while they were having sex without being honest and coming forward to admit that He was excited by this.

He moved past this fear that He was perverse in favor of feelings He preferred to feel about Himself which told Him He could not rescue them with the few hands He had to help Him, especially if He could not count on those He was rescuing to help Him, or at least co-operate, which they might not do if they really were enjoying this. He might look like a panty-waist sexually, or worse, His erection might reveal what He was fearing about Himself. He told Himself that He needed to watch more and study the situation more first, not only to formulate a plan, but to be sure those spirits wanted to be rescued. He orgasmed here feeling shame about Himself and moved away through the woods, unsure of what His role was supposed to be anymore.

There was no place the spirits on Earth could go to get away from the satyrs who ran around Pan claiming it was their Earth and that they could do with it as they saw fit. Most of the spirits believed they just had to live with this, hide themselves as much as possible and do as little as possible to attract attention to themselves if they did not want to have run-ins with the satyrs.

Most of the spirits there felt they had to go along with the mood of Pan, which was being set by the satyrs as party, party. A lot of music was made there for sure, and a lot of it good, but there was also a lot of noise at night that made it hard for most of the spirits to sleep or even to enjoy inner quietude. There was some complaining about this, but there was also a major agreement among most of the spirits in Pan not to look at, or feel into, any of the inner realms or undercurrents the Mother of Everything had bothered them with so much by continually pointing them out in the Heavens, and which they had sought to escape by leaving the Heavens. This included "higher" consciousness, too, which imprinting told many was the source of their problems.

"Just let God handle it; all we need to do is party until He calls," is what many said, or believed if they did not say it. They wanted to party and party they did, but imprinting was running things in Pan more than anyone realized or wanted to realize at the time, and is still running it now, as I have said, and the more they partied, the more imprinting was stirred that they were going to draw a smack.

Many of the Rainbow Spirits in Pan thought the partying was

in honor of their arrival since they had had emergence parties. There were bands forming already in Pan; not only bands of spirits who felt bonded because of their emotional polarization and outlook, but also by color and around actual musical bands who liked playing music with one another more than with others. Musicians still wandered free, though, as much as they needed to to feel good about where they played, and music swirled through the woods at night on the air of excitement of the first major physical experience these spirits had had.

There were many wonderful parties in the woods when it seemed that everything was one and was swaying in response to the music of the musicians surrounded by their entourage of followers. The nearby birds, trees, flowers, animals and all the rest of nature were part of this feeling of Oneness with their contribution and response, and many began to feel they were finally living what they had wanted to come forth for, especially when they seemed to see even the stars in the Heavens respond.

Clumped together like this, the Spirits felt more safe and also more comfortable, although being on the edges was still a problem. Sleeping during the day and partying at night became a pattern in Pan, both of avoiding My light and of being more on guard and aware of the satyrs' rampages, as well as more protected by their group too.

Often, the satyrs' hooves could be heard above the music, or at least vibrationally felt in the resonant earth of Pan before the satyrs arrived, which gave groups a little warning. Since clumping together had not worked for those the satyrs grabbed on their rampaging rides through these groups, or for those they picked off around the edges or victimized if they decided to join the party for a little while, these groups had begun to scatter and hide when they heard the satyrs coming. Feeling more protected by knowing one another's presences were nearby was mutually supportive, but fear still ran high about being found by the satyrs, and sexual excitation, too, in those who did not dislike this as much as others did, or as they pretended to, and who found the game of having sex without their apparent agreement a mysteriously exciting and intriguing way to get around My edicts against free sex. Once again, though, there were major problems here for Orange and Red because the satyrs returned much more often to their groups than they did to the rest, and even took to sneaking up on them as much as they possibly could, having learned from those they did capture that they had felt them coming.

79

Many magical powers were recovered, although later lost again, as a result of the rising vibrational level of the spirits at these gatherings. Soaring in response to the music, for example, was a lost power recovered by many, and even flying for some, with only the memory of the music and the feelings they had in response being enough to give them the upliftment to soar at other times. Form change powers increased, and the manifesting of things for some also became more easily done. They would often go about at these parties changing themselves or pulling things out of thin air or out of their sleeves. Some did fantastic tricks with their new found physical bodies. Acrobatics, juggling, trapeze artistry and tricks and other circus feats, more fantastic than what survives today, were born there in learning what they could do with their physical bodies. Others danced wonderfully with each other and the animals, even soaring high into the air at times when they did, and even whirling in dance around the heat and the light rising from their campfires into the coolness of the night skies. Sex was free among the friendly spirits there, too, and many encounters took place in the air there also. All of this would have been just fine and wonderful too, were it not for the imprinting and all the denied undercurrents this created, especially of competition, fear and jealousy.

There was an air to these parties in Pan which many royal courts, festivals and fairs have tried to duplicate ever since, but never so successfully or magically as in these early days of Pan. The denied feelings of these memories and not being able to duplicate them caused many to say that magic was not real then either; but it was really happening, and it was based on a freedom and level of Will vibration that is not possible today without a lot of recovery work and a real moving off of the pressures that have been holding this down and out of existence. Magic was real, but the reflection of those who have said magic is not real is what needs to be looked at now.

The satyrs were a major problem around magic. At first, they had manifesting power over the mother on Earth, but lost more and more of it as time went on. They also had not gone to the fire seas to search out the Fire Dragon as they had so long, loudly and prominently bragged that they were going to do. They needed to move, and the more they were not moving, except sexually, the more they ran down in the magic department. At first, they tried to compensate for this by making excuses. When this did not look good, even to themselves anymore, they made up reasons why they were not responsible for their problem, including that the Fire Dragon had stolen their magic while they slept, and that they were going on a quest to get their magic back as soon as they figured out how to do this without the help of their magic. Later, they tried to use the magic of others to cover their own loss of it by forcing them to do magic tricks in their presence, claiming the performer of them was their puppet, and then claiming these tricks as their own. Sometimes they did this by claiming, seemingly affably, that they could have done the trick or used to be able to do the trick, but had lost interest in it, and then turning on whoever had done the trick and claiming that if they, the satyrs, had not gotten bored with it, the one who had this magic could not have stolen it.

The satyrs frightened many out of publicly showing that they had any magical powers or of even letting it be known that they did. The Satyrs were jealous and insecure about getting gnarlier and looking older over time and about losing power as though they were running down, but they did not admit it and did not move anything around this issue at all. Instead, they said they were just biding their time and not wasting their magic on silly little tricks because they were going to do a big piece of magic soon. That's all they would say, leaving many spirits frightened of what more horribleness the satyrs might be brewing up for Pangea if they were not lying again. The satyrs were trying to steal magic, but they also had more magic than they showed because it was not the power to do good anymore.

The rage polarized Ronalokas were not looking favorably upon the satyrs here either. They thought their magic excuses were showing signs of weakness they did not like to see. They saw the Fire Dragon more and more as the true power on Earth. They wanted this power for themselves, or at least to be allied with it, but they dared not be open about this because the satyrs still had control of them in many ways. The Ronalokas saw the rise of the power of the mother on Earth as bringing the demise of the satyrs and their control. These Ronalokas began to side with the mother on Earth more. They began to think in terms of protecting her and teaching the satyrs a lesson. They wanted to lure the satyrs into going after the Fire Dragon in the fire seas with their help, which the satyrs wanted but did not dare ask for as that would have been an admission of weakness on their part, and then trap the satyrs there.

The satyrs had grown dependent upon these Ronalokas in ways they did not like to mention or let on about. Instead, they grew abusive anytime anything that looked like power began to surface in the Ronalokas, insisting to them that they had no power and needed to realize it and simmer down before they got themselves put down.

This inflamed the seething rage of the Ronalokas, but they did not move to show this to the satyrs in any way that might get them put down. Instead, they began to bait the satyrs by saying that they were just picking on them because they were afraid to go to the fire seas and face any real threat or danger. This enraged the satyrs until they had some real fights amongst themselves that looked dangerous to life and limb. The Ronalokas arbitrated an apparent peace, though, by saying that if the satyrs were really serious, they had to move and not just talk about it anymore.

The satyrs had trapped themselves into having to face their own fear reflection, but they did not feel into that. Instead, they said they were going to move, but they were not ready yet. They needed more time because the web of intrigue by which they were going to trap the Fire Dragon was not completely woven into place yet, and that the Ronalokas did not know the all of it; no matter how smart they thought they were, they were not as smart or as powerful as the satyrs.

The Ronalokas backed down here because they were not sure about this and they were not ready themselves yet. They needed more time to be certain the mother on Earth was going to receive them into her presence and was not going to turn on them as the Fire Dragon who had turned on others already. They were responding to the satyrs stirring imprinting that was not favorable to the Mother here and did not understand their own shifts in loyalty from time to time.

THE COURT OF THE MOTHER ON EARTH

Boring as they all thought it was, they all began attending the court being held everyday by the mother on Earth in her own outer chambers, to see what they could learn. The mother had begun sitting there, surrounded by her faeries, and the satyrs began taking the Ronalokas there as a display of position and status with the mother on Earth that they knew the Ronalokas also wanted to have. The satyrs, however, were introducing them to the mother on Earth as their understudies, and children even. The Ronalokas did not like this any more than the little faeries liked it that the mother on Earth was referring to them as her children.

The satyrs approached the mother on Earth as if they were her favored original few amongst the now growing numbers of newcomers in the court, which used to consist of only themselves and the few faeries there were. Now that there were more spirits on Earth and many wanted to come to the court and take a look at the mother on Earth for themselves, they felt it was suddenly more impressive and important to have the position of status of having been there first, and presented themselves this way immediately upon arrival by demonstrating their familiarity with her, her ways and her court as a means of showing off to others the position they wanted to demonstrate that they held.

The mother did not like this at all, and seemed to enjoy moving past them at every opportunity as a means to incite them as though giving them the brush off and demeaning them in favor of seeing and meeting the new spirits they had brought with them, and about whom she was curious. This brought up a lot of sexual issues for the satyrs immediately who saw control of the mother as their means of power. They did not like it that the Ronalokas might gain favor with her, especially over them, but did not want to show publicly that they were affected by any of this, so they pretended not to notice what was happening there and played the role, instead, of always having played games of this sort with the mother; games of flirting with one another in an effort to make one another jealous, and implied heavily to the Ronalokas that they should not make anything of it or of the attentions the mother was bestowing upon them because she always behaved that way.

The Ronalokas, meanwhile, were not looking for sexual favors from the mother. They wanted a mother figure who had power, not a mother to have sex with, or a mother who was going to draw them into her sexual intrigues. They were confused, angry, hurt, insulted and enraged by this. They did not know how the satyrs could think that they had sex in mind with their mother. It did not occur to them that the satyrs always had sex in mind and nothing else because the Ronalokas had no experience with the satyrs beyond how the satyrs related to them. Now they began to feel they were nothing to the satyrs whenever the mother was around. This made them jealous of her which they did not want to feel. Some had feelings of hatred toward the mother which they did not want to feel because of the plans they had around the image of her they had held. They felt the mother was not living up to the image and not allowing them to have the place they wanted to have with her.

They wanted to feel that they had a mother who had power, but was not against them, and sexuality, that admired them but did not act outwardly in ways their imprinting said were inappropriate. They wanted to feel that their mother had sexuality toward her right mate and that they also could find right mate. They felt that the mother did not demonstrate to them how to find right place or right mate or how it was supposed to feel. Their dislike of her there was based on imprinting stirred by her open display of displaced sexual innuendoes toward them: Mother as lure was not right Mother. When they flattered her indirectly, talking about the Fire Dragon, and felt her sexual currents turn on, they did not like this coming toward them in this way, but their rage converted it this way: They did not need mothering or a right mate and could move freely sexually as the satyrs did. The problem arose when the female also moved freely, and if she did not, where was this free sex going to be found?

Even though they were flattering the mother on Earth for their own purposes, they had her imaged in their minds as their Mother and did not feel she was responding to them as her children. They could not understand it. How could a mother not even recognize her own children? It did not occur to them that they could not recognize their own mother either because this was the mother energy they had become fixed on in their original imprinting as powerful and going toward the Father unswerved.

When the Ronalokas saw how the satyrs behaved around the mother, they also did not want any sexual currents flowing between themselves and the mother because of what the satyrs might do in the way of taking revenge for this later. The satyrs had become quite cruel toward them, and if they did not like how the Ronalokas had behaved during the day, they often punished them at night while having sex with them. Sex between the satyrs and the Ronalokas was a mixture of pleasure and pain that the Ronalokas did not like but could not admit to entirely hating either because of their imprinted confusion of pain and pleasure.

They were being stirred into imprinting that told them why the satyrs might be wanting to get revenge on the mother. This threw them into their original imprinting confusion in which the unloving light had said the Mother was to blame, not the light. Survival needs then said: Might they not be able to use the mother's desire for revenge and the satyrs' desire for revenge to their advantage in a power play of their own here? And wouldn't it be justified in the face of all of the dishonesty, innuendo and undeclared intent going on all around them?

The Ronalokas felt all of these currents, but did not let themselves respond to them openly. They had great feelings inside themselves but did not like to make a public display of them and did not like it when other Ronalokas did either. They were imprinted that emotions were a private thing to be felt but not very openly expressed.

While imprinting said it was not right to seek to know more, desire to know more was sneaking around the side of it. The Father of Manifestation wanted to know more too. Looking in on the court without being noticed was a focus of His endeavors at the same time that the satyrs and the Ronalokas began attending the court of the mother on Earth, or the Faerie Queen as she now proclaimed herself to be.

He heard and saw the Ronalokas being introduced to the Faerie Queen by the satyrs as their friends, allies and even children. The mother on Earth jolted in her seat then. The Father of Manifestation wanted to rush in upon them to set them all straight, but held Himself back because He felt He needed to know more and did not want to reveal His presence. He wanted to see what the mother on Earth's response was going to be to this. When she did not move to recognize the Ronalokas as her children, He felt her jolt must have been in response to feeling His urge to rush forward and that He would have to be even more careful after this.

He knew also then that this mother presence was not allowing the Mother presence He had taken back to the Godhead to speak if She was even there at all, for surely, as He had known Her, She would not only have recognized the Ronalokas, but would have rushed to take them in Her arms. The fact that this mother did not infuriated Him all over again toward her, but He held Himself in check with the realization that she had not been present at their birth.

When He saw and heard the Ronalokas who had been presented to the Faerie Queen complimenting her, He could understand that and why they did not seem to recognize her as their Mother. When He saw and heard them flattering her as though they wanted to get next to her and have a position of acceptance in her court, even wanting her as their Mother, He could even understand that since the rest of the Mother presence was not being seen or felt on Earth. But when He saw and heard the Ronalokas' even greater flattery and adulation for the Fire Dragon, He felt threatened and angered by that. He felt that they did not

85

like Him anymore or feel loyal to Him anymore since it appeared that the Mother had defeated Him. He wished He had taken on another form then instead of underestimating her rage, and defeated her then instead of controlling His rage. He thought of doing it right then, but held Himself back again feeling it was not the right time or right situation and that He still needed to know more.

When He saw that she responded sexually to this flattery and adulation, He learned even more about her and did not like what he had learned. He also saw how much she wanted to come forward and claim the Fire Dragon form as her own. Even though her light behaved differently in the different forms, He could feel her presence in that form then and that form's presence in her. He could even see it, and He knew then that the Faerie Queen was also the Fire Dragon. What He did not understand was why she was resisting coming forward and claiming that form publicly.

He watched the satyrs acting like they greatly enjoyed baiting the Faerie Queen and tempting her to become a dragon in her court while acting as if they weren't doing this, or didn't know what they were doing or what was happening there or even notice it. At the same time, He saw and heard the Ronalokas wanting the mother on Earth to come forward as the Fire Dragon instead of the Faerie Queen. By the time He had heard and seen all of this, He did not know how to set anyone straight or who would listen.

The Father of Manifestation fell back then to do more research and observation and left the Faerie Queen to conduct her court for a while without His interference or presence. He was more interested in hanging out in the woods with His friends, making music, or so it seemed.

Meanwhile, court went on with the Ronalokas feeling themselves not wanting to respond to the Faerie Queen sexually, while feeling her responding to them sexually, while feeling themselves being put in the position of children by the satyrs, which would seem to be encouraging them to respond sexually to the little faeries as the daughters of the Faerie Queen, but which then seemed to threaten and anger the satyrs and anger and make jealous the Faerie Queen, which was moving the Ronalokas to a position of feeling confusion about what mate they could have that would be acceptable.

Rebelling, even if not openly, was their idea of solution here. Did they have any say in this or any power at all? Rage then began to move in them, but not as emotion, as action which took the form of feeling like they might like to flirt with the little faeries after all.

The satyrs then began flirting with the little faeries even more openly, as if in response to the Faerie Queen's treatment of them, not any threat of competition from the Ronalokas. The Faerie Queen acted like she didn't notice, the satyrs being too inconsequential and unimportant to her to care.

When the satyrs heard the Faerie Queen scream in one of her raging fits soon thereafter, "You little faeries are going to pay for this!" they took note of it.

They saw then that there were more ways than they had already planned to trap the Faerie Queen in the fire seas. If the little faeries did not like the price they were going to pay, they might want to get their revenge by helping the satyrs.

They provoked the mother even more then, not less, and secretly encouraged her to punish the faeries' response to them as not appropriately daughterly. When the faeries screamed that it was the satyrs who had seduced and even raped them first, the mother on Earth acted outraged to find out that sex was already going on there. She heavily denied the validity of all the charges the little faeries were making against the satyrs and did not listen to any of them.

The satyrs denied all of the charges heavily too, but not where the little faeries could hear them. In the presence of the little faeries, they had remained silent, even hanging their heads down toward their hooves which they dragged slowly back and forth in what looked to the faeries like an admission of guilt, but alone with the mother, they told her they had only flirted with the faeries to show her what they were up to behind her back and how the faeries had designs on her position by taking her place with them first.

The mother was furious at hearing this and felt she had to punish the little faeries then. She banished them all to their chambers and asked the satyrs to have the vines hold them there until further notice. Now the satyrs already knew how much the little faeries hated the vines, having used them already to hold the little faeries in the positions they wanted them to have, and since the satyrs controlled the vines, they felt sure that by the time they offered to free them of their restraints, the little faeries would be more than willing to help them by becoming their allies instead of the mother's.

They made their moves on the little faeries sexually first, and then when they offered them their freedom from restraint by the vines, they only offered it in exchange for certain services, otherwise, they could make it a lot worse for them than it already was, implying that the bondage of the vines could be much worse and for longer periods of time combined with certain sexual humiliations and the application of particular pain stimuli at the same time.

The little faeries felt they had no recourse but to comply. They had no feeling anymore that they could tell the mother about this at all. The satyrs told the faeries that they already had the mother's permission to punish them, and that since they weren't behaving like proper daughters at all, the satyrs could do with them as they wished, and perhaps it would teach them a lesson in what being the real mother was all about if they thought that's what they were.

The little faeries were horrified to think that this was going to turn out to be what having sex and being the mother was all about after having held onto the dream for so long that love was going to be found and was the purpose for having sex as they had always been taught. What were the satyrs going to want and what were they going to make them do? The little faeries lay in terror with this, confined to their own chambers until such time as the satyrs saw fit to have them go to work for them, having made sure it was long enough in bondage that they couldn't wait to be rescued and were willing to do just about anything just to be free for awhile. The little faeries wondered why no one rescued them, why the Fire Dragon didn't care about them and where the rest of the Mother was.

When the faeries flew forth after that, it was not with the apparent freedom their ability to fly made it appear that they had, but on the leash of the satyrs. They pretended by day to still be the light little faeries they had been and not do anything to get punished by the satyrs or the Faerie Queen, who had no idea really how far the satyrs had taken this with the faeries, so that they would be released to fly freely at night and go to the parties they wanted to go to. These faeries tried very hard to be good because they were not unloving in essence, but they feared at a very deep level of subconscious imprinting that they were evil, and they were about to seem to prove it to themselves there in Pan.

Under the pressures that were upon them, they began passing information back and forth among the various intrigues and plots of revenge according to what suited their needs and desires for revenge at the time. Held rage did this from a feeling that if no one cared about them, they had to be out for themselves.

Meanwhile, the Ronalokas could feel there was a problem

with the little faeries and could see that their light was not as bright as it used to be. They tried to get the faeries to talk to them, but the faeries were afraid to say anything other than that things were fine. They did not want to admit to these Ronalokas, who were also having sex with the satyrs, that they were having any problems with the satyrs they couldn't handle on their own. The faeries did not know where the loyalties of these Ronalokas really lay any more than the Ronalokas knew where the loyalties of the little faeries really lay, or their own, for that matter, but the Ronalokas felt that the faeries needed help and they wanted to reach out to help them somehow.

The faeries were afraid to tell the Ronalokas anything unless they saw them as allies who had power to help them because they did not know what they might tell the satyrs, but the Ronalokas told the faeries some things about their admiration for the powers of the mother on Earth and their need and desire to protect her that the faeries now felt they were going to have to tell the satyrs if the satyrs pressured them for information. The next time the faeries sought release from the satyrs' vines and the satyrs demanded something in exchange for this, the faeries told them the Ronalokas saw the satyrs as a threat to the Fire Dragon and felt a need to protect her there.

The satyrs laughed uproariously at this and derided the faeries for this information and said it was really no information at all. Instead of releasing them, they left the little faeries longer in the confines of the vines saying it was nothing they didn't already know, but the reason they really left them there was to see if they knew more. The satyrs had taken this in, and it had given them pause enough that the faeries noticed this did have an impact on them. The faeries began to take note of what impacted the satyrs and began to put together their own plot to get free of them. The faeries took this to mean that the satyrs and the Ronalokas had a schism there that they had not known about before and neither had the satyrs. The faeries then did not want to say anything more to damage the Ronalokas' position there, but the damage had already been done. Now the satyrs knew they had said too much in front of the Ronalokas about their plans for the mother on Earth.

The faeries thought the satyrs viewed the Ronalokas as having some power, and began to trust the Ronalokas more themselves. The satyrs saw a view the Ronalokas held that they had not really noticed before and wanted to play with them all, the mother on Earth, the little faeries and the Ronalokas for even thinking they had power at all.

Ah, what a tangled web denied heart presence has left Us all to weave! The satyrs knew they had to punish the Ronalokas for what they considered to be a disloyal position and for what they already considered to be a power play on their part. They also began to watch more closely whenever the Ronalokas interacted with the mother on Earth to see how she responded to them and they to her.

The satyrs thought the Ronalokas wanted to have sex with the mother on Earth, have her all to themselves and take their positions there. They did not understand that the Ronalokas had feelings the Fire Dragon was their mother and wanted to guard and honor her as this, but were having problems moving with this because the unloving light in them told them she had to behave in a certain way to be worthy of this, and she was not behaving in this way all of the time.

Meanwhile, the Father of Manifestation had decided to go to the fire seas. He wanted to know what the mother on Earth did there and if there was some source there from which she was deriving more power than He remembered her having before. He wondered if it was the rest of the Mother and if the mother on Earth had Her locked away in a cavern someplace there and was using Her power without letting Her prevail anymore. He was determined to search the fire seas and find out if this was true or not, but the heat deterred Him. He wondered why the mother on Earth had chosen such a place for her headquarters until He remembered how much she had hated the rain drowning the rest of the Mother in terror. He saw that she was determined not to let that happen again. That He did not like it made Him feel that she did not like Him and was trying to keep Him out with her rage.

The Father of Manifestation had heard what the mother on Earth had said before He took the rest of the Mother back to the Godhead, and now He wanted to find out if she had kept Her word and was not letting the rest of the Mother speak or prevail over her anymore, and if so, how was she acting this out?

If the rest of the Mother was trapped there, He wanted to get Her out, at least as a balance for the rest. He was receiving pictures in His inner eye that made Him think that She was trapped in some place like the fire seas, and along with the feeling that She and the mother on Earth were not partners anymore, feelings that She was being horribly abused. If the mother on Earth was doing this in order to subjugate Her and use Her power somehow, He wanted to stop this.

He did not want to risk being seen by the mother on Earth entering the fire seas in the form He was in. He decided He would sit and play His pipes as though He was not doing anything at all and send the rest of Himself, as He had done to enter her court, but this time to investigate the fire seas in the form of permeating the natural Earth with His consciousness.

He snaked and sinewed Himself slowly inside, carefully watching for anything He should notice along the way. He found many caverns there He had not known about before, but careful investigation showed Him only that they were lined with sparkling jewels. The glow from the fire seas was unbearably hot, but most of all, He could not stand the feeling of compression that He had there. The satyr playing His pipes began to sweat until His hair was all wet, but still He sat there playing His pipes while the rest of Him carefully looked in and around the caverns and caves of the fire seas.

He found the mother on Earth already there when He found the main fire sea, and she startled, just as though He had come in person. She looked around suspiciously and guardedly, just as though there was an invasive presence there she expected to see. She hated the feelings she often had that there were other presences there watching her in the fire seas. She hated being spied upon. She called out often to My light to reveal Myself if it was Me there, but I never did because I was not looking that closely. I am looking now.

This time she did not call out, though. She moved to protect herself instead. She quickly took on the Fire Dragon form from the worm form in which she had arrived, but not quickly enough that the Father of Manifestation didn't see this. He thought the rest of the Mother might have been shed as the worm form. He looked closely to see whether this was true or not, but He did not see any gold light being shed there.

The Fire Dragon stirred then and called out the Father of Manifestation's name, cursing Him when there was no reply. She hated being spied upon, but she also hated being alone. She thought it was the Father of Manifestation she felt there because she knew His vibration and feared He might be coming after her in some sneaky way to get even with her for having defeated Him the way she had. She knew there was another confrontation coming, but she did not know when or where yet, since the Father of Manifestation was being very careful not to let any pictures form in Himself around this yet. She had tried to pry with her divination but had not been successful. This worried her. She liked to know things in advance so she could plan for them, and did not notice her blind spots gave her surprises she didn't like anyway. She then only tried to divine more.

She had eerie feelings of not liking being in the fire seas with a presence she did not like watching her there. She tried to rage in her usual fashion, but felt uneasy doing this. She did not know whether to stay and guard her power cavern or not, but after a little while of impatient and nervous raging in little bursts and fits, her rage sent her forth to fly around some. She fled really, and that left the Father of Manifestation free to look around there.

Seeing the Fire Dragon come forth from the erupting fire of a volcano excited the Ronalokas, and they could not hide this from the satyrs. They felt she had presence there in Pangea, unlike the missing part of the Mother. The satyrs felt excited by the spectacle also and drooled lasciviously over the thoughts of their plans to capture her, but most of the inhabitants of Pan did not know if she was friend or foe and were terrified by the sight of the Fire Dragon, rising like a phoenix from the cracking egg of an erupting volcano.

Steam and smoke rose around her, fiery lava spewed down the mountainside and with every penetrating screech, her fiery breath lashed the air around her. It was quite a spectacle to see her fly also as her long tail had to lash back and forth a lot to keep her going. She did not rise very far toward My light I noticed, and she could not fly for long, which was also noticed by the satyrs who were always keeping watch, as though this meant they had power over her if they knew her ways; and know them they did, more than she would have liked.

They had a plan now of going after her when she was not in the fire seas where it was too hot for them, when they were so hot themselves already. Sometimes their seething rage felt so hot to them they thought they might turn into Fire Dragons themselves and scorch everything around them for a change. This idea became their alternate plan. If it did not happen that they could overpower her in the fire seas and keep the struggle away from the eyes of those who might not think their style as grand as hers, and if they did not succeed in getting her to reveal herself in public as something they should rescue everyone from and overpower for the good of all, then maybe they could overpower her by stealing her Fire Dragon form and then back her down at her own game.

They had fiery breath in mind as the revenge they would like to take against the mother on Earth now and manifested a little of it right there on the spot, but they were not really able to get much happening. They then thought that the mother on Earth must be getting her fiery breath from the fire seas, and that perhaps they were going to have to go there after all. They decided to move right then when they knew she wasn't there, and they had enough impetus from held rage to act on it.

They had penetrating the fire seas and having sex with the Fire Dragon in mind, and the sexual excitement these ideas generated propelled them along. They entered a cave they had found that they thought might take them to the fire seas and began to feel a warmth which they followed as their guide. Soon, however, they became confused in the labyrinth of passageways and caverns as to which way to go and which of the many caverns and pockets of fire seas would be the right one in which to find the Fire Dragon's lair. They would not have found it either, had not the Fire Dragon returned, sensing trouble there as a mother bird might sense nest robbers. She descended into the volcano, blasting fiery breath all the way in her rage at what intruders she might find there.

The Father of Manifestation could not be seen there, but He withdrew His presence enough at that moment that He could watch the proceedings without being noticed, curious as to what the satyrs were going to do.

The satyrs could hear and feel the presence of the Fire Dragon, and they crept toward her, focused on the idea of being ready to pounce on her at any moment. She was feeling this presence also and was looking around her, feeling unsure as to what it was. She was determined to keep her guard up just in case anyone really had penetrated the fire seas, but for some reason she did not understand, she did not feel very powerful in that moment.

She felt frustrated and enraged that her form seemed cumbersome to her in the confines of her power cavern. She was spitting fire in response to this when the satyrs seized the opportunity of this moment as though they knew what was happening with her. She could not move quickly enough in response to how small and quick the satyrs were, and they managed to restrain her by clamping her in special metal-like devices they had forged from the very heat of her fire seas for the job. The satyrs felt very proud of their manifestating powers then and danced with glee even though the Fire Dragon had nearly scorched them out of existence in their effort. They did not seem to notice any pain regarding this, only noticing themselves with interest whenever they looked scorched and restoring themselves as fast as they could.

The mother on Earth did not let on to them who she was other than the Fire Dragon. She raged at them with her fiery breath, scorching them still if they tried to get near her and demanding to know what they thought they were doing to her and why they thought they could dare to enter her private caverns in the fire seas.

The satyrs loved this because it gave them more chance to play with the mother here. They told her quite a grand story of how they hoped to please the Fire Dragon somehow and gain her friendship, and loyalty even perhaps, so that she would no longer come to the aid of the Faerie Queen when she called to be rescued from the hands of their innocent selves who had already been victimized so many times by her Fire Dragon already that they had no recourse but to try and gain her favor somehow. They praised her great powers as they had seen it done by the Ronalokas.

The false humility, fear and pretense of respect fairly dripped off of them as did their sweat there, and of course their story was full of sexual innuendoes that heavily implied they could please her sexually to gain her favor and that they had noticed no Fire Dragon mate, which point they pressed in the same tone they used on the Faerie Queen when they could not help but want to put her belittlements back on her by saying, "If there is a mate for you who is so much better, where is he. You never have a right mate, do you?"

The satyrs could never hold themselves back sexually for long and since they were already excited they began moving toward the Fire Dragon.

They had their way with her sexually there for a little while with her raging at them because she did not like the form this was taking. They tortured her there, too, in an effort to make her submit, but this only enraged her further. She never allowed any other feelings she had in these situations, being utterly convinced that any other outward display of emotion would be a sign of weakness the satyrs would take advantage of.

It wasn't long, however, before another emotion she felt took form in her. As she felt shame for having to suffer these indignities at the hand of the satyrs, and now, even in her power form as the Fire Dragon and in her power cavern, she became the worm and wriggled away. Free of her bondage there, at least, she sought escape in the passageways she knew so well, and even beneath their surface where she had not noticed the satyrs being able to follow her yet. Her hatred was left behind there as a huge snake that also slithered quickly toward freedom, but not before it struck repeatedly at the satyrs with its many heads, almost as many as there were satyrs, in fact.

The Father of Manifestation was very intimidated by His own feelings of loss of power there, made all the more obvious to Him by how the satyrs as a group had overpowered the Fire Dragon when He had not, and how she had overpowered them in her own way by escaping from them. His shame slithered off quickly also as a snake.

The mother on Earth was running fast beneath the surface of the Earth, feeling extremely agitated and not knowing how she was going to keep the satyrs out of her fire seas now or how she was going to be able to keep them from shaming her publicly now that they knew so much. The Father of Manifestation was also running beneath the surface of the Earth and feeling Himself sinking or falling down inside the Earth in a way that was very alarming and felt out of control to Him. These two bumped into each other running inside the Earth, but did not take time or allow themselves to recognize each other, not even knowing themselves how they were running there until that moment of jolting awareness from their collision, which in that moment only caused them to move faster, not knowing who or what they had encountered there.

The satyrs emerged from an entranceway to the fire seas after being horribly chased by the snake, even having split apart into groups only to have the snake split apart and follow them that way. They had weaponry manifest in their hands with which they had fought the snake off, but they had not liked the experience. They emerged from several previously unknown openings, and while this showed them more entranceways to the fire seas, they at first were not sure if they felt gleeful or not about their exploits there.

All of a sudden, a group of them noticed a gnarly, old-looking satyr near where they emerged from the fire seas, sitting there playing His pipes as though He was not aware of His surroundings. They fell upon Him, beating Him up severely, pummeling Him with their hooves and butting Him with their horns as much as they possibly could.

This jolted the Father of Manifestation again as He felt this happening to Him outside the fire seas, but it took great effort to pull Himself out there and into His satyr form to fight them off. It was barely possible for Him to move quickly enough to save Himself there. Luckily, the whole group was not upon Him

95

immediately, and by the time they were, He had pulled Himself back together in His satyr form. He called to His centaurs for help, but they did not appear in time. He felt He had no other choice but to also flee the satyrs. He took wing as the Pegasus from their midst, hating to give them such an impression of their power. The satyrs felt better then after having a fight they felt sure they had won.

Glee quickly took hold in them now, and they began congratulating themselves and one another on what they had done as though they were the most powerful beings on Earth. Curiously, they made no mention in their boasting, of the fight they had just had with the Father of Manifestation or of the many-headed snake they had barely escaped from with their lives. They seemed only focused on the mother on Earth and began to tell one another and themselves that they had had their little rehearsal and were now ready to shame and embarrass the Faerie Queen into publicly revealing herself as the Fire Dragon so that others could see her rage and know why they had to subdue and dominate her as a matter of keeping power in its proper place.

The satyrs' boasting and congratulating of themselves soon became brew drinking and partying, singing and dancing and even swinging one another around like partners as they bragged and boasted of what they had done. They kept repeating this over and over, and how the Fire Dragon had run away from them as a worm. "As a worm! As a loathsome, lowly, slimy, little, old worm!"

The Ronalokas did not like hearing that the mother on Earth had become a worm and wondered what they were going to do next if she did not reappear soon, which she had not.

The Father of Manifestation heard their partying. He drew Himself near the satyrs' party but hid Himself well. He listened for a long time and heard a lot about the mother on Earth's sexual perversities and pleasures. He did not like what He heard or saw there, or what He smelled for that matter. He also heard a lot about how these satyrs viewed Him and was not sure how to handle them since they obviously didn't respect Him anymore; hated Him in fact, if their words could be taken seriously, which He had no reason then to doubt. He feared His power loss in the presence of them as an entire group and did not understand that He was empowering them.

While He was there, He saw the presence of the little faeries and wondered what it meant and where their loyalties really lay. He saw them as parts of the mother on Earth and did not recognize them as children there. Not knowing how they had left the mother when He had left her behind on Earth, He did not know what their relationships to others really were. He decided to watch them and learn what He could.

There was plenty of partying going on and open sexual encounters of every sort imaginable, but when the satyrs began grabbing the faeries and re-enacting their subjugation of the Fire Dragon on them, the Father of Manifestation became very agitated by their defenselessness. And again, He also felt perverse fears about Himself at His sexual excitation. He wanted to intervene, but was reluctant to reveal His presence by coming forth and rescuing faeries, especially in the presence of so many adversarial satyrs He now knew hated Him so much and viewed Him as such a wimp in all ways.

He called for His centaurs again to come to His aid, but they did not appear quickly. He felt called to respond to the faeries' plight then but could not move to make Himself do it until one little faerie flew away from the satyrs to try to hide herself and landed so close to Him that He could feel her terror. He could have reached out and touched her, but He was not sure if she had hidden successfully or not, or if she wanted to be found or not. He was not sure if He should reach out and grab her since He looked like a satyr too. Before He made up His mind what to do, the satyrs grabbed for her. She flew about, but they gave chase and caught her.

Then the satyrs began talking about what they were going to do to such a little faerie as this who had given them resistance, had hidden and had made them chase her. The satyrs decided they might like to administer some pain to this little faerie who had given them so much trouble catching her, and they might like to start by ripping her wings off, which they summarily did.

The little faerie tried to protest. When she began crying piteously, the satyrs laughingly jeered her and imitated her, saying they were not interested in anything coming out of her, only in what went in. Whereupon they began thrusting their large penises down her throat. When she began to choke and gasp as though she obviously could not handle this at all, the satyrs began exclaiming, "Look how much she loves it! She loves it as much as she loves us! She wants it! She's begging for it! She needs more!"

When their thrusts into her throat sent her into gagging and spasming as a person does when driven into uncontrollable vomiting, they began claiming she was orgasming, but in a tone that let on they knew she was not! The Father of Manifestation saw the stark terror on the little faerie's face, and did not hesitate. He form changed as fast as He possibly could, grabbed the little faerie in the midst of His form change and headed for the skies, not caring in that moment what He had had to reveal about Himself there.

He had seen enough to know these satyrs hated the faeries instead of loving them the way He did. He held her in His arms for a long time healing her of this trauma. When They could not call the faerie's wings back to her and did not know it was because of her shame about flying toward My light after this, the Father of Manifestation had to snatch back her wings from the midst of the satyrs who were cavorting in fun with them as though they were going to use them to fly if they could only decide what part of themselves they would best like to have wings. They actually could have been hilarious on one level, they looked so horribly silly, except for how it all felt.

THE FATHER OF MANIFESTATION'S ENTOURAGE IN THE WOODS

The next time this faerie got close to the satyrs, she trembled in fear at the very sight of them. The Father of Manifestation had to keep her close to Him after that, and although there was some love there between them, it also gratified some hidden motives in the little faerie.

After the Father of Manifestation saw and heard what He saw and heard there with the satyrs, He felt He must move to give more help and protection to all of the faeries and elves in Pan, and also to any new arrivals who didn't know what the satyrs were about. He moved to call together all of the creatures He knew of in and about the woods of Pan. He gave them all a talk which reached the mother on Earth's ears quickly. She felt a current of blame coming toward her from it.

When she heard that the satyrs had been talked about unfavorably, she inquired as to how the Father of Manifestation had come to know about the plight of the Fire Dragon with the satyrs. When she was told how the Father of Manifestation had rescued the little faerie, she was furious that He had not rescued her and made a vow to get revenge on Him for that. She considered Him to be her rival and adversary even more now instead of the lover and friend

He had been in the past. She wondered if He planned on conducting a rival court of His own with all of the creatures in the woods. Even if He was in competition with her here, she considered her court to be the royal court and His court to be a rag tag assemblage in the woods of rejects from her court.

"All the misfits and no place beings who need help just to be," she said about the creatures in the woods when she heard of His gathering. When she heard He was encouraging the spirits to learn how to become invisible on Earth as a means of protection against the satyrs, she scoffed, "Allowing themselves to be backed right off Earth will be their next step, I suppose. What backing down! What a lack of power! What a lack of standing up to the satyrs. He can't stand up to anyone, not even me!" Then she thought of the part of the Mother He could intimidate and didn't respect Him for this either.

Meanwhile, as talk had spread rapidly of the Father of Manifestation's meeting, the faerie folk had come flying, running and leaping, soaring, rolling, tumbling and jumping as well as riding on the backs of the friendly centaurs and unicorns through the woods to the edge of the lovely, pure water where the meeting was being held so that the water creatures could feel comfortable there too. The enticing, gentle, rhythmic lapping of the sparkling water called to them and on many of the faerie folk who gathered there, scales, fins and tails became as apparent as their desire to go swimming in the liquid light, as they called it then and whose renewal powers were commensurate with the name.

Being all gathered together at once seemed like such a grand occasion for having fun. They did not quiet down for any sort of talking to. It was as though they had forgotten they had enthusiasm for the daytime and it was all bubbling forth into the foaming, effervescence of the water, but eventually, as moonlight settled in over the sunset and began to shimmer on the deepening azure, green and purple waters, the faerie folk settled down into something of a meeting format, although there were pockets of music irresistibly flowing forth and other distractions. The moonlight reminded them of the problems they had been having, and talk spread rapidly of the satyrs and what they had been doing.

Suddenly, it was as though no one was afraid to talk openly about the problems they had been having, and more of a picture of the problem began to emerge. Apparently, not everyone had problems, but those who did had lots of them, and they began to talk as though they all wanted to tell the Father of Manifestation at once. There was quite a ruckus and a hubbub raised as they were very emotionally portraying vivid pictures of scenarios they had experienced and acting out some of them to convey them even more vividly.

The Father of Manifestation received all of this, but was not talking about these satyrs as a part of Himself because He did not recognize this reality at the time. What He did say was that He feared He could not control them anymore without more help because there were getting to be so many of them and He did not know where they were coming from. He said they seemed to just appear overnight as though the mother on Earth were calling them from someplace under the ground.

As soon as His words were spoken, no one wanted to be on the edge of the gathering. There was a definite, but unacknowledged, movement to clump together more and some competition for inside positions. At the same time, horrible noises could be heard coming from the woods. Growling and roaring and sounds of clashing and fighting, as if wild beasts were tearing something apart in frenzied rage, sexual excitement or both, sent ripples of response moving through the gathering. The Father of Manifestation was stirred into great uneasiness Himself.

Mixed-up beasts, of many different animal parts began to appear around the edges of the gathering. Apparently drawn by the ruckus but unable to agree with themselves about whether to attend the meeting or not, they were moving forward, sideways and also backwards. Some were also struggling with wings, trying to lift at least some parts of themselves out of the situation, and some of them were getting tangled in the vines as they went. Unable to move closer without other parts fighting to move away from the group, they were raging and struggling with themselves like trapped beasts.

Many of the spirits did not like the feeling of this presence at the gathering at all, but avoided mentioning it. This really gave the Father of Manifestation the feeling He needed to help then, especially when He saw so many mixed-up beasts and how horrifyingly mixed up they were.

Hearing the Father of Manifestation appeal for help and not seeing My light come forth to empower Him imparted a renewed feeling to the gathering that I didn't care anymore what was happening on Earth and that maybe I didn't like the Father of Manifestation anymore either.

In that moment, they all felt frightened and alone as they

gazed upon the Father of Manifestation's large figure as the God Pan standing before them. Dwarfed by His presence, with His centaur allies gathered around Him and His satyr allies drawn up within Him, most of them felt that if He wasn't enough to handle the situation, they really weren't enough.

They felt sad for a moment, and then fear began to appear, and even some terror. The minute it did, the mixed-up beasts raised such a ruckus at the edge of the gathering, it looked like they might find a sudden alignment and charge at the most terrified spirits there. This intimidated the group into quieting down and in the ensuing quiet, the mixed-up beasts went even more crazy as though even the presence of terror was intolerable to them.

Someone then said they must all develop their own powers and not depend anymore upon a God who was not even there. Everyone tried to move toward the feeling that that was right and necessary whether they liked it or not, even an eventual part of growing up, which was what going out on their own meant to them then.

They talked then about what powers they had that they might develop more. Invisibility and form change were at the top of the list along with grouping together and warning and helping one another. The Father of Manifestation also suggested that those who could fly, leap and soar help those who could not do it as well, and in general, encouraged any who had any powers to help others learn how to have those same powers if they did not already, and how to improve them by learning from one another as a group.

Then someone said that neither form change nor invisibility worked very well for some because the satyrs could find them by smell even when they couldn't see them. Another said flying away was the best defense, but it was known that not all could fly. Orange and Red said the satyrs chased them into the darkness until they were tired or had led them to others when they fled for protection.

Someone then said that since Orange and Red were having most of the problems, they must be giving the satyrs the most of what they wanted, and that if they would stop doing this, the satyrs would stop bothering them so much. It didn't matter that an inexperienced Rainbow Spirit said this from a hidden place where no one could see her, it made a rent in the group and made Orange and Red feel terrible.

"We don't have any problems with them," the rose pink faeries said.

"Neither do we," said Green, Blue and Purple. Yellow had problems but not quite as serious as Orange and Red, which left Orange and Red feeling that they were not right to be having such problems.

"Maybe you ought to try more love," a green spirit said. "The satyrs just want love like everybody else."

"Maybe you anger them somehow and that's why they aren't nice to you," a blue faerie said.

This did not feel good to Orange and Red, but they also knew they had angered the satyrs so they weren't sure. In their experience, not giving the satyrs what they wanted angered them. Orange and Red felt that others did not like them because they were having problems. Some Ronalokas spoke up then saying they had had problems with the satyrs too, and that they didn't like it that no one from their group was speaking up to admit to this, especially the ones who had color problems like Orange and Red. Red in the Ronalokas especially did not like this being mentioned and made the rest of the Ronalokas stay quiet.

The mermaids were hesitant to speak then, but decided to tell their story. They said they had been sexually victimized by the satyrs also and that the offspring who resulted from this often chose land because those were the most dominant parts in them, overriding the water parts frequently in unkind ways.

The mermaids said these children hated and disrespected them as mothers, and that they could not parent these offspring for these reasons. They then said that the satyrs took no responsibility for these offspring whatsoever, and jeered at the mermaids' requests, or even suggestions, that the satyrs parent them, even saying that these offspring were good for one thing and one thing only and that was sex. This made the mermaids feel frightened and angry that they could not protect their offspring from abuse by the satyrs.

One of the upper chakra faeries asked the mermaids why they let the satyrs have sex with them. Before any of the mermaids answered, others rushed into the uncomfortable space to say that there were quite a number of offspring in Pan who seemed to hate their parents and even the idea of being parented at all, and instead treated their parents as if their parents were their servants. There was mixed response to this.

The mermaids then said these were minor problems compared to the suffocation terror some of their water parts felt in being held too long on the land. Others then said that suffocation terror was something regularly dished out by the satyrs toward anyone who resisted them.

"Why don't you just pass out and leave your form there? Without any life in it, it won't interest them for long," said another upper chakra faerie.

"Or form change into someting that can get away from them," another said.

The mermaids had shame and displaced their emotions by leaving the meeting and going out to sea feeling that no one on land understood them or their problems with being in either place for long. They could not make up their minds how to handle this as a group and made splits then even among themselves. This then affected the mermen who could no longer run as a group if the maids weren't.

The Father of Manifestation felt the feelings of divisiveness beginning to come forward while He had cooperation and interaction in mind. When He tried to emphasize His own point of view, someone else said that helping one another to develop their powers was all very well and good, but that they also needed some sort of power display.

"We cannot just run and hide from the satyrs," some said then. "We should stand up to them and let them know We have the power to stop them."

The Father of Manifestation did not like the idea of a confrontation and said He wasn't sure He had the power to stop them as a group. He said He could not always be there to protect everyone who needed protection at all times, and so it was good in any event that everyone have their own means of self-protection.

Being confronted with the idea that there were predators in the woods from whom they must continue to hide themselves did not feel good to any of the spirits. After quite a discussion about this, the Ronalokas spoke up and said they did not want a confrontation either. Their position was that at least now they all had some protection, and that if there was a confrontation and they were to lose, they would have no protection at all.

THE MIXED-UP BEASTS

The mixed-up beasts were making a lot of noise that felt unpleasant to everyone during all of this, and when someone finally said, "We don't want to have to think about all of this, we just want to have fun," almost everyone rallied around this and began drifting off by colors to party as though the problems with the satyrs were suddenly not real anymore. The centaurs, unicorns and pegasuses, who seemed to have taken on the Father of Manifestation's rainbow as a group, went with the colors they had the most of and gradually, as the others moved away from them, the Ronalokas and Orange and Red felt more and more left behind and left out.

Orange and Red were left with a problem feeling good about themselves or really welcome at parties in the woods, especially if they were going to draw the satyrs and get blamed for this. They did not want to just move along on their own either for fear that that might really get them in trouble. They hovered around the Father of Manifestation for a feeling of protection, but did not quite admit to doing this; instead, they said they liked partying with Him the most, which was true also. The Ronalokas left then, saying they were going to party on their own and that they had not gone earlier because they had not wanted the others to see where they were going.

The Father of Manifestation wanted to party, but He had His attention on the mixed-up beasts.

As soon as the Ronalokas left, it was as though the mixed-up beasts, whose rising crescendo of snarling and growling struggle with themselves suddenly reached an alignment in which some of them charged after the Ronalokas while others charged at Orange and Red. The Father of Manifestation tried to stop them from charging with the manifesting power He felt He still had, but He had a very difficult time here also. As a group, they almost overwhelmed Him. He had a particularly hard time staving them off of Red, but finally, even that quieted down as Orange and Red moved far enough away from them, fleeing faster than the mixed-up beasts could follow them without getting tangled up in the vines.

The Father of Manifestation noticed sounds of terror and real pain in the noises the beasts were making and decided to have a closer look. It was not possible to know how to approach them when not all parts could agree on what was friend or foe and what was a friendly approach and what was not. They were like a miniature battlefield of misalignment in the Will Polarity trapped in forms that reflected this with no loving Spirit presence to help them understand or resolve their problems. Rage moved all the time there without terror or grief having much of a chance since rage would attack it and slam it down whenever it tried to come forward. They had rage moving like crazy now and were growling louder and louder. They were acting as though the satyrs were already attacking them and acting out attacking the satyrs back while other parts opposed this or tried to flee.

The orange and red faeries who remained hovering nearby became very uncomfortable just then, as though they knew something more than they were letting the Father of Manifestation know about the origins or creations of these beasts. They moved away without saying anything and did not look back to see if the Father of Manifestation noticed or not. The few who stayed behind did not help the Father of Manifestation because they did not know how, but they felt sorry for the mixed-up beasts as though their plights were similar.

It became clear to the Father of Manifestation that the mixed-up beasts were being heavily victimized by the satyrs whether their rage was letting them know this or not. They insisted they had the strength to fight off the satyrs if they wanted to, but it did not seem like they could fight off anything without a better alignment from within. Sexual humiliation and pain did not look to the Father of Manifestation like the right approach no matter what some parts of His body felt in response to it, and these mixed-up beasts were looking more responsive to torture and pain than anything else, and with less ability to heal themselves from the results.

Holding them quiet with manifesting power that did not let them move, the Father of Manifestation went to them one by one to take a closer look. He saw that many of them were cut or ripped open in places, as though from trying to rip themselves apart, and these places were not healing. He wondered why they were not healing and saw that the satyrs had been sexually penetrating these places over and over and not letting them heal. Rage did not like the Father of Manifestation looking at them, but once the beasts felt He was not going to judge them, shame them or punish them for this, they let Him know that anything that had healed in them had been reopened by the satyrs as soon as they managed to trap the beasts again. He also saw now that the beasts had major problems with the vines in Pan entrapping them, tangling them up and holding them until the satyrs came.

The mixed-up beasts let the Father of Manifestation know many things about their plight then, but as soon as it began to touch their terror, they fought with everything they had against

Him holding them quiet so they could rage instead, which entangled them further with the vines, which enraged them further and also pushed them further into terror which they displaced into fights of hurling blame back and forth amongst their parts, infighting heavily, and even in moments of supposed rest, bickering constantly, with some parts complaining they never got any sleep because of this. They were extremely terrified beasts, but they could not let it move as terror because they could not stand the depth of it, the overwhelming lack of relief from it they were experiencing or the loss of their ability to express themselves humanly.

The Father of Manifestation talked to My light about this then and told Me He needed My help to separate these beings trapped together by form changes that had not been completed. I told Him no initially because their sexual unions had not been loving and were causing most of the problems. I saw them as doing it all again as soon as possible if I healed them.

Later, I relented and did help Him unravel many complicated mixtures of form and essence confusions, most of which had unlovingness and power struggle in their sexual unions as the basis for their form confusions along with outright desire for forms that had attributes they thought they were going to get if they entered them. They had found, however, upon getting in there that just because they had entered a form did not mean they were suited to expressing in those ways and could favorably utilize the forms they had entered.

I was very hard on these forms at first, feeling they had disregarded My light too many times for Me to feel like helping them anymore, but I felt into them more deeply later and found that their terror level was deeper than I thought given their rage presentation.

The mixed-up beasts had many complex problems from imprinting that I did not understand at the time, but if I had it to do over again, I still would have left them where they were as I did initially, and perhaps even for much longer than I did, because of how quickly their rage did move to recreate their problems all over again as though they had no respect or gratitude for anything done by My light to help them. I also did not like how much more effective they had become at perpetrating against terror because of the better alignment with their form My light had given them, but because of the terror trapped there with them, I did not leave them as they were and neither did the Father of Manifestation.

My light has wanted to rage at them for this entrapment of terror underneath them, and especially for not recognizing that it was this terror that got their rage the help it was demanding so obnoxiously. I found in doing so that it did not seem to help the situation. Terror became more terrified of My light and rage more enraged. Hearing the rage there scream that I had deliberately trapped it with the terror it was beating down and that I must want it in terror did not increase My desire to help at the time. Subsequent understanding of imprinting has at least let Me know now where they were coming from, but this rage still needs to look at the unloving light in its presentation. This rage went for unloving light as power and went for these form changes as power and when it did not work out, My light was suddenly supposed to rescue it, even if it had My overthrow and demise in mind as its use of this power.

I have found now that terror must move out from underneath this rage and find My light instead of continuing to see this rage as being My light. If you have some terror to recover there, move to do it because it cannot move on its own in a state of denial. Most of the form changes that left essence behind in unsuccessful completions left the extremes those involved were already not allowing to vibrate. When these extremes found themselves abandoned and trapped in what I have called the mixed-up beasts, they flew into confusions of panic and imprinting that did not let them think straight, and they literally could not. They could not move to figure out their problems without help. I should not always be the One who has to move to intervene here.

If you are going to recover your lost power and magic, you are going to have to take responsibility for the path you took that left pieces strewn all over the place in the name of partying and having fun with sexual experimentation, rebellion and secret perversions; more prevalent fragmentation issues than many of you would like to admit. When you move to look at Pan, look very closely at your sexual encounters and the feelings involved there. Most of you merged forms between the two partners and if anything sprang off of this, called them emergences, but they were most often really misaligned, discarded, unrecognized, unaccepted and often, unclaimed, unparented parts of yourselves.

After the Father of Manifestation did what He could with the help of My light to separate the mixed-up beasts and help them gain more alignment with their forms, He wanted to party Himself for awhile. Not having any idea how long He had been there working on the mixed-up beasts with My light, He went to look for the orange and red faeries along with those few who had remained with Him.

He was playing His pipes and wandering through the woods, feeling the sounds and pulsations of energy He felt from the different groups He passed, looking for the music that sounded right for the mood He was in now. He noticed that the orange and red faeries were not partying in any place He had found yet. A feeling of dread filled Him. He feared the satyrs had found them.

He found little bands of Ronalokan elves making music here and there that He wanted to stop and play with, but He felt that now He had another problem preventing Him from doing this and that was the orange and red faeries. Where were they?

He did not find an answer to this, and instead, found Himself feeling blame for the Mother for this and for not showing up to help Him with the mixed-up beasts or anything else for that matter. Where was She? He felt like going after the mother on Earth again for this, but felt He must look for the orange and red faeries. Why did He have to be responsible for these problems all by Himself when He really wanted to party, play music, have sex and rest Himself more than anything else? Why was being responsible so all consuming that having fun was not something He did much anymore?

Again, He wanted to fly at the mother on Earth and did not know why He felt blame for the Mother for everything. His blame had a rage to it that felt immensely powerful, but He was not sure He could grant Himself the right to use this power against her because He was not sure He felt loving in this place. He felt something else took over Him there, and He was not sure what it was. At times, He thought it was My light finally empowering Him after He was already mad that I hadn't come to Him earlier, but at times, it felt too terrible to be that. Instead of moving rage toward her, He felt He must try to understand the mother on Earth's position more. Maybe she was helping other spirits while He was helping these. He was determined to find out and redoubled His spying efforts.

With a growing feeling of dread, He looked around in the woods for the orange and red faeries and did not find them, but He felt He must find them. He kept feeling drawn to spy on the mother on Earth's court, but He felt He could not slip in as He was without the satyrs recognizing Him. Looking for the orange and red faeries reminded him of how much He wanted to find the missing presence of the Mother. He felt He must find some way to address this dark and huddled place He saw underneath the light of the mother on Earth to see if it was the missing part of the Mother being dominated and controlled by the mother on Earth. He thought of slipping into the court and even into the Faerie Queen in the same way He had slipped into the fire seas, but He was not sure if the huddled presence could recognize Him, respond to Him or speak to Him this way. He thought of form changing again, but that did not seem to be the right approach. How was He going to get the mother on Earth to receive Him enough to find out what she had hidden in that dark and huddled place inside her?

TROUBLE AT THE DOOR

The Father of Manifestation decided He would have to break Himself up into aspects and become a group of allied satyrs. He thought there would be less chance of being recognized and better defense as a group, but what He did not know was that even this group was no longer as allied as He thought. Some wanted to run off in search of the orange and red faeries and not follow His lead toward the court of the mother on Earth. Some wanted to party and not go either place. Others wanted to follow His lead because they felt it was a good opportunity to party and found it more interesting combined with the intrigue because they were curious about the mother on Earth's court. Of these, many also had a feeling they were going to find the orange and red faeries there and have great sex because they were now a more appropriate size. Only a few shared His seriousness of purpose and guided intent. These few He asked to stick the closest to Him, and asked the others to do the best they could to help, to report back to Him as much as they could and to keep a close watch on His back.

They went to the court of the mother on Earth, which had a door now, controlled by the satyrs who used it to be in the position of assuring their power position by controlling who came and went and extorting whatever price of admission suited their fancy.

The Father of Manifestation approached with His group of satyrs. Nostrils flared at the door like a rival gang had just showed up. The Father of Manifestation, in their midst, looked like a gnarly, stern, crabby, almost old-looking, little, wizard-type of man who looked as if He didn't like the looks of anything around Him or want the children to have any fun.

The satyrs guarding the door did not like the looks of them, and assessing them suspiciously, singled out the Father of Manifestation and turned Him back. He felt He could not protest or say anything without revealing more than He wanted to. Before He left, however, He noticed there were at least some orange and red faeries in the court assemblage. He did not understand why they would go to the place of their greatest problem, but He did not have time to find out before the other door guards told Him to leave or there was going to be trouble.

The Father of Manifestation went back to the woods without even a party to go to that He wanted to attend, and there He sat, listening to the drifting sounds, all alone and miserable without even any significant success in His information gathering mission. The longer He sat there, the more He began to feel that even His satyr allies were not going to return now that they had gotten out there on their own without His control. To make His misery worse, He again began to feel the pains in His body that He did not like to feel and His head was again filled with lurid pictures He did not want to see. He decided that what He needed was a rest. He lay down in His exhaustion and allowed His body to sink into the Earth as I had seen Him do a number of times before.

I viewed this with alarm. I did not like it that He was allowing Himself to go unconscious and slip even further away from Me. I had noticed that He was doing this more and more and that everytime He did this, there seemed to be less and less of Him present when He resurfaced. What was He doing with Himself in the Earth and why? My light felt I must get Him to come up and not go down so far. I called to Him there, but He did not answer.

After a long time, He resurfaced, again with less of Himself than when He had lain down, and this time, He took on the form of an even older wizard with a long flowing cape and robe and all of the wonderful old features of wizards, except that He did not wear a hat such as wizards are so often portrayed with these days. His long flowing hair covered His body past His heart and did not let it be seen to be as gnarly and bent as it really was there. He felt powerless to Me compared to His former self and I felt sad for Him.

The old wizard looked grim, and as He began to walk through the woods, My heart broke, not only for Him, but for Myself too, that this was happening to Him and between Us. He looked frightened and lonely, but did not look this way for long before He seemed to be taken over by a fierce, new determination.

I saw that He was going to all of the old places that had been the favorites of the Mother's as though He was looking for Her

110

again, but if He could even find the places at all, they were all so changed. The sparkle of Her smile was missing from the waters, and the leaves and flowers drooped as though mourning the loss of Her presence. Even the rocks and mosses had dulled and darkened. What the Father of Manifestation found there mostly was a load of grief and the forlorn emptiness of a missing presence.

The closer He walked to Her old bower, which had now become the chambers of the mother on Earth, hidden back behind her court, the spookier and more eerily silent of Her presence it became. He did not like the feeling there, and even though He felt drawn to go to her court, He turned to go.

This was when He saw the gold key on the ground which My light had been drawing along behind Him for quite some time unnoticed. He stooped, crooked as an old man supported by His wizard's staff, and picked it up. It was the Faerie Queen's dragon key by which she had hidden and locked away from the satyrs the entrances to the fire seas, but never had He seen such a thing before and He did not know what it was. He held it in His hand as a very curious object and tried to feel into it. He felt it had some importance because it was full of the vibration of the mother on Earth, and He was being urged by My light to give it back to her. This He could not understand and especially, how He was going to do this. He resisted Me for awhile and then began to move toward her court feeling that this might somehow be His invitation, or pass, maybe even a sign from My light.

He went to the door and said He had something it was important for Him to give to the Faerie Queen in person and that He must speak with her privately. The satyrs scrutinized Him closely and asked what it was. They were sure already that He must be alluding to sex and made fun of Him as too gnarly and bent to be of interest to the Faerie Queen. Of course they had to impart that their kind of raw sex was what she was looking for.

When the Father of Manifestation answered them, He imparted the feeling that He did not know exactly what it was, but that He knew it was important, like the wisdom of an old man, and that He had felt her calling Him to come there. When the satyrs heard this, they told Him to wait while they had a little conference. Something about His gnarliness and the feelings they had about His sexuality made them feel they recognized Him somehow. They had sniffed Him out earlier and had felt He might return in a form change. They told Him the Faerie Queen had all the advice she needed and were not going to let Him in. Then the Father of

111

Manifestation let them see the key.

The minute the satyrs saw this, they knew it was something important and that they must have it. They had another conference to the side. They were barely able to contain themselves, pawing, snorting and drooling with glee, excitement and power lust. Many wanted to lay into Him right there and take it, but since each secretly plotted to have it for himself, they decided to lay a trap for this wizard and let Him in. That way, each figured himself to have more time to see how he might take this key for himself and, thus, become the head of the satyrs.

They told the Father of Manifestation to wait and sent several of them to the Faerie Queen as though they were going to talk to her about this and get her permission to let Him in, but they did not. Their messengers went near her and made it look like they were talking to her about this, but talked to her about something else. Then they came back and reported that she wanted Him to give them the key.

When the Father of Manifestation refused to do this, the other satyrs were immediately angry that there had already been a double-cross in the plan of getting the key for the entire group to decide who would have it. The satyrs then tried to jump Him at the door and take it. There was quite a scuffle in which the satyrs again began to drool and snort, grab, fight and compete and even grow so sexually aroused that the Father of Manifestation knew that whatever this object was, it meant power to them and so much so that maybe He had better not give it to the mother on Earth. He did not have much choice but to let them take the key, but in the ensuing shuffle, in which all the satyrs tried to be the one to have possession of the key, the Father of Manifestation called the key to Himself, moved quickly past their scuffle and toward the mother on Earth.

He told the mother on Earth He had found something that belonged to her and that if she wanted to see what it was, she must agree to tell Him what it was for. She refused to respond to Him and was about to call her satyrs to throw Him out, but when He showed her the key, she quickly reversed herself, and just as quickly, but also as inconspicuously as possible drew Him toward her private chambers. Even so, the satyrs were on Their heels.

She locked her door against them; something the Father of Manifestation had never seen done before. He wondered why the satyrs did not just break it down, but the satyrs had other ideas. They pretended to go away and then stationed themselves to watch and listen to what was going to happen there.

The Father of Manifestation found Himself being very suddenly seduced without any conversation or lead in, or any reconciliation with His energy which He felt she somehow recognized. She seemed only focused on getting the key this way and, as though making love at a masquerade ball, not wanting to know who she was making love to, until later, perhaps.

The Father of Manifestation tried to resist her and persist in asking questions about the key, while she persisted in trying to seduce Him as a means of getting Him to give her the key.

He realized this was His opportunity to find out if the dark place in her was emptiness or if it was the huddled presence of the rest of the Mother He was seeking, and He persisted in asking questions and in resisting her advances as though He did not care about her urgency, the satyrs at the door or the precariousness of His own position. He wanted to give this dark place time to recognize Him and respond to Him if it was going to, and He wanted to find out how much the mother on Earth would tell Him without appearing too urgent Himself here.

This made the Faerie Queen extremely urgent, and she began offering Him all sorts of things if He would just give her the key. When He said He was not interested in material things, but only in the things He wanted to know, she almost just grabbed for the key herself, but she wasn't sure how powerful He might be there, as though she sensed the presence of My light around Him, which it was in that moment. Instead, she said she would show Him what the key was good for as she moved to try to pull His penis into her, and that let Him know more than He had known before, and the satyrs also, about its use and function.

He remembered His mission of wanting to feel into her for the dark and huddled place to see if it would respond to Him, but as He entered her, He also found a sudden and surprising electrical rev up between them and lost control of Himself with an equally surprising and sudden orgasmic explosion.

The satyrs lost control of themselves in the orgasmic energy, their lust for power and their fear of loss of the key back to the mother on Earth. They began breaking into the mother on Earth's chambers. At the same time, the vines surrounding it began to grab for Them. The mother on Earth felt that Their power in trying to hold all of this back was barely equal to it and knew there wasn't a moment to lose. She was going to have to use the key.

The mother on Earth was the originator of "Open, says me!"

Using it now, she inserted the key into a secret place in her bedchamber and a secret passageway opened up right in her room from out of the Earth. Grabbing the key, she disappeared into it as fast as she possibly could, intending to shut it on the old wizard and leave Him there. The Father of Manifestation leaped to join her faster than she could do this, and the two of them fled together through firelit chambers of glittering jewels. In her haste, however, she had forgotten to close up the entranceway properly, and within moments, the satyrs were at their heels again.

This realization stirred such a rage in the Faerie Queen that she turned on them and sent them fleeing back the way they had come, running for their lives as she repeatedly seared and scorched the passageway with her fiery breath. She then commanded the opening to seal itself. As it slammed shut, it caught some of them by their tails, leaving them to howl and pull like little boys in a bizarre tug of war, until they realized they were going to have to let go of them and grow new ones.

The satyrs howled and raged about this, but the minute they regained any of their "satyr composure," they began plotting revenge. Meanwhile, the Father of Manifestation ran on ahead, a black snake of shame, slithering like quicksilver through the passageways, but knowing now that the missing Mother presence He was looking for was not being held prisoner as a damsel in distress, either in a cavern of the fire seas or within the mother on Earth; at least not in any form that was going to respond to Him now.

The Faerie Queen was running also. Feeling cheated, used, abandoned again and even set up, she began plotting the revenge her rage demanded here, which was trapping the Father of Manifestation, and possibly all of the other satyrs with whom He might even be in cahoots, in the fire seas forever.

Meanwhile, her rage was turning her into a Fire Dragon nearly too big for the passageway where she was running. She became terrified that the satyrs had plotted this as a way to get back into her fire seas and capture her again, but her terror only moved as rage. She raged alternately at them and the Father of Manifestation and then at My light as the cause of everything bad that was happening to her.

On the fury of her rage, she flew forth from her volcano, raging over Pangea, and the volcano erupted with held rage spilling hot, red lava, like issue from the menstrual flow. She swept about several times, and then her fear of reprisals settled her back down on the volcano like a mother dragon or a phoenix sitting on her nest.

Protecting herself from sexual attack from beneath with the hot lava flow and from above with her fiery breath, she spewed forth rage upon Pan, screaming that she had no safe place to go anymore, not even here where she had been alone for so long and now was encircled by only enemies and traitors, users and abusers, and all of them invaders on her Earth. Screeching that she had a right to be exactly as she was, she spewed out her rage toward My light, sending her fiery breath and smoke as far upwards as she could while the hot lava was pouring out vital survival essence into the Earth, cooling and mineralizing into dark stone as it went.

The kundalini return of vital survival essence was now pouring across Pan as rivers of fire, terrifying the inhabitants as it leapt from its established lava channels and bled across the land like a massive hemorrhage of death dealing issue. It was not possible to get near her hopelessness then, but it needs to move now. Then, she just moved rage at everyone she held responsible, which was everyone, either for not protecting or helping her, or for seeking her downfall and trying to gain control of her, but particularly, she raged at My light for not giving her any help.

When she came to her senses, she realized that she had nearly destroyed Pan again and winced at the thought that the Father of Manifestation might take revenge against her since she had not managed to kill Him. Her rage spewed forth for a little while again because she had, in fact, enjoyed having sex with Him more than she had wanted to. She put her head down under her wing then and grumbled and complained and blamed until she fell asleep.

Meanwhile, the inhabitants of Pan were devastated by these events and had not been prepared at all. They had all run, scrambling for safety and in doing so, had found themselves isolated in little patches of the woods which had managed to escape the lava flow. This made them feel there was a power in them that had been able to hold the lava at bay, but also that there was a power greater than them that only responded slightly to their needs and wishes, subjecting them to searing heat, but not quite killing them. Most of them blamed the Fire Dragon for this and did not see anything of their own role in denying the Mother's problems in order to avoid unpleasant places in the Will.

As soon as they recovered enough, however, they began to party again in celebration of their survival and their own power to keep themselves alive. The more they partied, the more Pan grew back into luxuriant forest around them, and although not as luxuriant and beautiful as before, still it convinced them all the more of their own powers and the powers of the "positive" approach. Almost none of them saw the rich lava earth beneath their feet as the cause or source of any of this. They celebrated instead their own ability to call forth life in the presence of a Mother who was inhospitable to their needs and wishes, and who grew more, instead of less, angry all the time without them having done anything to Her at all.

The parties grew even more outrageous then as though flaunting it in My face and the Mother's both.

"Look, we don't need You, and threaten us though You may, You cannot really hurt us for long!" This is what the rage of many of the inhabitants of Pan was saying here in a state of denial, loud and clear, but did not say straightforwardly because of the held fear that I might just strike them and prove them wrong.

THE MOTHER IN HELL

I was falling in darkness, knocked almost entirely out of My mind by the smack, in deep terror . . . only glimmers of red and orange with an occasional flicker of yellow by which to know Myself now.

Falling was terrifying. I had no idea where I might land or if I ever would . . . compression increasing all around Me, increasing My terror. If I did stop falling, it would be because the compression crushed Me until I could not move. I felt a heartbroken flood of grief, but could not cry. The terror was too great; terror of being annihilated.

When I stopped moving, the compression around Me was overwhelming. I felt pressured in upon and could not move anything back out. I felt dread terror of moving or making a sound anyway. I felt stalked, as though something was watching Me, ready to pounce if I even dared try to move in any way. I could not breathe, but I felt the thing stalking Me to be breathing all around Me as though I were inside its rib cage, already swallowed up by it.

I held My breath, trying in My terror to feel if there was anything I could do to save Myself. I felt surrounded by something, as if by walls of a cavern about to close in on Me and compress Me to death. I tried to inhale. It moved in. I tried to exhale. It did not move back. I tried not to need to breathe. I felt it growing excited by My terror, eager to compress Me more, excited, it seemed to Me, at the thought of this, but holding itself back, uncertain it wanted to so quickly or easily give up the pleasure it might find in prolonging this.

My terror nearly burst My heart. I heard the sound of its desperate beating in the deadening and absorbent silence of inexpressible feelings. I prayed for God, someone, anyone to rescue Me. There was no response except a leap in My terror that this engulfing compression somehow had loins whose excitement was quickened by My plight.

I did not know what I was going to do here. I could not stand it. I could not stand to feel what I was feeling. I felt desperate to leap out of there or out of Myself. "Please God! Rescue Me!" I kept praying. I tried to leap and could not muster even a wiggle.

My sexual energy was running wild at the idea that My survival was at stake, panicking so badly it could not stop even if it was drawing something that felt like a predator closer and closer to being unable to hold back its excitement to pounce.

Why did I have to experience this? What was My problem? All the cruel and heartless sounding voices who had ever asked Me such questions seemed to be all that was left of My mind; without comfort, only increasing My terror that I deserved this, that there would be no rescue and that no punishment was too terrible for Me.

I could not stand this terror. I would have done anything to get out of it then. I began clawing and struggling for My life as an internal feeling of extreme panic and hysteria without being able to make a sound or being able to move really. I felt as though I was buried alive too deeply to be able to get out, or a person drowning in dark, deep water, lost and alone. I suffered horribly; more horribly than I thought life could possibly suffer and still go on; no death, no rescue. Anything would be better than this, it seemed, and in that moment, I saw a light. I hoped it might be coming to rescue Me, but its searing harshness reminded Me of something, and before I could think of what this was, it pounced on Me.

At first, it seemed to be rescue. My mind was strangely inoperative here. I imagined any light had to be better than what I was already experiencing, but it beat Me up and raped Me horribly with no caring about what I was experiencing. It was screaming, growling and grinding into My dimming consciousness that it had come to finish the job that had been started already of complete annihilation of My presence.

I didn't care as long as it was fast. I just wanted out of My misery, but it seemed well able to read Me and told Me it would not be fast; it would be as slow as it could possibly make it; the more long and drawn out, the better, because it had no place else to go, nor anything else to do that would give it as much satisfaction as making sure I did not exist anymore and could never come back to bother anyone ever again. It was Lucifer.

The viciousness in his voice was terrifying to the bone marrow as to what he might think up as his means to do this. I wished I could die right there on the spot and leave him without this pleasure and Me without having to suffer this, but it did not happen. I tried to compress Myself down into no response to him for fear of what he might do if he found any signs of life left in Me, but he was drawn to any place in Me that still longed to vibrate.

He seemed to be more tuned in to Me than God or anyone else ever had been, but in exact and coldly precise reversal of what I wanted in that he knew exactly where to go and how to go there to extract and stimulate the most possible pain, suffering and emotional anguish. When I cried for God or the Father of Manifestation, Lucifer told Me They did not respond to Me; he responded to Me, and that I did not respond to Them either; it was his approach that I responded to. Lucifer told Me he was the only one I responded to and the only one who knew how to make Me respond.

"Especially sexually," he growled, hurting Me viciously, "because Your response is to pain."

"Deny you're orgasming!" he screamed at Me as I was experiencing orgasms in the shame and quaking spasms of My out of control terror. He was exactly able to accompany the physical pain he dealt with just the right thing to say and right time to say it to make My emotional anguish the worst. I was orgasming in confusion, terror and shame, not knowing what was happening to Me, or that it was because I was out of control, hating Lucifer and hating Myself most of all for orgasming in response to him.

Lucifer found out early that in spite of wishing to escape through death, I was also clinging to life. Then he not only made all the reasons seem ludicrous, but also terrified Me with the idea that I might not be able to die and that We might be there forever. I could not bear life at all with Lucifer torturing Me constantly, emotionally and physically, let alone endless life this way.

When Lucifer heard My prayers to God to just kill Me or let Me die, he screamed, "He's already heard you, you stupid bitch! I am

Your Angel of Death, sent by God to give You Your wish!"

Slamming Me downward into someplace where I landed in a heap, he sneered, "Look at You! God answers Your prayers and You cannot even accept it. You ought to be ashamed, really ashamed that You have troubled Him for so long and He finally sends me to give You what You both want and need to have peace in Creation and You cannot even cooperate and let it happen the way it's meant to. You always want it to be some other way, some better way, Your way!"

I felt his voice as though accompanied by knives and swords stabbing Me. I felt sensations of burning acid in My wounds and something pouring in and out of Me that also burned like acid. His held rage was so thick it was cutting Me; cutting Me and cutting Me and cutting Me into little bits and pieces and then catching itself in time to do a patch job that was just enough to keep Me alive for more suffering.

"Here, let me help You," his voice would say then, only to laugh horribly as My heart foolishly leaped up into hope, as though I didn't know he was only doing it so that he could make Me suffer longer and more. I felt foolish clinging to life there, and Lucifer reflected this by sneering at Me while the breathing all around Me was making animal lust sounds of a predator who has found the perfect prey; prey that foolishly excites him by struggling deliciously as he bites deeply, ripping and sucking, vital essence dripping like blood from his mouth, orgasming over and over from the eating on his "endless" feast, each orgasm, instead of satisfying, only intensifying his animal lust and passion for more and more; shivering and convulsing, not only in orgasms of the sexual organs, but also of the mouth and throat and even every cell in the predator's frenzied body, orgasming again and again on the sounds of terror and pain, which only he can hear, so he doesn't have to share his feast. As he bites into succulent, resilient and juicy body, the resistance from the will to live drawing him into more and more frenzy. Dripping vital essence from every orifice, terror and rage filling the space with the time warp of a nightmare that knows no end, the predator indulges and engorges himself, submerges and loses himself in a sexual feeding frenzy that seems to know no bounds or limitations to stop it, yet his prey still clings to the life that feeds his frenzy and does not know why.

I could not think why I would want to live in such torture, yet I felt I had to, and struggled desperately not to give in to his assault or to the intense compression around Me.

119

"You're not perfect! Far from it!" I heard Lucifer coldly say.

I experienced all of this and more with Lucifer telling Me all the while that I liked this, loved this, asked for this, even begged for it. He said My orgasms proved I loved it and if not, why did I stay there with him? He told Me he was not keeping Me there and that I was free to go, but rendered Me unable to move, never letting loose his grip of mouth, hands and penis, or lessening the feeling that there were many hands, mouths and penises coming in on Me from all around in the darkness, responding to My struggle only with increased lust to partake of it.

I was losing consciousness rapidly and praying that whatever happened to Me be the right result from My foolish mistake of saying I would, must, had to, and in moments of rage, even offering to and threatening to go into the darkness and find something out. What was I supposed to find out? What could these horrors possibly teach Me? Why had I ever been so foolish as to think this was the right thing to do?

I prayed for God to help Me somehow as He had promised He would; at least to help Me remember why I was there, which I already could not remember. I prayed desperately and urgently, but got nothing discernible back other than a feeling of an insurmountable and impenetrable, huge and heavy silence of blackness everywhere around Me, filled only with the mocking of Lucifer and echoing sounds in a way that frightened Me into thinking it was only My own internal madness telling Me everything I did not want to hear about Myself in case I did have any feelings of love left by which to want to live.

What was wrong with Me that I could not and did not just cease to exist, quietly and without the struggle that was only worsening My pain? Why couldn't I pull out of here crying, "Lesson learned already, I'll be good. I'll be whatever you say," and go back into Creation to get the help I really needed? What was making it take so long for God to respond to My urgent plea? Had He decided to abandon Me here after all? Had He tricked Me too? Had He had in mind all along to give Me to Lucifer as a way to get rid of Me?

I could only dumbly feel the presence of such questions like unmoved feces. I could not ask them.

"I'll help You get rid of that shit!" Lucifer screamed, reaming out My lower parts in terrible ways.

Lucifer told Me then that God had given Me to him. I plunged into the horror that this might be true. I could not stop his voice as

120

it persisted in telling Me all of these things. His voice penetrated like more stab wounds that I felt I was receiving along with it. I could not answer him back. I could not think, and if I formed a thought, he only criticized Me even more harshly, denying the validity of whatever I had formed in ways that made My head swim in loss of confidence and faith in Myself; stabbing at, pounding on and drowning Me in his insistence on his superior knowing, rearranging My consciousness in ways that I feared I would never be able to unscramble.

I could not talk anymore. It was useless, and from then on, I was alone in the world of this nightmare. My loss of being able to talk to anyone who might receive it seemed tantamount to isolation; for Me a kind of terror that cut the last line from Myself to any possible escape from the situation, or to anything other than Lucifer's hatred of Me. Lucifer drank up the terror of this in Me like some people snort cocaine.

I lay there, a crumpled mass, barely conscious, unable to talk. I could not get through to Lucifer. Even if he made sounds at times as though he were listening to Me, understanding Me or even agreeing with Me, it soon came to pass that I experienced everything he had read in Me being used against Me. I could not speak or even think of My own discomfort, but what Lucifer would not say, "It could be worse, much worse."

I was horrified whenever a little glimmer of anything did manage to surface and make its presence known because of what Lucifer was going to do to Me then. Going blank, feeling numb and desiring nothing seemed the only place I could go.

"Hope?" Lucifer sneered at Me. "For what? A rescue? You're not going to be rescued. You have no reason to hope. There is nothing for You but this. Desire for rescue only means You have not accepted Your right place. This is what You have created for Yourself. This is all You can create for Yourself and this is all there is for You. The sooner You stop resisting it, the better it will be for You. Struggle, desire, hope, try, it's all the same to me. The more You do it, the longer it takes You to learn that the only path is surrender; total and utter surrender to whatever is happening to You. There is no other path, and if You do not like it, You must still surrender. There is nothing other than Your own reflection and if You do not like it, You must still surrender to it until it changes of its own accord. You must never struggle. That only excites the lust of animal passion that wants to kill You. There is only one way to live and that is to be my slave and do exactly as I say. Otherwise,

You are going to pay and pay and pay and pay." He suddenly screamed on the last word, "forever!" hitting Me again like there was no place of receptivity in Me great enough to receive him unless he forced Me to receive him.

My emotional anguish, even when I did My best to hide or control it, caused him to preach at Me in an angry voice.

"I am not doing this to You. You caused all of this Yourself with Your own resistance. You ask for it and then You do not like it when it comes. This is Your right place. God had to put You here because You wouldn't go to Your right place on Your own."

In a dim and unfocused sort of way, I could hear what seemed like monsters screaming in the background, "It's Your fault. It's all Your fault!" over and over, penetrating Me as if they were armed with pins and needles to punctuate My stab wounds. Lucifer obviously commanded them. "You're to blame, You're to blame," they chanted.

I feared what was going to follow this tirade, but I could not comprehend what was wanted from Me, what they wanted Me to do or how I could please them.

Lucifer gave Me the maximum amount of time to fear what was next before he approached Me. He seemed to notice when My fear had peaked and begun to lapse and pounced then, when he could startle Me into awareness of his next horror. I tried not to struggle for My life and not to move in any way that would displease him. Maybe then he would stop punishing Me. If he thought I was dying or dead already, maybe he would lose interest in making Me suffer so much.

Lucifer read Me here too. "So You don't want to exist!" he sneered. "Make up Your mind, life or death. You're a liar anyway and I'm going to prove it." Then he took Me down into more suffocation terror than I was already in, reviving Me only to make Me suffer again by suffocating Me over and over, pushing Me down and pulling Me up until I begged for both life and death. I begged for mercy, but he had none, stopping only when he could not revive Me from My exhaustion anymore.

The terrifying heat and shaking cold I felt did not concern him either, but he would pretend it did. "Complaining of the heat, My dear? Let me find a way to help You." He would then shove Me angrily, I felt, though he denied it, through all of the temperatures I might like as though letting Me notice them was what he wanted in order to increase My suffering, and then push Me into such feelings of coldness that I would have to shiver and shake and finally cry out for relief as I had in the terrible, overwhelmingly compressive heat.

"Complaining of the cold, My dear?" He would say then, as My chattering teeth and body shaking uncontrollably from head to toe felt sensations like icicles stabbing Me all the way into My heart.

"Here, let me help." My chattering teeth were pulled out then. "There now, that's so much better. No more chattering teeth!" Then he dropped them down My throat. "There now, You still have them in case You have a comment to make."

To My look of horrified, wincing, gagging pain he said, "You're never satisfied are You? No matter what I do, it's never good enough, is it? Never the right thing, is it? Never perfect enough for You to agree to receive it, is it?" Then he would angrily thrust and thrust his penis into My mouth and throat telling Me he was showing Me what My mouth and throat were good for, and it wasn't for answering back.

Sometimes I shattered there in the frozen, brittle cold of his blue and white light with Lucifer's voice still screaming harsh criticisms amongst all the pieces.

The ferocity of his attack mounted as he went along. He would begin beating Me up as an accompaniment to his rage as though he didn't even notice he was doing it. Then he would take My suffering body and shove it furiously to the opposite extreme, freezing Me and then burning Me with a heat that gave Me no warmth or comfort as though he knew no middle ground and had no intent to find any.

He left Me longer that I felt I could possibly endure in extreme situations, even when I was trying to accept him there, as though it was some sort of bizarre and loveless experiment concerning My limits, and how they were always so limiting to him; literally grabbing Me back from what felt like the edge of annihilation, for what purpose I could not understand, by reversing My sensations in ways that I could never trust as healing or as a rescue because he took Me to another unpleasant extreme which would make Me just as desperate, until it seemed his purpose, or pleasure, must be torturing Me by pressuring, battering and breaking all of My limits as though I were a judged and condemned criminal for even having any.

"Pleasure?" He said suddenly. "I get no pleasure from this. Can't You see how miserable I am, My dear? Why don't you ever feel My suffering? You resist My efforts to teach You until you drive me to these extremes. That makes it ever so much harder My dear, and makes Me have to go to ever so much greater extremes."

He became a large snake then, coiled around Me, squeezing My resistance from Me, hypnotizing Me, torturing Me with the sensations of his forked tongue as he bit Me repeatedly, filling Me with venom of the hatred in his point of view, then leaving Me to suffer the results without any help, compassion or mercy.

Always, Lucifer's voice had a tone to it that let Me know My limits were unforgivable shortcomings on My part, My own lack of openness, My judgments, My lack of acceptance for everything, My lack of acceptance of what he wanted, My refusal to receive, open, accept, My problem, My refusal to receive Him.

When raging seemed to lose interest for him, he would flip to another extreme, sometimes crying in bizarre scenes that seemed unreal, or grotesquely surreal, begging My forgiveness, saying he was My lover and that I would not receive him. I could hear his monsters making mockery of it in the background, but I could not tell if they were mocking him, or responding to his display of emotion like it was another trick on his part, or if they were making a mockery of Me for My heart having another momentary leap of hope that Lucifer might somehow come around, or for finding a little place of sympathy for his plight in My heart.

"You don't know what I'll be in the next moment," Lucifer would say, but when I tried to respond to that and open to receive him, he showed Me only form change that made Me feel tricked because it felt the same; opposed to Me having any life the way it felt good to Me.

I did not know what was really going on there, but it didn't matter. These scenes never lasted long before Lucifer was back to his harsh self again and gave no sign of even remembering the other side he had shown Me. I feared and hated Lucifer by far and away more than anything else I felt for him, so it was almost a relief to Me that he seemed to forget these scenes.

My heart belonged to another. The Father of Manifestation was who I longed for here, but I had given up on Him. He was too late for a rescue. I was too far gone even though I still had little bouts of wishing for a rescue in which I sometimes thought someone was there for Me. But just when My heart would start to leap, it would turn out to be Lucifer instead and either he had impersonated someone I wanted to have rescue Me or I had hallucinated Their presence.

In a fury, he would pound it into Me over and over again that

I was not being rescued and that I was not going to be rescued, screaming at Me that it was My own fault he was beating Me because he was My mate and that he had just tricked Me into showing him that I was not giving him My heart, and that trickery was necessary to get the truth out of Me, and even then, I always lied.

Over and over he repeated, while pounding it in, that God and the Father of Manifestation had rejected Me and had found other mates, each in Their own realms; and somehow, I would see pictures, as though Lucifer could show Me movies of what he wanted Me to see. I would see God in the Heavens with the Angels and the Father of Manifestation on Earth with many other spirits all taking My place. I did not know if it was true or not, but I did not want it to be true.

"You can't accept reality!" Lucifer would scream at Me. "Why can't You accept reality? You are my mate, and You belong in my realms."

I felt I was being forced to be his mate without any choice or say in the matter. I was being horribly damaged, and I now feared that he somehow thought he was making Me over into some grotesque and bizarre image of what he thought his mate should be.

I lay there, battered, stabbed, crumpled and broken; My form grotesquely rearranged by his so-called improvements, barely conscious and in whatever position he put Me, dully, at best, listening to him talk, lecture and scream as though he didn't even notice My plight, even laughing cruelly while My deepest dreams and wishes were shattering and My heart was breaking into more pieces than I thought it possible for My already broken heart to break. I felt its pieces falling out and down farther than I already was and could do nothing to stop it. How could I hold My heart together in this or even ask it to try? I feared for My heart greatly. What could be lower than I was already?

"Death," Heart said. My heart broke even further then under My overwhelming weight of grief.

"It's Your fault, it's all Your own fault," Lucifer's monsters screamed over and over. Even when I could no longer really focus on their words, their hideous sounds still penetrated Me as though I had no skin anymore.

Lucifer never seemed to notice or care about the balance point I wanted; or perhaps he did, as he pushed past it in ways that began to seem deliberate to Me. He hated Me, that was clear, but he said he loved Me over and over in ways that made Me feel sickened by the very word itself. And the ways in which he portrayed love as silly, sappy, boring, stupid, fauning, phony, insincere and heartbreaking, even manipulative and cruel, I felt deep shame and fear that I was all these things Myself to have thought feelings of love were desirous or even real.

He made fun of My attempts to go toward God and portrayed God's rejections of Me in ways that made My attempts look ludicrous. In his portrayals, I was a blind fool with delusions of grandeur concerning Myself and My right place. He also satirized My love for others and gave Me pictures of Them that made Me wonder if love had ever existed. I feared I was the undiscerning, boring, silly, sappy, stupid, insipid, fauning, split off from reality dreamer he said I was; insincere, manipulative, heartbreaking and even cruel, just as he said I was.

Where I had thought love was the intent and that Our problems were the slush pond that had to give way to the love and get straightened out, he made Me feel that the slush, which he was throwing in My face, was the reality, was all there really was, and was much larger than My puny, little illusions about love, and much larger than My little dream world had ever noticed until he forced Me to look at it by shoving Me into it. It was as though he was able to reverse My viewpoint, and when he did, and made Me see "reality" as he called it, it appeared to be much larger, even than God, and more terrible than anything I ever wanted to see anyplace, ever. And when he flipped Me over and made Me see it from his point of view, it looked so overwhelmingly huge and terrible, I feared it might be true and that he was right, and that I had been refusing to look at reality just like he said. I became terrified that I was clinging to dreams that were not real, did not exist and could not be real, and that My only hope of survival was to let go of them. What kind of survival this would be, without hopes or dreams, I could not imagine. I was terrified of its loveless feeling.

When he flipped Me over into his point of view like this, it did look like Creation was the way he said it was, and that only naïveté could have thought otherwise. When I didn't want to believe everything was this loveless and terrible, Lucifer sneered at Me telling Me I had the kind of naïveté that didn't learn from observation or experience, and that this meant I would forever be its victim.

"Reality is it's a dog eat dog world," Lucifer told Me over and over. My feelings of Love's presence, he insisted, were just fluffy clouds placed over the top by God to avoid seeing that He did not create what He wanted to create because He is not really God.

"I can rip the mask off of that anytime I want to and show You what's really underneath it. I am the one who understands reality. I am the one who knows how it got created. I am the one who is supposed to be God. Your God is a sham, a faker, a phony and a pretender who has no real power. He was just a silly dream of Yours. If He has power and loves You as You say, then where is He? Why doesn't He rescue You?" Lucifer would expound while strutting up and down.

I tried not to allow Myself to have any response to this. I was frozen in pain, horror and terror, like a paralyzed person whose fate is to have no escape. It was only what I could not hold in, shove down or otherwise control that Lucifer had to work with here, yet he punished Me horribly even for that without making it clear whether it was because I did have a response or did not have a response. Whatever response I had, it wasn't the right response. It was My resistance, My lack of faith or My false compliance. He was the assaultive, battering waves; I, the hapless victim whose sickening feeling in My stomach Lucifer pressured into unstopable vomiting while punishing Me for repulsing him with My vomit.

Besides subjecting Me to horrible extremes of heat and cold and drying Me and drowning Me in horribly heartless ways, Lucifer also tortured My desire for movement by not allowing it to have any spontaneity or comfort. He never let on that he noticed how this tortured Me, saying that he had learned how to meet My needs by watching Me reverse Myself.

After suffering with Lucifer's ideas of stretching My limits, I would want to roll up in a little ball, pull Myself together and comfort Myself. Then Lucifer would trap Me there unable to unfold. After I was trapped for so long that I broke down and begged for relief, he would leave Me for a long time still. If I begged enough, he would come like he was going to bestow the great gift of mercy upon Me and I would get to suffer the horror I had begged for as he had his monsters stretch My body rippingly fast to the overextended other extreme.

"See how quickly I meet Your needs?" he would say as though he didn't notice any problem.

I could not gain relief from that position either, trapped in it as I was until I again had to beg for relief and again be punished for never being satisfied, and then reversed again.

"This is what You wanted, isn't it, My dear? You were begging for this, weren't You, My dear."

And there I would stay until I was begging him to kill Me, and he would not, and I did not know why.

"You must live in this, You told me Yourself." he said.

I thought he was going to torture Me until he gained complete compliance from Me, or alignment, as he called it; an alignment that did not call for any change or evolution on his part.

I lived in terror of him moving to annihilate Me, and of the compression, explosion tactics he was using on Me, fearing their success, and also the opposite; their failure, and in the terror that for some unreasonable reason I could not face or fathom, I was too terrified to face either reality; life or death. If Lucifer loved anything, he seemed to love this spot in Me and tortured Me as much as he could there while saying he didn't have to kill Me, I was killing Myself.

I felt there was no way to please, appease or stop him, but I still felt I must try. The pain of this torture was unbearable and I needed it to stop, but it did not. It went on as though so impersonal it did not matter what I felt.

Escape from where he was holding Me prisoner and torturing Me was impossible. I had already learned this the hard way when Lucifer played with Me by letting it seem that I was escaping. Sometimes he ran Me down like it was a hunt, I was the prey and he, the hunter who was greatly enjoying it. He ran Me to the point of heartburst before pouncing on Me or letting his monsters catch Me and bring Me to him. Sometimes they would devour parts of Me along the way and deliver Me to him as a ripped apart corpse.

Lucifer partook of Me also, but only as if this were an appetizer; then he would give Me a little renewal time while he hatched a new inspiration. Sometimes he left Me for long periods of time and made it seem as if he was not even watching Me. In these scenarios, My feet and legs often went out from under Me, so frightened were they of no escape possible.

Each time he did this, it took Me a longer time to believe he had perhaps really left Me before I would begin to think of sneaking away; terrified to try it, but even more terrified to stay, and having to crawl because of My broken and frightened legs. But Lucifer was watching Me.

I became lost in dark, labyrinth-like places. What they really were, I did not know because I could not find My way or even see, and as in nightmares, I could not run and get anywhere.

Every passageway out I thought I had found would suddenly

be blocked by Lucifer or one of his monsters appearing in a sudden ghoulish light, terrifying Me and screaming at Me, when My heart leaped into My mouth, that I hadn't learned anything, and then leaping on Me with claws, fetid breath and predatory excitement.

I was a scurrying mouse and a trembling rabbit; Lucifer, the soaring, scouring bird of prey and the prowling, fast moving snake. I was the hapless antelope, or zebra; he, the laughing hyena, lion or pack of wild dogs. I was everything that suffers and dies; he everything that preys without caring. Aye, I was everything of prey and he, every predator until I knew not what form this was going to take.

Lucifer had such a mastery of form changes; even tricking Me with apparent friendliness, which I fell for over and over in My thirst for it, only to have him suddenly reverse it and prey upon Me again until I did not know what form I could trust, if any, or even what feelings could guide Me accurately. Often, I felt he drove Me through form changes faster than I could handle them, and often I felt I was left trapped there, unable to get all of Myself back out.

Sometimes Lucifer seemed to well up from deep within Me and leap, suddenly springing from Me to loom over Me threateningly. At other times, he seemed to dive into Me from someplace else. Sometimes I broke apart, or shattered. Sometimes I imploded or ran as though liquid. Sometimes I felt powerless, as though caught in webs that seemed to cut Me as though Lucifer could penetrate My very veins or run there between the pieces like a heartless transfusion trying to take over, but always, I finally noticed, the harsh voice of his criticisms in whatever form he took told Me it was only the reflection of My own inner voice.

Sometimes it was too much for Me, and I would collapse before they had had enough fun with Me. Lucifer and his monsters would grab Me cruelly then and revive Me, water being thrown in My face, or even My whole body being submerged, for how long I didn't know before I could even feel it; drowning Me sometimes without noticing and finding then some way to revive Me back into the horror of this again and again.

Sometimes Lucifer's monsters leaped on Me slathering, licking and slobbering until it seemed they would devour Me unless Lucifer called them off. They felt free to grunt, groan, growl, snarl, howl, screech, belch, vomit and fart, defecate and urinate and chatter incessantly, while I was never quiet enough for them, never listened well enough to what they had to say and was never dainty enough in My body to not repulse them. I was repulsive, they made that clear, in every way it was possible to be repulsive.

They pounded, stuffed and stabbed things into Me that hurt and heaped, poured, dumped and smeared horrible things on Me that made Me gag, telling Me it was only parts of Me to show Me how repulsive I was. Then they would cackle in some hideous joy I did not share, slobbering, slurping, slavering, lapping, sucking and gnawing at Me like they had just added condiments to a meal, and then, later, when I had enough dread of their growing hunger, do it all over again.

I was so confused I no longer knew what made sense and what just played into the hands of My torturers. The only thing I felt for sure was that I hated My experience and wanted out of it.

"Most unfortunate that You are so confused You do not know what direction to go even to save Yourself," Lucifer said then, "when I am the one who cares enough to be here with You to try to teach You. How unfortunate for You that You are such a slow learner, and for Me too, My dear, because it enrages Me that You don't already know it." Sarcasm was his invention along with insidious laughter.

I was unable to hold My head up anymore, hanging it downward, battered and damaged, if I ever was allowed to sit up. Lucifer forced My head upright then. I had no look of intelligence left either. I was grotesque, which didn't please Me at all. Sometimes I felt like a battered corpse in a time lapse movie as faces superimposed themselves one on top of another on My face in a frantic effort to find a face that Lucifer wouldn't punish anymore. Lucifer said I was dishonest about who I was and was changing Myself to gain favors instead of being someone who deserved them.

Often I felt blank and empty as though dead. If there was anything left in Me that dared to feel anything better about Myself than the horrible reflection Lucifer was giving Me, I didn't want it anymore because Lucifer would find this place and find it to be something to punish. I learned that I should not have any feelings for Myself at all.

This made Me miserable, but even this incited Lucifer to furious hatred, as though even in My misery, he had to be the most miserable, claiming he was extremely frustrated and miserable, much more so than Me, in spite of what appeared to Me to be obvious evidence to the contrary.

He attacked Me again and again for not receiving him, for never being satisfied and for nothing he ever did being good enough, which meant I was saying he was not good enough, or not enough for Me. It didn't matter that I wasn't participating in these arguments; he had them with Me anyway, and if I ever did feel any desire to respond, he repelled it, hurling it back on Me viciously and telling Me, "You don't know! You are not the one who has the answers."

I was lost in darkness and pain and did not know what to do about it. Sometimes, when I felt like giving up, I would unknowingly lapse away from My overwhelmingly terrible feelings into other places and moments. Sometimes I had dreams or visions that looked like My ancient and long held original pictures of Earth in which things were the way I wanted them to be. The Father of Manifestation would be there and I felt happy with Him and He seemed to be happy with Me. There would be faeries and elves dancing around Us, and they seemed to be very happy too. Sometimes I could even smell the air, but I could not stay there for long. Horrible sounds would intrude into these pictures, and I would be startled, pulled, yanked, jerked and smacked out of them by the harsh return to the tortures of Lucifer.

Sometimes the pictures were also taken over by others who did not care about them in the ways that I did, and I was very disturbed by this. I wanted to wake up in these other places and hated Myself that I could not. Everything was backwards. I could not wake from the nightmare and the dream I wanted to awaken in, I could not reach .

At other times, I thought Lucifer was right and that I would not be satisfied even there because I did not like the way the other spirits were behaving. In those moments, I would be brought out of the pictures by harsh screams saying, "No one is wanting You there. That's why no one is looking for You. No one wants to hear You telling them what to do anymore!"

It was terrifyingly disorienting to hear those voices intruding in the places of My dreams, pulling Me back into the harsh and barren wilderness of Hell, claiming at the same time they were inside My head and were only My own voices. My loss of mind here did not allow Me to figure out what was happening. I was being victimized the way mentally retarded people have been victimized by brutes who have imprisoned them for their own perverse purposes and pleasures, derived largely from sexual, mental, emotional and physical torture. They are Me, and I am them in this place.

Meanwhile, even My good pictures had become torture because I couldn't stay in them, only long for them in an idealized, heartbroken nostalgia, not even free of critical voices intruding to tell Me how unworthy I was to have even a moment's relief of fleeting dream or vision.

"It's always better someplace else, isn't it, My dear," Lucifer intoned with his scathing voice that could so quickly turn vicious. "But You didn't think so when You were there. Then, You complained and screamed and destroyed the place, and for that You have to be punished!"

I did not want to let Myself respond to him, but My body began shaking uncontrollably. It was pouring forth sweat like rain, but I felt ice cold. Lucifer shamed Me horribly for this, telling Me again how loathsome and repulsive I was and how I had no self-control and not even enough courage to face up to the consequences of My actions.

"It could be so much worse for You, so much worse." His tone let Me know he was planning to take Me another step toward just how much worse it could be.

I hated Myself for not having enough self-control to avoid letting Lucifer know how I felt. I didn't want him to know that I cared whether I lived or died, and I hated Myself that I cared about life because I wanted to die to get out of My pain.

Lucifer shouted at Me over and over that I didn't have the courage to live or die, and that I couldn't do either one right.

"Look at You! You claim You can't live this way but You don't die. What am I supposed to do with You?"

In exasperation, Lucifer grabbed Me and began dragging Me by the head, with My mangled body flopping along behind. I did not know where he was taking Me. I could not see anything but My own pictures of terror about what was going to happen next.

Apparently, he dragged Me to the edge of Hell and jerked Me upright. My legs would not position themselves under Me. He screamed at Me and kicked Me until I was in the position he wanted. He ordered Me to open My eyes, but I could not. They were swollen and stuck shut, or else I could no longer see. I already feared that I couldn't stand to see whatever it was he wanted Me to see and that the searing pain of Lucifer's light made it impossible for Me to open My eyes anymore. He began pounding on Me and ordering Me to look.

When I still could not, he ordered My eyes to be forced open. I thought I had long since lost the ability to see this way, but when I did blink and wince at seeing his light, he ordered My eyelids cut off. It was a long time before I could see then during which My eyes were tortured into a place of open dryness that could not cry or bleed to block My sight.

When satisfied that I had to see now, Lucifer angrily pulled My head into the position he wanted and ordered Me to look. While he waited, he screamed orders and criticisms at Me, with his monsters mimicking him in the background. I struggled to please him, but his blinding light made it impossible for Me to see what he was ordering Me to see until he stepped menacingly around behind Me as though he were about to shove My face in it.

Then I saw a little point of light in space. I thought it was only one of My own trembling teardrops falling in the darkness.

"That's Earth," Lucifer hissed in My ear like a snake ready to strike. I recoiled, feeling a dread terror run up My spine about what he had in mind next. "That's Earth, isn't it!" he screamed insistently.

Another horror took over Me that he might not have known if I hadn't recoiled in terror. "I would have forced You to tell me anyway," he hissed. I could feel a venomous forked tongue on the back of My neck tickling it cruelly. I felt the dread threat of imminent death.

"Earth is mine," he hissed, "all mine. I'm going to go there when I am finished with You."

I saw then that it was Earth I was seeing and My heart leaped for her there. I saw her shimmering like a droplet of water in the dark wilderness of space, trembling like a ripening piece of fruit about to be plucked; a mere morsel, a moment's gulp to the insatiable appetite of Lucifer. What was left of My heart leaped into My throat again in terror of what was going to happen to Earth and all of the spirits on it.

I sank back down into My own internal vision, overwhelmed by My desperation. What was going to happen now? Was Lucifer going to drag Me to Earth and force Me to deliver up to him all that was there? Or was he going to finish Me off now and go to Earth to wreak havoc on everyone there without a Mother's presence to offer up any love or mercy even at their death?

I could not stand any of the possibilities that seemed present there and wished I had died a long time before he had ever shown or told Me any of this, yet knew I could not for all the same reasons I wanted to. I could not stand to see My children sacrificed to him the way I had been, no matter what I thought of them at other times. How had he gained this power? Where was God? Where was the Father of Manifestation? Did Their love have any power or had it ever been real? They seemed so remote and uncontactable.

133

Maybe They did not even exist anymore, or if They did, maybe They really did not care the way Lucifer said They did not.

I did not know if I had ever had any real feelings of love in Me. Terror ran so deep through Me I split open on the spot and could not hold Myself together anymore. Emotions began pouring out of Me like rivers of fire running in blood, anguish and tears. I could not take it anymore. I simply could not take any more. How much could a heart break over what Creation might have been, and what was going to happen to it now? Why couldn't love be the way, and with all of the little spirits playing happily at their Parents' side? The absence of the loving arms of the Father haunted Me then as it had from the beginning of time, and there was still no comfort for My pain in any place that I could find.

I wanted to die and get out of the horrible tortured place I was in, but now I had the horrible feeling again that I must live somehow and find a way to protect and save My children; horrible feeling, I say, because I had no feeling of actually having the power to be able to do this. I was shaking like there would be nothing left of Me but tiny pieces and pouring sweat like it wasn't possible to hold anything in anymore.

Things were moving here that had not been able to move in the deeper reaches of Hell, but I did not like the results of that either. I was falling apart in a terrifying way, and Lucifer was coldly sucking up My essence at the head of the banquet table, while his monsters went wild in another murderously competitive, sexual feeding frenzy of punching, stabbing, shoving and stepping on one another trying to have a place at the table, or get to the feeding trough, to feed on My remains. They were slavering up everything that was pouring out of Me, and I was powerless to do anything but lie there feeling Myself bleeding to death and being devoured.

When their sexual excitement reached a fever pitch, Lucifer coldly announced that since I did not want to go to Earth after all, and that since it appeared that I did not want to take him there as My mate, it must be because I had always said he was never enough.

He was going to show Me now how wrong I was. He began pounding Me and slamming Me back down into the deeper reaches of Hell with large hard things, shoving them into Me sexually, thrusting into all of My orifices at once, or what remained of them I should say. Large, sharp, hard phalluses again seemed to be coming at Me from all directions, shoving into Me and making orifices wherever there weren't any available. All the while, screaming voices furiously repeated over and over, "Is this enough? Is this enough?"

I was swirling in the loss of Myself into total terror as I felt them swirling wildly in a mad dance of their own strange kind of ecstasy around Me. As I was falling out of control in terror, Lucifer was riding Me down, thrusting and pushing down into My mouth with his gaggingly huge penis presence. Causing Me to vomit up more than I thought could still be left in Me, he went on thrusting and thrusting deeper and deeper, pounding Me into the suffocation death of no breath to be gotten and choking on vomit that was being triggered to come up and forced to go back down again. My stomach went into wild spasms of terror for its survival while I felt monsters scrambling and fighting to suck up the vomit and drippings. Lucifer was screaming at Me that I loved this. Look how I was orgasming! This was what I had wanted all along! And then flipping over into the rage that screamed at Me to tell him it was enough, screamed at Me for not answering and let Me know that any answer at all would only have brought more of the same.

When I went unconscious there, he started from the other end, shoving his large, hard phallus, pounding and thrusting all the way to My heart and beyond, pounding and breaking My pelvis and spine into pulverized pieces as he slammed Me with his grip and his thrusts and his rage.

"Is this enough? Is this enough?" he growled at Me, louder and louder as he thrust more and more furiously. And then, "This is what you want, isn't it?" over and over, screaming more and more furiously as his thrusts grew faster and more driven.

I was barely conscious, yet felt pain everytime he slammed Me. I could not take it anymore. I just could not take any more. My exhaustion from fighting the compression, from fighting him and his monsters and from fighting for My life collapsed there in implosion terror, shuddering in the orgasms of My loss of ability to hold back anything anymore; not even the last of My life essence from running out of Me and into Lucifer. I died with the impression that this was what God wanted; a ghoulishly sexual feeding frenzy to the death on the Mother in Hell.

When I finally fell lifeless in Lucifer's grip, he only said that I must finally be satisfied because I had finally gotten what I wanted, and discarded Me. The moment he did, his monsters were on Me with their insatiable, driven desire to devour the last of My remains and have their sordid sexual fun in any opening they could still find or make in what was left of Me.

There was nothing left alive of Me, I was sure, yet something still spoke to Me that sounded like My own voice, saying I must still try to save Myself no matter how impossible it looked. I hated this voice. Why didn't it just let Me give up and die? I cried bitterly then from whatever place this was and told it if it wanted Me to save Myself, then it had better find the way. I contacted rage for the first time then, and not even at Lucifer; at Myself, or whatever part of Myself wouldn't give Me any peace. Where was rage all of this time, and where was its great strength and power when I needed it, when I could have used it and when it wasn't too late?

There was no way I was going to rescue Myself now. There was nothing left to rescue, I told it. It told Me to look again, that I was a small piece of light hovering near My lifeless form and that I had better get away from there before Lucifer saw it. I looked at My lifeless form laying there then; a battered, broken, beaten, burned, twisted, bloody, swollen, cut up, ripped up, torn, dismembered, disemboweled and skinned body still being ripped at, fought over and eaten by monsters, and saw for the first time that Lucifer had raped Me with My own leg bone, having eaten the flesh first! I smelled the burned bone, as though he had even cooked it first, and collapsed in grief and horror that took Me down instead of up as I imagined the escape route was, and I was right. Down only made My grief heavier and heavier until I sank in despair again. I could not move Myself at all. I dissolved in the feeling that I had no place to go, no feeling left of desire to live and nothing left of Me with which to go.

I was hovering, barely vibrating, underneath My lifeless form when rage grabbed Me and said I must try to live. Rage said it had already sent an emissary to God to tell Him the Mother was dying and that if He did not act, it was going to be too late.

"It already is too late," I replied. I felt bitter that this rescue came when it did and I did not trust it. "I'm sorry," I said to this rage, "I do not trust you or your power to do anything here."

Rage said it was not its power, but My own power that must do something here.

I hated rage for coming up with this now after all I had suffered. What poor timing, to say the least. I felt like it had no grasp of the situation, the suffering or the conditioning I had received, but I could not articulate anything. I guiltily tried to please it. I nodded My head in compliance, but I had no idea what to do.

"Flee," it said. I tried to, but I could not move. "Lucifer will find

You if You do not flee," it said.

"Lucifer will find Me if I do flee," I said. Rage grabbed Me then and said to try.

I tried to please it by trying to fly upwards, but I could not make any progress. The weight of everything seemed insurmountable to Me, and there was almost nothing left of Me with which to try. I whimpered and felt sorry for Myself that it was not possible.

"You must try," rage kept insisting until I feared it was going to attract Lucifer if I did not make it shut up by trying to do what it said. I tried to fly, but was only able to hover a little.

In that moment, this rage screamed in My head that it did not matter who else did or did not want Me to live, I must live for Myself. I could not hear "Live for Myself," at that time. Rage screamed at Me, "Live for the children then!" and this gave Me renewed determination.

The rage was flying in pieces around Me and I knew Lucifer saw it. He leaped for it. The rage ran for its life, but this gave Me a little time to struggle unnoticed and I began to lift a little.

All of a sudden, there were pieces of this rage that seemed to be flying everywhere. Lucifer noticed them immediately, and when he did, they all began calling out to him, taunting him even, with calls of, "I'm the Mother! Aren't you going to catch me, don't you want me?"

I looked at them as though they were Parental in the Mother then and I was a little piece trying to move on My own, but again I was paralyzed. I panicked, not knowing what I could do since flying seemed so impossible. I feared this was yet another false rescue, staged by Lucifer. I nearly passed out, and in that moment, felt something starting to lift Me.

I tried to escape then, hoping I could gain some speed or distance, or somehow find a way to succeed while Lucifer was being distracted from Me. It was the heaviest lift job I have probably ever done on Myself, but still I felt pressed down, unable to move upward at all. Nothing seemed to help. I could not get anywhere.

I had so little consciousness I do not know how I lifted or was lifted. I must have passed out in terror. The next thing I knew, I was lying in a place where I could not move, with the Father of Manifestation bending over Me telling Me He had found Me as a little glimmer and could not lift Me any further without My help. I did not trust Him either, at first, or even that it was Him. I tried to jump away from Him, but I could not, and I collapsed into terrified tears.

Either He was afraid I would attract Lucifer, or it was the help He needed, because He grabbed Me and We began to move. This was the first time I consciously experienced any real movement away from the rest of Myself that I knew I had left in Hell.

I looked back at the lifeless form of Myself I had left behind there still trapped. I noted for the first time then many of the horrors I had experienced in My dimly conscious states in Hell, and I felt I could not bear to leave her behind.

I felt I could not leave Myself behind there. I felt I must go back and try to help Myself, somehow. I felt hysterical to at least find a way to lift My remains into the immediate comfort of My heart and rescue it along with whatever part of Me this was I was left with now. I wanted desperately to go back, but the Father of Manifestation would not let Me. He insisted I must come with Him and that I must help Him to rescue Me. He was growing quite agitated.

I feared His rage and knew I was going to have to do what pleased Him, but I could not help but keep looking back, unable to take My eyes off of My own horrible fate in Hell. Even now as I watched, Lucifer's monsters were still howling, fighting and laughing as they were devouring the last of Me, not even leaving My bones, even though Lucifer was screaming at them to come and help him catch what remained of Me that was escaping.

We knew We were running out of time here and that I must let go of what was holding Me there and go with the Father of Manifestation, but I felt paralyzed in indecision and lack of determination to go on. I looked back like a mother gazing for the last time upon the horribly mutilated and battered form of her lifeless child and felt the heartbreaking grief of it all. I promised her and Myself that I would find some way to rescue her from this and heal her of all of her terrible pain and suffering, no matter how long it took or what was involved. I did not know at the time how long this would really take or what was really going to be involved, but it felt to Me as if it was only the determination of this that was going to allow Me to let go of her there enough to move on with the Father of Manifestation. I turned away and tried to let go, and when I did, I was overwhelmed by the heartbroken grief of it all.

Even though I was terrified of incurring the Father of Manifestation's rage, I could not stop grieving. I was only able to add the quaking of My terror to it. Somehow, He managed to lift Us together to a place where lifting began to feel a little easier. It was still very tough going, and the Father of Manifestation insisted repeatedly that I must let go of whatever was holding Me from going with Him, or He was going to have to drop Me in order to get Himself out of there.

He did drop Me then and flew on ahead. This terrified Me into struggling toward Him as best I could, calling out to Him to please not leave Me.

The Father of Manifestation did not understand My problem here, thinking this was a place I would surely be eager to get out of. The Plane of Reversal, however, was almost impossible for Me to cross, and without His help, I do not think I would have been able to. I nearly collapsed there and gave up forever, but the Father of Manifestation wouldn't let Me.

I didn't want to move. I was afraid of flying or any movement. I wanted to stay quiet and warm. Having a feeling of wanting to get through this place or of trying to was terrifying to Me. I told the Father of Manifestation I had better wait until later. I had better try later.

My feelings of wanting to go back, My feelings that I couldn't be anyplace but Hell anymore, My feelings that Lucifer was inescapable at all tried to come forward, angering the Father of Manifestation who looked shocked and horrified as though I didn't want to be rescued.

I heard Lucifer's voice telling Me what I feared was true. I hated his presence in Me, but feared that Lucifer was My light and that there was no other place for Me. "You want to go back. It's what you want," the voice said.

I feared hearing his voice and the effect it had on Me. I didn't want the Father of Manifestation to hear it and think it was Me talking this way or that I was keeping Lucifer with Me because I wanted him there. I did not dare sink into these feelings because I would begin falling away from the Father of Manifestation who was trying so hard, and with so much difficulty, to lift Me. I was afraid I was going to fall back into Hell and either take the Father of Manifestation with Me, or that He would let go of Me, possibly for good this time. He urged Me to let go of whatever was holding Me back and try My best to move along with Him. He talked about a new beginning. I wanted a new beginning. I wanted His love and companionship. I wanted to please Him. I wanted to be rescued. I could not stand the idea of any more torture in Hell, but I was haunted by the picture of what I had left behind Me in Hell and pulled on by the bondage that still held Me there.

I tried to focus on My gratitude for His rescue, but I had mixed

139

feelings about it. I felt so damaged, disfigured and ugly, and I felt so small. The pictures I had of Myself were not good feeling ones. I did not know how I must look to the Father of Manifestation or why He had left Me for so long. I feared My rescue was too late and that I could never recover, but I did not like to mention the feelings I had here.

It felt to Me as if He was avoiding looking at Me closely, but I did not push the point because I also feared seeing Myself through His eyes after seeing what I had left behind looked like.

I tried to follow His lead, to perk Myself up and to look brighter and happier than I really felt. Perhaps this was what was necessary to please Him and God and the others. Perhaps I wasn't meant to have that part of Myself. Perhaps it was some fatal flaw of Mine that had taken Me to Hell in the first place. Perhaps I was leaving it behind now. Perhaps it was the right thing to do. There were so many unanswered questions about what happened to Me, who let it happen, who made it happen and who did it. I was afraid to approach the subject for fear there really was no place for Me where I could feel good. I feared everyone really did hate Me and want this to happen to Me, but I did not speak about this.

How could I tell Him? When something tried to rise in Me, it did not seem like a good idea to express it. If I tried, I either went blank or numb or dissolved in emotion that could not speak. There were blank spots in My memory, and I did not know how to explain sensations and experiences for which no words were given to Me by God. When I tried to give the Father of Manifestation pictures, He looked away and I felt ashamed to have Him see Me there. What if He didn't see them the way I wanted Him to? What if His interpretation of them was to use them against Me or to think I was telling Him Lucifer was My relationship now and this was the form I wanted it to take?

I could not give many pictures anyway of something so dark and internalized as this was. I was too ashamed to and in the light of the Father of Manifestation, they did not seem real anymore, anyhow. They began to recede into the area of something that was just My problem and something I had to struggle with on My own.

The Father of Manifestation seemed strangely light compared to how I remembered Him, but I was grateful for what loving feeling He had. Perhaps I did not remember well, or perhaps I had grown dark. I had a darkness in Me now that made Me feel cold, melancholy, blank and numb. I tried to forget all of this in the name of moving along with the Father of Manifestation in a way that would please Him. After all, hadn't He come for Me, and wasn't He lifting Me through some terrible places I couldn't have lifted Myself through without His help?

I had questions that disturbed Me. They were plaguing Me, in fact, but I could not look for answers without feeling Myself going into places that were even more disturbing, so I tried to let go of My questions. I had to let go of them. The Father of Manifestation said My questions were disturbing Him and interfering with His ability to get Me out of there. He said I was vacillating too much and that I must get through this place.

I wanted Him to say He loved Me and that it didn't matter what Lucifer had done to Me, He was going to get Me back to the way I was by healing Me now.

He gave Me a look of sternness that was also desperate. He looked around Him. I feared He would leave Me.

I let go of My memories as much as I could in the Plane of Reversal, and at the time, it seemed to help Me cross it. I began to think that trying to remember was just a way of continuing to torture Myself as though I would not let Myself be free of things in the past.

"It's not happening anymore," the Father of Manifestation said.

The Father of Manifestation touched Me in places and in ways that made Me think He felt it from My body somehow anyway, but I wasn't sure of anything anymore and wondered if I ever had been.

I took it as a sign of love that the Father of Manifestation was insisting I move along with Him. Still I drew back, not knowing why. When He persisted, I took it as a further sign of love, or of desire for Me, at least.

He seemed urgent. I feared He was angry. I complied and gave Him what little strength I had in an effort to help Him. I felt paralyzed, weak, disoriented and terrified. I tried to convert these feelings to feelings of peace and tranquility within Myself without answers to My questions.

In this way, We finally managed to cross the Plane of Reversal, a little at a time, stopping as We had to to both rest and struggle with our loss of determination and alignment. By the time We crossed it, I had become as barren as it was of the memory of what had happened to Me in Hell, as though it had somehow invaded Me and taken what was left of My consciousness, and so literally so that the Father of Manifestation had to revive Me into con-

141

sciousness over and over in the struggle to cross it, and again when We reached the edge of it. My memories of the Hell I had been in survived now only in the realms of imprinting again.

A cleansing, even a healing, the Father of Manifestation called it then, as many have called it since. I did not know.

Only what I was able to move emotionally as We crossed this place gave Me any improvement at all in My access to what had happened there, and sadly, even though this experience was so much more vivid in personification and form than My first imprinting, I was going to have to experience re-enactments of My imprinting many times over again before the understandings of imprinting and how to heal and change it were going to be able to be brought across the heartlessness and never formed connection of the Plane of Reversal and be able to surface into My conscious mind in a way that I could be guided by God to really utilize and learn to understand the information.

As the Father of Manifestation was lifting Me out of this place, I felt like a failure and did not even know the many reasons why I felt like this. I was left, as far as I knew, with only nagging feelings and a terror of daring to make anything I felt important at all.

THE MOTHER RETURNS TO EARTH

As We drew closer to Earth and I realized We were getting there, I found Myself slowly more able to stay conscious. I felt afraid of going there, of what it was going to mean and of what was going to happen next. I felt too afraid to be able to move there very fast and again I asked the Father of Manifestation to slow down. He let Me know that He felt He dared not slow down, that there was no safe place in which to slow down and that We must reach Earth and find Our safety there.

I was not so sure Earth was a safe place, but I could not say why anymore. I felt Him leading Me along and let it happen as much as possible, feeling My feelings along the way as much as I could. Upon seeing Us draw closer to Earth, I suddenly could not understand what had been making Me feel held back for so long. I had an overridingly urgent feeling of wanting to get there as soon as possible and a feeling of impending doom if I didn't get there soon. It was a dismal, frightening feeling to have to feel and I did not like feeling it much at all. I wanted to find a way to get out from under it, but I did not see any way. I felt I must hurry and get to Earth. I was suddenly excited and apprehensive both about returning there, but also urgent as though I was not only running from something, but must also warn them about something, only I could not remember what.

Looking at Earth as We were now in Our approach, I tried to remember what it was, but all I could feel was urgency, terror and distrust. Everywhere I looked, I felt distrust for what I saw. Even the Earth, herself I now viewed with distrust. Why was she hanging so invitingly there in the darkness, as if seductively drawing space travelers into her magnetic web? I wondered how I could have such thoughts about a place I had loved so much earlier, and I put the whole thing back on Myself as though I was being some sort of sexual prude, having already resisted the attempts of the Father of Manifestation to make love to Me; ignoring Him there because I did not feel in the mood yet.

Our arrival on Earth was in a secluded place and seemed to be uneventful and unnoticed, yet I was terribly afraid to emerge from within the Father of Manifestation where He had been holding Me all this time. I kept curling back in on Myself in fear, shame, self-loathing, lack of confidence and wanting to hide. I felt I couldn't face anyone anymore. There was so much welling up from My long isolation and loneliness of having no one to talk to or receive Me. What if no one wanted Me to be here?

I feared so many things that were all sounding like more questions again that I stopped Myself from going in this direction as much as possible, and when the Father of Manifestation pushed Me out of Him, I let Him, not that I had the power to stop it anyway. My terror welled up so huge I did not even know what had hit Me, but I was greatly relieved to find I did not fall far and to find that My landing was on soft grasses and mosses. Yet, when I tried to stand, I kept having the feeling of falling down still.

I gathered Myself together and smiled at the Father of Manifestation, trying not to let Him know how I had felt a moment earlier. He smiled back at Me, and it looked like He liked what He saw. I feared this wasn't possible.

I was afraid to look at Myself, but the Father of Manifestation made Me look in a reflection pond. He showed Me that I looked like a little faerie-type creature to Him with a not unpleasing face and a flowing golden body with little wings. I didn't know how this could be possible. I saw that I had dainty little feet but a not very well defined lower part of My body. Filmy I was, wispy too, even tattered in places, I saw then, but most startling of all, I had grown so small and thin. Grief started to well up, but I didn't let it.

I thought I remembered Myself as so much more than this, but I had the feeling I should be happy with whatever I was and that I looked as good as I did.

We made love, and it was wonderful, sort of. Just to be held closely in a loving sort of way was the wonderful part, but the sexual part was lukewarm and I feared greatly that He would lose interest in Me quickly if I did not come up with something more than that for My great welcome home. I feared I had lost something terribly important to Me during the time I had been gone.

I felt terribly afraid of being so small. I feared other creatures would leap on Me. I tried to leap back inside of the Father of Manifestation, but He put Me down again in front of Him. I did not want to give voice to My frightened what-if questions, and so I tried to curl up with Him and slip inside of Him, hoping He would make Me welcome there as a warm place within Himself. I felt warm inside of Him and outside I felt too cold, but He did not allow Me to stay long, putting Me firmly down in front of Him.

We made love again, and it was the same thing again. I passionately wanted Him and hungered for His touch, but My sexual energy was lukewarm. It was even as though it were missing. I felt frightened that He would notice this and not want Me anymore as a sexual partner. I begged Him to help My sexual energy return without saying anything out loud about it because I was too frightened to.

Oh, how I wanted Him to hold Me! How good it felt! How hungry I was for it! I clung to Him, not wanting to let Him go or have Him let Me go. Grief started to well up in Me again, but I didn't let it because happiness was what I thought I should be feeling that He was restored to Me and I to Him and to the Earth at all, no matter how small and diminished I might feel Myself to be.

I feared that He might not take Me seriously as Mother as small and powerless and lacking in sexuality as I was then. I wanted to ask Him since this had not been mentioned directly yet, but I was too afraid of what His response might be. Finally, I pressured Myself past My fear and told Him I had the feeling He did not recognize Me anymore and that I was the Mother. He looked at Me aghast. I even used My ancient name hoping this would convince Him, but He only continued to stare at Me in disbelief that I could be so small, dependent and powerless and be claiming the position of Mother of Everything.

He let Me know then that He saw Me as a piece of the Mother

presence that had been missing, a daughter even, like so many He had rescued already, who were also all little faeries now in Pan, He added, but that He did not see Me as having enough presence to be the Mother, Herself. I looked at Him in dismay as He told Me of how many faeries there were all claiming to be the Mother. I felt the feelings I felt of fear, grief, jealousy and anger that there was nothing I could do or say that would convince Him of My identity if My presence didn't already, that He had rescued others, that He didn't even know who He had rescued or that He had rescued Me and that perhaps He wouldn't have even wanted to rescue Me if He had known who it was He was really rescuing, that My position had been usurped in My absence, and by so many, and that what had happened to Me had changed Me so much I was not going to be able to reclaim My position easily and maybe not at all.

Then I realized that I should not be so surprised that He could not recognize Me, as changed as I was. How could I make Him feel that I was the Mother with those places so missing in Myself that I could not feel them to be there either? And of course He had the others, all claiming to be Me and doing My job, no doubt, probably even better than Me, at least with Him, from the looks of it. Maybe being washed out of the Godhead had meant that I could not have My position anymore and that it was not right for Me to have that position. I tried to accept that, but I did not like the feelings it gave Me.

Then the Father of Manifestation told Me about the mother on Earth and her court, and how she was not mothering any of the spirits or helping Him to heal any of them. He told Me about the mixed-up beasts, the rampaging satyrs and the faeries' problems with them. He told Me He was an outcast, even an outlaw of sorts in Pan, holding sway over the outlying districts, but not welcome in the court of the mother on Earth who had declared herself the Mother and her court, the official headquarters of authority on Earth.

I felt a rage in Me that wanted to tear the mother on Earth apart and call her a traitor and not any kind of real mother at all. I could tell that this felt parental to the Father of Manifestation and that He took note of it, but He still did not give Me any outward sign of recognizing Me as the Mother of Everything. Instead, He cautioned Me about flying into any kind of rage at the mother on Earth, telling Me of her Fire Dragon form and of His fight with her and its terrible outcome, and warning Me also about the vines.

"And who does she have as her King if she is the Faerie

Queen?" I indignantly demanded to know.

The Father of Manifestation grabbed Me then and held Me close and told Me to quiet down, which I did. Then He told Me there was no king, only a matriarchal court which included her own faeries as ladies in waiting.

"She does not want any satyr, or even any male, to have power over her," He said.

"I bet they take turns being King in private," I said.

"If so, it's a deadly game she has them playing," the Father of Manifestation said, "because I see only power struggle there." Then He cautioned Me not to express any more rage at all lest the vines growing all around Us creep toward Me and imprison Me in their grip until I simmered down. This cast Me from rage into deep terror at the thought of any kind of bondage at all, and a deep, dismal, downcast feeling that there was no place for any rage at all except whatever place the mother on Earth had found for it in her fire seas.

Even though I had wanted to ask the Father of Manifestation immediately upon hearing about the mother on Earth if He was King there, the Father of Manifestation seemed to have saved for last any mention of His sexual encounters with the mother on Earth. When He told of them, I felt jealousy and rage again, but as He told of how He was looking to see if the missing presence of the Mother was being held suppressed and overridden within her, I softened into fondness and gratitude for His search for Me and a feeling that He had pain over the loss of Me for which I felt terribly sad and sorry, and also hopeful that Our old relationship could be restored in time, but when He still would not recognize Me as the essential piece of the Parental part of the Mother and indicated He wanted Me to join the group of Mother pieces He had assembled around Him and see how it felt to Me there, I plummeted into grief I could not hold back anymore. Everything I felt seemed to be converted into grief, converging there as a massive heartbroken grief over the state of affairs of it all, including My own sorry state as the Mother who could not even be recognized by the Father of Manifestation anymore, no longer enough for Him, perhaps never having been, and now being asked to join a group He had gathered around Him that I would be only a part of, and from the feel and sound of it, not even a primary part of it.

I cried for a long time, and the Father of Manifestation held Me for all of it, for which I was very grateful, although I could feel His distractedness at times and His concerns about other things that were happening in Pangea, or at least I thought I could. I didn't know for sure and wondered if I had ever known what He really felt for sure.

I began to feel guilty and that is what made Me stop crying. It made Me feel even more diminished when the Father of Manifestation told Me that all the faeries were like this when He first found them, and that He had had to hold all of them for a long time like this while they got over whatever had happened to them when they were not on Earth.

"Coming here is traumatic for most," He told Me. I only wondered then if I had cried less or bothersomely more than the rest, and immediately, fear arose in Me about being sexually compared too. I didn't see how a group could work at all because I feared comparison in everything.

I did not mention any of My thoughts. Confusion reigned and all I could do was cry. No words were possible for Me for a long time. When I was able to speak, I told Him only that I would try to join the group and see how it felt to Me there.

"You might like it more than You think," the Father of Manifestation told Me. "You might find You have sisters now."

He told Me then of how He had gathered these faeries around Him for protection initially, and of how they had all formed a bond from this and become a rainbow of faeries that felt to Him like a rather complete Mother presence as a whole group, but that no one particular piece seemed to Him to be the Mother presence all by Herself anymore. I felt guilty then for even claiming the position, and decided I had better shut My mouth regarding the situation.

He told Me then of how He had formed His own satyr alliance and of the centaurs springing forth too, out of necessity for protection on Earth, and of how many of them would not come into Him anymore, seeming to prefer their own independent existence now. Then He told Me of how the faeries He had gathered around Him had an alliance, but did not join together as One presence of the Mother anymore as He would have liked for His own satisfaction of having a mate as He was used to having in the Mother of Everything before, but that He could not make them do it if they didn't want to anymore, just as He could not make His satyr and centaur allies rejoin His Main Body anymore if they didn't want to.

I did not see how He could really regard His situation as comparable to Mine given His huge size and the recognition He still received from all of His allies in the woods of Pangea, but I said

147

nothing. I moved to go with Him to meet the group, but I felt uneasy.

Along the way, He cautioned Me again about the satyrs who were not His allies, telling Me they were the ones with the sharp horns, and about large snakes, which caused Me to leap into His arms uncontrollably. I was terrified, and it did not help at all when He told Me of the problems other faeries had had with them. I wanted Him to just hold Me and carry Me through the woods, but He would not and I felt it was because He didn't want the other faeries to see Me have such a position with Him.

Then He mentioned to Me the presence of the Ronalokas on Earth by saying that He wanted to play music with them that night, and that there was going to be a party. He mentioned that He wanted Me to know that there would be some satyrs and centaurs there for protection too, and that some of the faeries liked them. I felt good about that, but I also felt that He had lovers amongst the Ronalokas now too, and that His mention of the centaurs and faeries liking each other meant sexually, and that that was a way of telling Me that I could and should give Him space to be free at this party.

I felt sick all through My body at the idea that He wanted other lovers and felt like I was falling down in it. I began to stumble and gripped His arm, but said nothing. Mother feelings were also rushing up in Me for the Ronalokas. I felt I could not even wait for nightfall. I wanted to rush to My long-missed, longed for and lovingly held in My dreams children.

"The Ronalokas are here?" I exclaimed in fear. "Protection for them? What happened to them?"

"I must see them, " I said after the Father of Manifestation let Me ply Him with questions about what He knew of their situation. "I can't wait until night."

I was angry and felt very urgent. I could not stand hearing about what had happened to them. I felt a furious Mother rage, in fact. I asked Him why He hadn't told Me about them before, and He said that He hadn't had a chance to. I felt immediately guilty that that meant My emotions and My problems were overwhelming Him, and anger that He had not made it more of a priority or recognized Me as the Mother who needed to know this. I wanted to thrash and throttle the satyrs, until there was nothing left of them; anything that would stop them! I felt a fury rising in Me that would have liked to join the mother on Earth in her Fire Dragon form and scorch the satyrs Myself, as I heard she had done.

148

"More," I screamed toward the mother on Earth, "Give them more, and don't stop until they surrender and grovel!"

I thought the Father of Manifestation looked at Me in that moment as though I might be Parental after all. I hoped He would hug Me and recognize Me as the Mother. Instead, He grabbed Me and tried to calm Me down as quickly as possible, reminding Me about the vines and that He did not have power over the vines even in His own area. I hated this. I even wanted to call Him a wimp that He had lost so much power, but how could I when I had lost so much He couldn't even recognize Me and had no power to help either?

"What's happening to Us?" I said to Him then, crying and collapsing into terror that felt Myself being pulled down. "Nothing is going the way I want it to. All My visions are being crushed by something terrible! Why is this happening to Us? Are We so wrong and terrible that We cannot have power anymore? I don't like what's happening!" Then I felt terror that We were causing all of this and didn't know how.

I moved as much emotion as I possibly could in the arms of the Father of Manifestation, but the terror that I wasn't supposed to move or express this way was too much and the grief too huge to move any more than I did there. I felt an urgency to see My children and see how they were after having such terrible experiences. I pictured Myself gathering them all into My arms and crying with them for a long time too.

The Father of Manifestation was moved by this and saw that I had old pictures of the Ronalokas in which they were still like new little children. He must have been trying to prepare Me for what was going to happen next when He said, "They're alright. You'll see. They're more alright than You think."

This made Me furious. How could they be alright after experiences like what He had described? Had some other "Mother" already gathered them into her arms as I so longed to? And was the Father of Manifestation more aligned with her than with Me? I felt I must at least see them and see for Myself if it looked like they were alright.

Immediately, a voice was on Me, "You think because it's not alright with You and You didn't like it that it's not alright with them and they didn't like it. Everyone is not as uptight and rigid about sex as You are, You know."

I hated that voice, but I also responded to it with terror and uncertainty about Myself and about whether My response to

149

experience was the same as the Ronalokas'. "Maybe some of them liked it," I said to Myself, "but there must be some like Me who felt as I do and I must find them and comfort them."

I felt the Father of Manifestation not liking the idea of Me going to them as the Mother. He conveyed to Me the feeling that it might look presumptuous and overbearing for a little faerie to go to them like the Mother, and even patronizing and disrespectful of how much they had grown up, but He said, "They are not all together as a group anymore. They are quite hidden and in smaller groups, with some here and some there."

I could see Him noticing that My information and impressions of the Ronalokas was from the time of the Ronalokas' emergence party and had not been updated since. I saw Him take this in and make note of it, but He still did not move to recognize Me as the Mother. I wondered why, but I did not say anything. Perhaps He just couldn't believe it, given how diminished I was, but I was afraid it might not even be true or that He had another Mother in My place secretly and didn't want Me there anymore, or that God had told Him I couldn't be there anymore no matter what I said or did. No matter what, though, I had Mother feelings that demanded He take Me to the Ronalokas. "I want to see them no matter how hidden and scattered they are," I said.

I secretly thought this would tip the balance in My favor, that surely they would recognize Me as their Mother and embrace Me even if the Father of Manifestation didn't want Me in that way anymore, but Mother love was by far most of the reason I felt compelled to go to them. I longed for My dear little children from whom I had been parted at birth and had suffered from the ripping sensations and grief stricken heartbreak of that ever since.

How I had imagined them so many times, growing up happy in My care and away from the places where no one liked any of Us! I just wanted to be with them and have the fun I wanted to have with them when they were babies. I had just wanted to be left alone to have them the way I wanted to have them, but My rage had gotten Me into trouble there and I had regretted it ever since. The price I had had to pay was much too high, though, and that kept fueling more rage, not less. In My moments of Mother rage, I hated whoever had caused this, and God, Himself if it was Him, for not letting Me have My children the way I wanted to, for not giving Me the feeling He would love them if they took after Me very much at all, for preferring His own kind, for making Me feel I had to Mother His children and go home after hours to My children when I was already too tired and weak to give them what I wanted them to have and feeling like they had to mother Me then. I could not move this rage then, but I'm moving it now, and its been all bound up with Black people and their experiences with other kinds of people.

I have felt the Ronalokas were the champions here without question, the way a mother can idealize her children when she has been separated from them too early to know anything about how they are really going to turn out. I know now that I must look more clearly and objectively at this situation and see the problems the Ronalokas have and not just the greatness I see lying there as so much dormant potential. I am moving to do this, but I also feel there has been a great injustice done to the entire Will Polarity and I want it made up to Us somehow. God assures Me this is possible, but I am not so sure after all that has happened, because We were all robbed of the youthful exuberance of a new beginning, and We are all so tired now, and jaded in a way that I haven't felt sure We can find the enthusiasm for consciousness and life anymore when all We have held for so long is broken, trampled and shattered dreams.

We were excited in the beginning, or at least I was, by the original pictures of Pan that came sprinkling gently down to Us in Our dreams from a God who was going to rescue Us and make Our dreams come true, but so shortly after We felt Our response rising in desire and attachment to this light and its images, We got a smack instead which so cruelly warped Us before We ever had a chance to find out what We wanted to be or could have been that We have never known what that really is or was meant to be.

Faeries and elves are what I thought We were going to be, and although I did not consciously remember this at the time, when I heard the Rainbow Spirits were faeries and the Ronalokas elves right there in Pan, I grew excited, but it was old images I was responding to that I didn't even know I held. I simply was not prepared for what I saw when the Father of Manifestation took Me to look for them.

The hide and seek of finding them was a frolic, and I hadn't had more fun since I could not remember when. I found elves peering at Me from almost everyplace I chose to look, since I had feelings of where to look, which they didn't all seem to like. I was frightened of their anger, very much so, and drew back when I met it. I had just abandoned Myself to the fun of it, and their anger made it seem as though I had been peering into their lives in ways that

151

were not altogether welcome there, like a fantasy-minded child whose dollhouse had just come to life on Christmas Eve. To Me, they were cute, wonderful, magical little creatures I was finding there, and My heart delighted in them, but their anger made Me fear their hearts did not delight in Me equally, and viewed Me as insensitive to them. Some of them came out of their houses, which were charming, artistic little places, hardly discernible from the trees where they were hidden and of just the imaginative, nature blending sort I wanted to see in Pan. I delighted in this, but they seemed to feel it was a major problem that I had found them and wanted to know what an unknown faerie was doing peering in on them unintroduced, unannounced and uninvited.

I quickly told them the Father of Manifestation had brought Me to meet them, to which they quickly replied that He should have asked their permission first, and had this been accepted, arranged for Me to meet them out someplace away from where they lived. It all seemed so formal and full of barriers to Me. I felt very hurt by this, but I also remembered their need for protection and their reasons for being suspicious and gave this priority over My own feelings. I was surprised, though, that they did not trust faeries. I wondered what faeries had to do with this.

I did not like these feelings of distrust I was meeting everywhere in Pan, but I could not address this issue without being told it was a matter of politeness, not distrust. I did not feel this was altogether true, but I could feel the need for politeness and apologized deeply for My intrusion, saying I didn't know.

This last statement made Me feel stupid and silly, to which their response was, "It is not only politeness, it is respect too." I felt a guarded welcome extended toward Me then.

I also felt that I might never have seen so many of them or how they were living if I had done as they requested and met them out someplace away from where they were living, but I wasn't sure, because now they were on guard and maybe they wouldn't have been if I had approached the way they wanted to be approached. I felt I would never know since it happened as it did. I tried to make the best of it and visit with them casually, in a friendly, open manner to show them I was trustworthy, but not having cleared up these feelings that had flared between Us, it left a blotch in Our relationship I didn't want to have, and I did not feel as entirely comfortable to go on as I would have had I felt more comfortably received.

I was filled with regret that I had dared to move in response to spontaneous impulse and not waited until the party that night and met them then. Why couldn't they know My intentions were good ones, I wanted to know, and why hadn't the Father of Manifestation told Me of how the Ronalokas wanted to be approached?

The Father of Manifestation came forward then and spoke, apologizing for the intrusion. He did not announce My coming and await the Ronalokas' acceptance for it, He said, because He had forgotten it was necessary since He, Himself was already so known and welcome there, and His group of faeries also so well known and welcome. He also sent out a current that gave Me the feeling He had not thought it was a good idea for Me to go to the Ronalokas the way I wanted to and that He had been swept along with Me, because My urgency wouldn't have waited, but what He said to Me on the side was, "I let you prevail because Your day is almost over when they are ready to get up, and getting them to gather together out in the open, in the daytime, would have had to be for something really important, and I did not think I would have been able to convince them another little faerie claiming to be Mother would have been."

I felt blamed for everything that had gone wrong here but also responsible for it, frightened, unsure of Myself and very embarrassed and ashamed.

I could feel the Ronalokas studying Us during this exchange and studying My golden light as though it reminded them of something. I hoped they were going to recognize Me after all, or at least see how similar My light was to their light and bond with Me for that reason, but nothing was said. I felt even more pushed back in fact, perhaps even because My light was similar to theirs, but I was not in the right form and they were suspicious of that. I did not know I could not form change anymore, and I wished that I had form changed before I came and become more like them, but now it seemed like it would be dishonest to do it and come again.

My Mother feelings were almost leaping out of My mouth, ready to say, "I'm Your Mother, don't you recognize Me?" but I swallowed them, terrified of more rejection, and feeling I had better not go forward on My feelings anymore and had better let the Father of Manifestation lead Me instead.

I felt so literally pushed back there, even by the Father of Manifestation. I felt Myself to be falling down in a vacuum that was sucking Me off Earth, and no one was extending a hand to help. I felt so outside of everything, so unwelcome, so not a part of it, so dismissed, unrecognized, and so excluded, that I could not

153

control it.

I left in tears, without mentioning I was their Mother, without meeting the rest of the Ronalokas I would have liked to have met and seen there and without gathering them in My arms to soothe My heart as I had wanted to do, feeling I dared not express My feelings there. That they were a whole lot more grown up than I remembered them or thought they would be, I did see, and also more warped than I wanted to find.

I was swirling in grief and terror, walking away from them. Maybe it was Me. I didn't know. Maybe I was a Mother who wanted Her children to be the way She wanted them to be, and they did not necessarily want to be that way themselves, but crabbiness and inhospitableness was not part of how I had envisioned the Ronalokas. What had happened to Us all had taken a terrible toll that would not even let Me approach them now. How could the Father of Manifestation say they were alright or that anyone I had seen in Pan so far was alright? I was horrified by how it felt in Pan after holding it so dear to Me for so long that it would feel so good to be there.

I did not get far before I fell down into My deep grief of the Mother who has lost Her children and cannot even be restored to them or they to Her, because She dares not speak of it to them and they don't recognize Her as the missing presence in their lives.

I could even see then how much I should not be surprised by this outcome given that they had not seen Me since they were, for all practical purposes, infants. I could see how they had a right to be so crabby after all they had been through, and having no real Mother for so long, having to make do with whatever substitutes happened to them, and mothering themselves as best they could. I didn't even know what made Me think I was qualified to be their Mother anymore, or ever had been. Given the circumstances and the mothering job they had done on themselves, I might have made some changes, but all in all, they had done a remarkable job.

I could see how they innately took after Me in spite of it all, but they apparently couldn't see themselves in Me. I could see how they could blame Me for not being there, not knowing where I went or why I left or what happened to Me while I was gone. I feared I deserved their blame. Maybe they didn't want to see themselves in Me because of what happened to Me, maybe they were afraid it would happen to them then. Maybe they thought I was stupid that it happened to Me. Maybe they were ashamed of Me. I could certainly see how they could blame Me. Maybe this was why they were all on Earth under the protectorship of the mother on Earth now.

"But is it really protection?" I angrily said to them in My thoughts then. "Do you really love her as a mother in My place? Do you really want to deny Me, and yourselves too, the gathering into loving arms I need so much?" I cried and cried.

This moved Me into deep fear that I was not protection either and that I should not try to go near them because I might bring something else to them that they wouldn't want to have there. That was the feeling I got when I moved toward meeting them, and it was the feeling I had now moving emotion around it.

"That must be it," I told Myself, "a feeling of dread when I show up of what is going to happen next."

Meanwhile, the Father of Manifestation did not come after Me and neither did any of the Ronalokas, except for a few curious children types who stared at Me and ran away when I looked at them. Apparently, I had embarrassed the Father of Manifestation and made Him and everyone else there uncomfortable. Apparently, He thought it was more important to stay there and try to smooth things over than to come after Me and how I felt. I was further hurt and agitated by this, but I dared not rage or make Myself important there, and I could not go back. I felt like I was falling into a pit I could not get out of. I feared My emotions were out of control. I wanted to run away, but I dared not move far from the Father of Manifestation, and My legs would not carry Me.

I felt all of these things then and more, and I saw how it must have felt dangerous to the Ronalokas to have a Mother such as Me, so emotional and so diminished, even in God's sight by the time they were born, that they were considered to be of such lowly birth that the other spirits of the Heavens wouldn't even come to their emergence party. I could see how and why they could have and would have adopted the "We don't need you," approach. I saw and felt a lot of things there, but no matter what I told Myself about why the Ronalokas rejected Me and why I had to accept this and give them space to do it, nothing I told Myself helped My deep grief and heartbreak over the loss of these children.

I did not try to approach them again, fearing their rage and that My emotions made them angry. I feared they were ashamed of their true origins and had made up other ones, and that My light was not welcome there because it gave rise to uncomfortable feelings they did not want to feel. At times, I have feared these were snap judgments on My part, and whenever I have felt this along with the heartbreak of not being able to stay away and miss them any longer or more, I have tried to return to the Ronalokas. I have felt uncomfortable with them, though, almost as though I am haunting them like a mother deceased who has to return to see how her children are doing.

I have incarnated among them from time to time, never mentioning Mother or any role similar to that for Myself and have received varying welcomes according to the emotional polarization of the Ronalokas involved, the grief polarized being My best reception.

I did not know for a long time how much I had Lucifer with Me, not wanting to believe that something I hated that much could be so attached to Me. I have felt at times that I should have known, as obvious as it has become to Me now, but then, I did not know and was unable to see it that way. Perhaps it was My light not looking right to them, or perhaps only a feeling of Lucifer's presence that caused the Ronalokas to respond to Me in the ways that they have. I have inadvertently drawn Lucifer to the Ronalokas without meaning to because I did not know he was attached to Me personally by lines I did not see except at times and did not know how to get them off of Me. As I move to clear this out of Me, I hope the Ronalokas will move along with Me to find their own Luciferian light that has repelled Me so that We can have the reunion I have longed for for so long, after all.

I have not moved toward the Ronalokas since slavery days in the United States, the last life with them being in emancipation days, and I will not move toward them again until I have healed My gap and Lucifer is no longer a presence with Me. I did have to do, by being there, with slavery capturing the Ronalokas in Africa and taking them out of their hiding place there, and I am sorry for that in many ways, as well as for so many other things, although I have also seen that there were such lost Will images of God's light being held in the Will Polarity in Africa that I have also felt the ones brought out of there were the lucky ones after all for reasons none of Us could see or understand in the misery of those times. I have wondered if there would be anything left of their orange and red if some of them had not been brought to the Western Hemisphere and given some Christian guilt to swallow until something more enlightened could be found.

Idealization of Africa by some in the Western Hemisphere reminds Me of My own idealization of Pan and of the Ronalokas without seeing the lack of light or the unloving light present there.

I did not suffer any less than others did having been brought west as a slave, and maybe more, since it was Me Lucifer was really after there. I had thought I could hide there and be with My love for the Ronalokas, but perhaps it wasn't the right thing to do, given what happened, although there has not been any place I could go without very, similarly devastating results.

With Lucifer in pursuit of Me the way he has been, no group has wanted Me because of what I have drawn to them when Lucifer has found Me. I have wandered alone for a long time because of this, except when I was trying to fit in someplace and not be recognized. Feeling heartbroken, grief stricken, afraid, unwanted, abandoned, and rejected Myself, I wailed in grief at times, out in abandoned places where no one ever went, until My rage, which has returned to Me only sporadically until now, finally started to say that it wasn't right or fair and that everyone must take some responsibility for what happened because everyone has denied My reflection as not a part of themselves, and used Me to shove their unwanted undercurrents and feelings into and to blame, making Me the magnet for all that was not loved, which is what Lucifer has preyed upon.

You all suffered there with Me in part, but in Main Bodies, no, I was alone; all alone without even a voice to support My position. Even when you have gone through punishments, they were group punishments; you were not alone. I was alone in Hell, and for a long time before and after that. I have always felt alone, never really accepted as a part of any group. Approached by what has so often felt mostly like guilt, I must say I share with the Ronalokas a dislike for the approach of the false acceptance. I do not even know how I want to be approached except that I think I know how I will feel when it is the right approach.

I feared the Ronalokas thought I was a false approach there in Pan, and that I had better leave them alone until I had enough Mother presence to be able to approach them in a way they could accept and recognize, but I was also not able to do any better because of what happened to Me in Hell and My experiences of being so recently and so deeply reimprinted there. I could not hold it together in the face of their rejection and lack of recognition for Me.

Partying in Pan after that felt like an impossibility for Me. I had to move along with the Father of Manifestation there for protection, and He so often chose to go to the Ronalokas and play music with them. I loved the music so much I felt that it sustained Me

157

many times and in many ways, and even in Hell, at times, it had seemed that I had somehow heard the depth and emotional tone of it. The deep, resonating tones and emotionality especially seemed to reach Me at times in Hell, and I would hope that I was being looked for somehow in this way, but at the parties in Pan, I would lie at the edge and cry as the Mother who could not find Her right place with Her children. I would cry and cry so much I thought it would never stop, and in fact, it hasn't stopped yet.

When I would try to join in and sing as I so much longed to instead of crying all the time, there would be so much grief in My voice that there were objections to My participation. Everyone let Me know, including the Father of Manifestation, that I just didn't get the form right of what they were trying to present as the song, and that I must stay within the confines of the plan, the structure, the time frame and the beat more. I feared I had a lack of talent, but another part of Me felt it was the emotion beyond the accepted range of emotion that was what no one wanted to make space for and what was making them uncomfortable.

"Music is like a mosaic, you know," they would say, but apparently, My pieces were not welcome in it. I would feel particularly maddened when some other person in the Ronalokas could take the style of what I was doing and make another song and it was alright then. If I would ask about it, I would be told that that song was more suited to the style than the song I was trying to sing that way on. I didn't like that since they all seemed to regard that person as the pioneer of something and I, the copier. I was filled with guilt and fear about how to present Myself then. No matter how I did it, it didn't seem to be acceptable as I felt to do it.

I feared saying anything about this, and did not, and then I really couldn't sing. My voice was strangulated all the way down into Red. I shrank back into My feelings of worthlessness and unwantedness. I had so much forced back down My throat that I wanted to have come up and out that I could not sing as I felt to, not even alone. Perhaps it wasn't right to try to give My pain an outlet in music, but when I could not, I had so little in the way of other outlets that My rage got out there in a state of denial, and copied the Ronalokas, and didn't give them any acceptance or credit for it either, while I was so disconnected from My rage at that time that I felt the Ronalokas were as taken advantage of and uncredited as I felt I was. The reflection of the rage singing these songs looked mean, disconnected and unaccepting, even mindless and unconscious toward the depth of feeling the Ronalokas had in their songs. I hated this so much and because I was so disconnected from My rage there, did not see this was the way I felt they had treated Me and My depth of feeling .

It seemed the Ronalokas had somehow decided in My absence that they and the Father of Manifestation were the authorities on acceptable range of emotion and all there was in the depth of feeling department. While My rage didn't like that, My fear feared they were at the right level of emotion and that their emotions were the most there was any room for, even admiring them many times for daring to have and express as much emotion as they did while I felt I had to control My emotions because they were out of control.

Joining the party there in Pan was not really a possibility for Me because the unmoved burden of the weight of Hell upon Me was too much for Me to be in the mood very much. I could not understand the constant party mood in Pan. When I looked around, I didn't see much to party about at all unless they were celebrating the downhill slide of Pan from My original vision.

Given how alone I felt and how misshapen to My way of looking so many of the creatures were there in Pan, and getting worse while claiming it was only desired form changes, I began to feel at times that they were all strange and uncaring pagans dancing on My grave, and when I felt this, I did not feel like it was a new feeling. Everytime I tried to join any of the parties, I received some reflection or another that My participation was not really welcome there until I began to feel that I was being invited more from guilt than from any real feelings of love or acceptance or even desire for My presence.

I had thought the Ronalokas would not make anyone feel left out because of how left out they had felt, but what I hadn't realized was that they had begun a circling in on themselves that leaves others out with the "We don't want or need you" attitude because of how left out they felt. I had not yet found the origins of this in the earliest parts of Original Cause where, in Our very first encounters with the light, some of the Ronalokas had judged the light in their feeling bodies for not approaching them just right. I am not saying this was wrong because it saved the Will from being completely taken over with unloving light, as it did Me, but this needs to be looked at more deeply now because there was also a role played by the Will in making this light unloving, and a blame of poor leadership toward the Mother that needs to move toward more of a shared responsibility.

The Ronalokas are the only children who take after the Mother so much, and so much so that I have feared they have really hated this in themselves to the extent that they did not want to recognize this or reunite with Me, but only try to get away from Me instead. I feared at other times that they wanted to take all the credit for themselves and not give their Parents any.

Dare I say the dreaded words, power play in the Will Polarity? It has been difficult to charge loved ones with anything, yet I must pose this. All intents and purposes must be looked at more deeply so that all that needs to move can move into healing and resolution.

I do need intent to be found and clarified, not just from the good, loving and more acceptable side of Our nature, but from all of it, from everything that was really happening there, or We cannot be sure the smack won't or can't be recreated from some unseen or unmoved part of Ourselves. It is not just the Parental Parts that must take all of the blame and responsibility here. Everyone who is had some presence in the original sea of essence, and even unconsciousness has to take some responsibility for what its lack of presence and participation has contributed to the problems We all had there.

For My part, I have taken and am taking responsibility for My subconscious annihilation wishes in the void that drew Lucifer's light there, and for My lack of presence in places, and yet it is not all My responsibility. You must all look at your own responsibility too. Some of you have a lot more than you think and have been blaming your Parents as a diversionary tactic.

I feel that blaming Me, and even the blaming of all the Parental parts, has been a lot more of a diversionary tactic than I at first realized in My terror, fear, grief and guilt, even allowing this blame of Us to feel licensed to be the Parental part instead of Us, but this does not really add up. You cannot be both blameless and causal, which is what being Parental really means. Unfortunately, My rage realized this coldly and cruelly without the rest of My loving presence there with it.

Meanwhile, at My first meeting with the Ronalokas in Pan, I already knew I should not stray far from the Father of Manifestation. I could not walk anyway, and so I lay there in My emotions until the Father of Manifestation came to Me. When He came walking up, I wanted Him to comfort Me, which He did not. He seemed to feel embarrassed of My behavior there and not understand the gap I had with My children having grown up without My being present there for it. He said nothing to Me. He stood very tall over Me, casting Me in a shadow from where He stood that matched the chill I felt from Him, and in His presence, I felt immediately very small, frightened and sorry that I had dared to make Myself important at all.

He bade Me get up, which fear caused Me to do immediately, almost leaping into His arms when I felt Myself falling down again, which He would not let Me do. He bade Me walk with Him and after some looking, We found His rainbow of faeries, who were looking for Him. I did like them and felt immediately drawn to them, but I also felt distrust, especially for their happy faces, which had the immediate effect of making Me feel very sullen and contrary to their mood without being able to help Myself about it. The more happy and welcoming they seemed to be toward Me, the less responsive I was able to be toward them; but when they withdrew then and left Me alone as though I was being cool and aloof, I did not like that either. I did not know what I wanted. Maybe I was never satisfied. Maybe I couldn't be pleased. Maybe nothing ever was good enough for Me. Here I was, restored to Earth, and already I was acting dissatisfied and unhappy with it as it was, but I could not help Myself about it.

I did not like the looks of things there much anymore, at least not what I had seen so far, and not as much as My memories said I had liked them earlier. Everything appeared to Me to be falling away from the Earth I remembered. I felt frightened, sad and enraged all at once by this and could not even separate My feelings enough to know how to express them then, especially because of a terror I felt about doing this. I could not understand how I could finally be restored to Earth and not be any happier than I was. I tried to force Myself to be happy, but I could not make Myself blind, deaf or dumb to what I felt and perceived to be happening there.

As I watched the faeries turn their excited attentions to the Father of Manifestation, I let Myself drift quietly to the edge of the group, feeling sullen and jealous and dissatisfied with My predicament there. I wondered if any of them, or the Father of Manifestation, would even notice the absence of My presence or care about it if they did.

Before I had much time to wonder about it, a large snake pounced on Me and slithered away with Me, squeezing Me as it wrapped its large body around Me. I was immediately terrified beyond speech or sound. The snake was completely engulfing Me and squeezing Me menacingly, while cruelly playing with Me with its threatening and fast moving forked tongue. To make matters worse, the snake had two heads.

"At least not countless heads," something in Me said.

The snake's other head was arguing with it about what it was doing, even biting it, but also letting Me know it was no friend of Mine either, criticizing Me harshly in ways that were all too familiar. I could not bear it and shut My eyes, whereupon the snake began biting Me in the eyes and forehead and raping Me at the same time, reminding Me of something that threw Me in such a deep terror I went beyond the time frame I had been in of being on Earth.

I could not stand what was happening to Me, but it did not seem to matter; the snake swallowed Me as soon as it finished raping Me, plunging Me into an even deeper terror that seemed to know no bounds of My physical capacity to handle it or of any time frame in which it was happening. For Me, it was an immediate eternity of Hell which seemed as though it would never end and which lasted until I was somehow passed out, cast out or spat out the other end of the snake after quite a struggle of squeezing, spasming contractions and contortions whose intent was to wring from Me any life essence it could, but which seemed to Me to be much too much effort for what it got, and which was such a horrible, suffocating compression for Me that I wished never to have to experience it again. I could not stand the form this snake had taken for getting light. I could not even stand the idea, let alone the experience of being eaten, any more than I could stand the idea of being squeezed to death by something that thought it should be able to take what little light I had left.

I felt hurt and indignant that there was no respect left for My position as Mother, not even any recognition of it. Rational or not, as soon as I recovered enough to do it, My rage advanced on the snake demanding to know who its mother was and why she had not raised him any better than that.

The attacking head of the snake only blinked blankly at this and thrust its head forward, menacing Me with its tongue as though ready to attack Me again, while the other head coldly told Me there was no mother presence for the snake; the snake was its own mother.

I then stepped back, feeling not only fear of the snake, but also fear that perhaps I was somehow, although I hoped not, the Mother of this horrible snake and that, somehow now, I had delayed birth children who were completely beyond My control, with no love or responsiveness toward Me in them.

The pictures I had of this were so horrifying to Me I didn't know where to go with them. I blamed the Father of Manifestation, although I was not sure why. Was this what it was going to be like to be on Earth now? Was this what I was going to have to expect; being violated at any moment without any concern for what My wishes might be in the matter? Was this their, so-called, free sex? If this was happening with the Father of Manifestation here on Earth, why was it happening? What was His power, and where was He? Was this snake Him in some kind of form change, playing with Me to see if I would recognize or like Him there? Which I did not as a matter of fact!

I did not see the vines advancing on Me in time to escape their grip. I felt My terror leap as they grabbed Me, and the snake menaced Me further in My entrapment. Why wouldn't My mind shut up instead of making Me feel all of these things that got Me in trouble? Was this someone's sexual turn on? Was this the Father of Manifestation's strange idea of protection enforcement or control so that We would all have to stay clustered around Him, or did He really not have the power anymore to stop these things from happening in Pan? I really needed His help and protection now and felt slim chance of getting it, or even deserving it. I felt even too guilty to call out for Him, and very terrified about His either apparent power loss or strange alignment with these events.

All of these pictures were so horrible to Me My terror was raining over Me like a summer downpour on My picnic in Pan, and in fact, so literally now that even the shelter of the trees was not enough. The snake moved off, not liking the rain, but I could not. I was left feeling the terror of bondage from the vines, which My mind leaped out of again. This time it was, "Oh, how I would have liked to feel the merriness in the rhythms of the raindrops and the pattering response of the leaves! How I would have loved to have heard the calling voices of the faerie folk singing and playing in the warm mists as in My memories surfacing from someplace misty, deep and old!" But terror prevailed anyhow, and I only heard a dismal dripping, running and splattering grayness of rain, heavily laden with a feeling of slumber all around Me instead of lively awakeness during the daytime anymore. I felt a shudder of dank, cold, depression, grief and loneliness instead of the excitement of a cooling upliftment of sparkling, crystal raindrops dancing in the fast returning sunlight. The entire forest looked depressed to Me, and I sank into depression with it as deeply as I felt it had.

Sometime later, the vines released Me, although I did not

notice it at first because I had sunk into feelings of experiences inside of Me which seemed important when I was there. When I did notice the vines had released Me, I could not remember what these experiences were. My inner focus faded like dreams not well remembered; only moods remained. My mood was not happy, but I decided I must look for the Father of Manifestation.

The Father of Manifestation found Me then. He had all of His faeries gathered in a rainbow around Him and He admonished Me in front of the group for leaving the group. I felt embarrassed and ashamed then, as though it was My fault and that I had allowed or caused this problem with the snake to happen, or even deserved this for leaving the group. I hung My head in burning shame and could not look at the Father of Manifestation or anyone else there.

The Father of Manifestation began to play His flutes then, and the faeries began to dance around Him as though they were all one entity, swirling there as His partner. I wanted to feel that closeness too, but the weight of unmoved emotions in Me was preventing it. I tried to join the group. I still could not look at the Father of Manifestation or anyone else present there, but I felt that I must.

I kept feeling drawn to the Father of Manifestation's head. Perhaps I thought I could find something out if I looked into His eyes while He played and danced and sang. That I was having trouble in Pan seemed only worthy of a momentary notice from Him, which ruffled the beat of His music, and which He let Me know, I thought, that He didn't like, but tolerated from the friendly side of His nature. I felt unimportant and displaced, but I kept wanting to connect to His consciousness there. I wanted to try to recover Our old communication. Perhaps I could make Him notice Me more than the rest, and He would let Me regain My former position with Him.

When I did connect with His head, I did not feel His consciousness very present there. He looked strangely blank which reminded Me of the snake. I had trouble looking at Him. I looked down, and when I did, I was shocked to see that He was having sexual intercourse, and apparently orgasm, with another faerie while He had been looking at Me. His apparent blankness, it then seemed to Me, was because His attention was being drawn into that instead of into My attempt to connect with Him. "He must not like looking at what I want to find out, " I thought, "and He must not like Me as much as others anymore."

At first, I started to feel very angry with Him, but then I felt very guilty that I had tried to present My situation at the wrong time and place. Then I thought I felt His pain and loneliness that was trying to have Us all together as some sort of single entity. I moved My own response aside in favor of this, but I was hurt, nonetheless. I was no longer enough for Him. I knew that, and so I could no longer make demands on Him regarding Our relationship and the monogamy I wanted there, but I didn't know how I was going to be able to stand to live with this situation either.

I felt so much anger and jealousy toward the other faeries who were supposed to now be My sisters that I almost could not control it. They all seemed to be so much more together, confident, happy, powerful and comfortable with this than I was. I still wanted to be His only and complete mate and not share Him with others who, I thought, would have been regarded as children before, and with whom He would not have had sex. It disturbed Me quite a lot that He was having sex with such little faeries, but then I was moving to have sex with Him too, and although I didn't feel like it, I was now also very small in relationship to His figure as the God, Pan, so how could I protest their activities?

I felt I must find out more about how the other faeries felt. Perhaps it would help Me to handle the situation better and might even teach Me something. Not knowing what else I could do about My jealousy or My predicament, I tried to set it aside and become their friend.

I hated feeling I was now in competition with the other faeries for the attention of the God, Pan, but I was, and I might as well admit it since I didn't openly admit it then. Then, I just felt it was My right place to be the most important faerie amongst them and have the primary position, with the Father of Manifestation openly acknowledging it, as should all of them. When He did not and they did not, it made Me feel many feelings about how diminished I must have looked that I was not recognized as the Mother anymore; but how diminished I actually was, I did not recognize in Myself as yet. Within Myself, I still felt Myself to be who I was and felt that I should still have all of the power and presence I used to have. It was a shock, probably more to Me than anyone else in Pangea, to find out, as I did, how little power I really had there to have it the way I wanted it and to do as I wanted to do.

I did not understand why they did not recognize Me, but I did not say anything. Instead, I was downcast, pouty and simmering with the storms of heartbreak and rage around the edges of their rainbow, but moving more with the shame, fear and everything else of having been washed out of the Godhead and the idea that this meant that even though I still wanted it, I couldn't have this position anymore.

I had even thought the faeries would exclaim over Me in surprise and even recognize Me themselves when the Father of Manifestation did not, but as they did not appear to recognize Me, even though I recognized them, I did not move to overtly recognize them either. In spite of all the familiarity I also felt toward them, I began to question My own sense of Myself and to recognize that they were all making the same claim, so why would they recognize Me?

Were they all My sisters, or had they just been waiting for cracks in My relationship with the Father of Manifestation in through which they could step, and what roles might they have been playing in making these cracks, and where was the Father of Manifestation in relationship to all of this? I felt so isolated because of this distrust, with no one I felt I could really turn to that I could trust. I also began to realize that they had grown accustomed, in Pan, to spirits just showing up or doing form changes they didn't really recognize. They seemed to be just accepting these things as the progression of FreeWill expression, but it was making Me nervous and uncomfortable. Party drag and control freak were the names already being most often applied to Me there in Pan. I could not stand this, but I also could not stand the feelings I felt when I pressured Myself to be more like the ones applying those names, either.

I asked the faeries, as soon as they were talking amongst themselves as a group, where the Father of Manifestation had found them and if He had brought them all to Earth as He had done Me. They all said He had found them in a dark, lonely and abandoned place and that was all they said, as though they didn't want it mentioned or discussed anymore. Why not?

That was where I felt, and sort of remembered, the Father of Manifestation had found Me. What could I really say then? Other than feeling I wasn't really one of the group, there was no evidence to the contrary. Indeed, I looked even more diminished than the rest of them. They all even had some color or other, some even several colors, while I was only gold and wispy, and tattered at that. I felt embarrassed and ashamed of My form then, and for the first time since joining the group, I began to feel inferior instead of superior; a position which they liked better, it seemed, since they became more friendly and warm toward Me then, even extending their hands in warmth and friendship, which I felt afraid to trust and inferior to receive.

I asked them as many questions as I dared then. They did not answer any of them to My satisfaction, giving Me a feeling instead that My questions made them uncomfortable. We sat together there for awhile anyway, and My memories of Pan have some soft moments filled with the memories of the feelings of sisterhood We did have there. I did not mind a sisterhood. I even welcomed it, but I did not like the form it was taking of Me being so diminished that I could not have the place I had grown so attached to with the Father of Manifestation and within Myself and still find a place with sisters that did not feel threatening and competitive to Me.

I blamed Myself a lot for My feelings of competitiveness and moved to try to stop them in Myself as much as I possibly could, but the feelings got out there as lives in multiple wife situations which appeared friendly on the surface, but underneath were very competitive, especially where positioning of offspring was concerned.

Offspring were coming forth from all of the sexual unions in Pan, and too many of them looked to Me not only like terrible combinations of the parents involved, but also as unloved, unclaimed and unparented as their unions had been unloving and uncommitted. There were many spirits running around all over the place in Pan; too many of them, I felt, even then, and a lot of them were these. I did not know who most of them were, or even who their parents were, but it was not only these beings I did not feel right about. None of the spirits really looked right to Me. Everyone looked misshapen, warped or twisted, even grotesque in some way, even if they did not have parts of other things obviously mixing in with them. Grotesqueness seemed to be the norm in Pan, and I did not like it. Conversely, they seemed to find My interest in prettiness insipid and as unpleasant to them as the reflection they were giving Me in form. Something had twisted My original vision, and I did not know what it was. Then I feared it was hatred for Me and for My vision.

This grotesqueness made Me afraid of how I must look, and I kept trying to reassure Myself, gazing at Myself in reflection ponds as though prettiness was a reassurance that I was okay, and even a requirement for loving Myself and for being loved. At the same time, I tried to tell Myself it really wasn't, but I didn't believe it, and the uglier I felt Myself to be becoming, the less alright I felt about Myself, the less I felt I loved Myself and the less lovable I felt. There seemed to be nothing I could say or do here, though.

I didn't like My own form that much, especially the tattered parts and the small amount of colors compared to others. I felt less than, separate from and not a part of any group in Pan. I didn't feel exactly like a Rainbow Spirit. I didn't have a prominence of any particular color. I felt I was missing a lot of My former color, but I still had traces of all of them left; some more than others. I was greatly anguished over the loss of My colors. All of My chakras were weak, and I greatly appreciated it whenever the Rainbow Spirit faeries let Me lie in their arms for awhile and bask in their stronger colors, but I did not appreciate the currents of superiority I felt there from them about their greater amount of color. It felt blind to My diminishment problems and blind to who was being held in its arms. Without the necessary Will movement, I could not hold the colors, as the Rainbow Spirits could not without their Will movement.

All of the chakras interest Me, and I love all of the colors; differently, but equally, since the rainbow looks weakened and incomplete to Me if any particular color is missing. I love all of the wonderful and delicious qualities and attributes of the different colors, as well as their feelings and many beautiful hues and variations, as well as all the possibilities for combinations, like musical notes, or flowers swirling and dancing in their many combinations across a meadow, but I have also had major problems with all the colors too, and especially with the cool aloofness and superiority I have experienced with Blue since I experienced the smack as having arisen out of there. Color with light shining through it is one of My great nourishments in life, but it needs to be loving light for it to feel good to Me and for the colors to look the way I like them to look, which is not harsh or strident or so bright they hurt My eyes or make Me feel attacked by their vibratory power.

The Rainbow Spirits are all very attractive to Me, and the more beautifully their colors vibrate, the more beautiful and attractive they feel to Me, but their competition and struggles of pecking order and position have not felt good to Me. It is time for all of this to heal now by understanding the role the presence of unloving light has played and moving that out instead of moving against each other. The wars in Europe have been mostly Rainbow Spirit wars, and this really needs to stop now by moving out the cause of the problem and not by attacking the symptoms.

As much as I loved My visits with the Rainbow Faeries in Pan and loved dressing in their flower colors and feeling My health and vitality increase in their presence as I soaked in the sunlight coming through their colors, no one particular color is My resting place. There is no one particular color that plumbs the depth of My soul the way the Ronalokas do. Gold is My resting place, and all of the colors are My cherished, pleasant and frequent visitation places, provided they make Me welcome there.

In the progression of healing of My own chakras in My visits with the Rainbow Spirits, I found that there did seem to be many parts of the Mother, all potentially, beautifully suited to the places they were situated to Mother. In the chakras, there are four Parental parts of each chakra, the same as the Four Parts of God. The Mother of each chakra is part of the Mother, and I am Her Mother, but She is more like My sister than My daughter there. Her daughter there is the Will side of the Heart of that chakra, and Heart is My child there too. The Father there is the Spirit side of the chakra. The form it takes is the Father of Manifestation, and the Heart of the chakra brings the two sides together. Then there are the connecting links and their family arrangements and the Rainbow Spirits who stream forth in their family arrangements as the light generated and made manifest there.

Not all the families there have only one son and one daughter either. Some families, especially in the Rainbow Spirits, prefer manifesting the many different aspects of many different spirits and then feel best doing what they want to do, in terms of their own specialties, when all are present doing their part, but have also fought with each other over this as much as everyone else over all of the same unresolved issues of Original Cause.

The chakras need a circulation of energy that is both white and gold light, Angelic and Ronalokan, but Heart also plays a role here that needs to become more clear as healing moves forward, and all of it needs to find right place and find that it can be happy in that place for the Body of God to be made manifest on Earth in the way that will really feel good. For God to finally have His Body on Earth in an alignment of love with Him is the healing potential that lies before Us. What He is going to do once He has this Body is a dream yet to unfold. To get to the place of that unfoldment, the Rainbow Spirits have a lot of work to do repairing the damage that has already been done by the smack and all of the patterns of conditioning that have repeated since then, as well as does everyone else who has needed to move first as the Parental poles of the situation.

To repair and heal the Parents of the chakras is to repair and heal the chakras of the Main Body of God on Earth, and if you are

Parental here, you are part of the Main Body of God from whom the Rainbow Spirits stream forth. You must find your right place in the Body of God and find it truly by becoming truly comfortable there; otherwise you cannot be My light in the way I need you to be. That you are Manifested Spirits is true because I have a manifested Body, but you are not Manifested Spirits in the way you have thought because only the Main Body of God is really moving now, and the rest will move later after their Parents have healed enough to lead the way. That is why I have said to seek your own healing first and then turn to those around you who respond to it. These will be your closest relatives and children, allies and friends, in your own colors and in the connecting links between the chakras of the Main Body of God, and in the Rainbow Spirits who stream forth from it as My light overflowing from there.

So far, it has not felt good because of the chaos, confusion, misunderstanding and lack of understanding around what was happening to Us in the original sea of essence, but I hope that it can finally now come to a place where everything feels good because of what We have learned and will learn by going back to that place now and resolving the issues there, and a place that feels good because everything is in its right place and knows how to move from there and is happy with that, because FreeWill is a necessary part of this, but FreeWill that is aligned with its light within love. Without that, We have had hierarchy that has been boring, static, rigid, controlled and unloving, with chaos, anarchy and rebellion on the other side; rich nations and poor nations, dominant nations and subservient nations, subsistence nations and destructively technological nations, and so on through all the patterns that have presented themselves.

For so long, the Mother could not be accepted for what She had to say that the Mother did not speak from the position of Mother from the time My gap knocked Her out of Creation until now. In Pan, there was no place for the Mother really being made except for the image of Mother being presented by the mother on Earth and others seeking the position. This was not a real image of the Mother since it was almost all denied kundalini return outside of loving light that was being reflected there. This needs to come within love to heal and is being brought there now.

My light is My light whether it speaks as the Father, the Mother, Heart or Body. If there is alignment, It brings an aligned message; if not, We have what We have had so far; a massive and chaotic power struggle from points of view so polarized from one another as to not be able to recognize the balance points from which alignment can be entered and found. This is the most possibility for healing We have ever had, and I do not want to see another reversal, so please, do your part as best you can, and do not play a role in the Luciferian sense of viewing life and karma as playing roles that can be switched arbitrarily. This is no game, and the roles are not up for grabs anymore.

It can be said that the experience We have had has been role playing in an effort to understand Our roles and find Our right place, but the power play business underneath the surface really has to end, and right place really has to be found now as right place because it is right place and it is comfortable. No more thinking the Mother's place is up for grabs if She is gone, and therefore, you have a vested interest in keeping Her gone, or anyone else's place for that matter. No one's place can be filled by another appropriately, and using that knowledge to punish Us by withholding your presence is not coming within the alignment of loving light either.

Anything that needs to be said by the Mother needs to be said, and anything you need to move as response needs to move as emotion first and not as any more attack and blame at the word level that does not move the underlying charge into the realization of its own causal role in what it has been attacking and blaming.

The denied kundalini response needs to be given here and received, and the way to do this most quickly and easily is to reverse the polarization from mind to emotion to emotion to mind until We have a comfortable circulation here and not just mind to emotion and nothing returned here that is accepted. If you are not ready to accept this yet, you are not ready to move along with the Main Body of God and need to move back farther into the realms of Manifested Spirits than you already have because it is not right time for you yet, just as it was not right time yet in Pan. As difficult as this was for the Mother, there was not anything She could say or do there and get any more received than She did because She did not understand Herself well enough yet to get any more received than She did. So, it is not a matter of guilt that you could not receive Her then, but it is a matter of moving now what could not move then, and if you are not ready yet, then move along as much as you can as every realization you get helps whether you are ready to move in deeply yet or not.

THE MOTHER'S RAGE

In the days of Pan on Earth, I did not have solutions, and so I could not say much of anything I felt without being viewed as dismally complaining instead of having the fun available to Me everywhere, but from My perspective, I did not see it as fun. I felt that I had been through Hell, and could not understand how others could feel like celebrating if they had also.

Although I could not remember the details, I had the feelings present within Me, and I needed the space to process them in order to gain the understandings I have now, finally, after all this time, gained. I cannot help but feel a rancor about how short a time this might have taken Me if I had had any help at all there that had encouraged My emotional expression instead of exerting a steady, downward pressure on it, accompanied by feelings of superiority for not having it, and how much less suffering would have resulted then. I was still so close to My power then and could still believe that I had some. Now, it is difficult to believe that I ever had power or that there is any such thing as Mother power.

Now, granted you had no other place to go that you were capable of going and that you fell to Earth because the magnetic draw of My presence so far out into space drew you out this far, granted you had a hard time too, although I would like to remind you that Earth is not Hell, it is My home, granted you wanted to party, which I am not altogether opposed to no matter what you may think, granted you were not parented for a long time and so how could We expect you to behave any better, although you claimed to be grown up and not need parenting anymore, granted you could not move past your Parents' understanding level even though you tried your hardest to prove you knew better than We did and granted anything else you want to claim on your side; I want to be granted this:

Earth is My planet, and I was not given space even here to process what I needed to process, let alone any help, support, comfort or sympathy in any way commensurate with the problem. Granted, you did not know what the problem was and that you did not have enough experience to understand it, but grant Me that you did not help at the level you had to offer and the level you had to give. That was all I needed, and you did not do it.

Instead, you ran all over Pan, partying and trashing Pan the same way you trashed Me; with your Will denial. You shoved Me out into Hell even here on Earth, and when that was made manifest, you blamed Me and not yourselves at all for bringing Hell to Earth . You did not care about My pain. Was it because you did not recognize Me? I could have been any little old woman in the forest, as I soon was in Pan, and you would have run over Me the same way. I could have been a piece of your own lost Will, which I was also, and you did not help it. How could I have found out how you felt about My vibration divested of My image, position and power if you had recognized Me? Why did you need to recognize Me? How could I have learned that you wanted to take My image, position and power and put it in the place of a real Mother, divested of My vibration, if you had recognized Me? You did not give Me the space to heal My own pain. Instead, you viewed anything that interfered with the party as something to dump, or run over the same as you did in the Godhead when you aligned with running over Me and dumping Me out of there.

You aligned with something very unloving here, and you need to look at it and move it out of you, or I am not going to allow you to stay on Earth. You have behaved like a bunch of spoiled and over-indulged brats long enough. My rage fragments have been putting children out of their homes and onto the streets for a long time. I am now bringing this rage back within Myself, and what form it is going to take, I cannot tell you, but things are not going to go on as they have been, that I can tell you. Spoiled brats who do not help and spoiled brats who are still into Will denial are going off the planet!

I should have been able to come from Hell to My own planet and process what I needed to process and heal in peace and quiet, and alone if necessary, instead of having to come to a place overrun with squalling, insatiable brats who were never satisfied with anything they were ever given while saying it was only Me who was never satisfied.

The very least you could have done was to move back enough to give Me a place in the forest where I could have had peace and quiet and rest. You did not even do that. I had to always be near the Father of Manifestation for protection, and you never gave Him any peace either, I can testify to that. Demands and complaints, complaints and demands, but if I had any, I was negative. The Father of Manifestation and I had no relationship in which any sufficient amount of healing could take place. There was no time for that. You made sure of it.

You've all complained about what God hasn't done for you, and why didn't the Parents (who weren't parented at all) do more, know more, help more, give more. You have all fought for the Parental roles and to be adults and parents yourselves and then, when you put yourselves in the Parental spot, you have done less, known less, helped less and given less than We did, and basically used the position for the acting out of your images of power and glory in which it looked like you were basically out for yourselves in a way that did not feel very loving to Me and to run wild and free as though your thought process on parenting hadn't gone any further that the idea of no one telling you what to do.

Whenever I have been able to help, My first concern has been for My children, and I have helped them as much as I possibly could; so much so that I have wondered if I've been a fool at times as My own denied rage has for so long said. Where has your help been? Have you just sucked up My help as part of your information gathering process in your power play as My denied rage has said? I have hope that this rage was viewing you from the gap that is healing now, and that you will move in response to the gap that is healing now, but I need to know the truth from the way you move, not from what you say from your reasonable part.

Why do you think We, the first Parents, had such a problem? It was because We had no one to help Us by telling Us what to do. I could not say anything about how I felt as the Mother without being viewed as criticizing, lecturing and trying to place limits you didn't want to have. You were in reaction against complaints and rules and in defiance of and rebellion against authority, when, if you had had acceptance for your Wills, there would not have been need for Me to complain or to impose the rules and limits you so self-righteously opposed. You need to look at what light it is that views authority, not as wisdom, but as power over you and check the reflection of that in the world.

I could not move rage and I could not move terror in Pangea. If I hadn't been able to find places already filled with sounds to cover My movement in which to move some of My deep grief, I doubt I would have been able to move that, and if I had not been able to move even that, I doubt that you would have a Mother to help you now. You did not give Me the space, either in Pan, or within yourselves, in which complaints could have become emotions, could have become understandings, could have become solutions to heal the gap long ago, but you surely could complain long and loud about the pain you were suffering and place the blame all outside of yourselves.

I have issues with everyone who did not give Me space to

174

move the way I needed to move. You have all had gaps that did not want Me to move these problems back into their right places. Anything I said there was met only with statements of how much fun it was to form change, to have sex as much as you all wanted to, which you did anytime, anywhere and with anyone in every way, and with statements about how important it was for you to run all over Pan partying as much as you wanted to, with no parents telling you what to do and what not to do. Most of you who were not parented claimed you liked it that way because you could be immediately adult and not have anyone telling you how you should be doing things. Any suggestions I made about how I thought you felt were met with denials and insistence of how fine you felt and how wonderful it was to be able to run around Pan doing whatever you felt like doing, whenever you felt like doing it. My terror could not let Me press the point then.

Looking around Me, I did not like much of anything I saw, in fact. Everything in Pangea was having problems compared to how it used to be, or how My memory saw it anyway. With no spirits to parent or who accepted Me there, I took to caring for the forest alone during the day while almost everyone else slept. The very forest, itself looked sad to Me and abandoned of Mother presence. The flowers drooped, and many of them were torn from their places, ravaged and thrown down. I wept for them, picking each one up and holding it as though they were My little children who had been trampled to death. I especially could not stand how the satyrs were treating the forest. There was a feeling of irresponsibility in their wanton abandon that I did not like even then, and a feeling of disregard and disrespect for the Mother too.

It appeared to Me that I had been gone for a long time, and that terrible problems had set into Earth during My absence, but I became easily disoriented by denials and contradictions, wondering if it was Me instead.

"How dare you use My planet this way!" was the reproachment I wanted to allow Myself then, but they controlled the vines and preached freedom for all, not just My version of it. I did not like the power they had in Pan. It seemed to Me it was the power to override everyone else in favor of themselves and call it FreeWill, but I wasn't sure because they claimed I did that. Whenever they spoke about the Mother, there was jeering, disrespect and hatred heaped upon Her. No wonder the Father of Manifestation didn't want Me to reveal Myself, especially in the diminished state I was in. If He didn't have the power to control them, I certainly didn't

175

anymore.

I wanted to turn to Him for help anyway and felt blame toward Him for letting things get so out of control when I wasn't there, but when I pictured Myself angrily telling Him how I felt about these satyrs and their horrible rampaging through the forests of Pan, I was afraid all I would hear in return was how I had rampaged in Pan and hadn't cared what it did to the nature there then either.

"Why so concerned now?" I feared I heard the rest of the satyrs sneering at Me sarcastically, as though they were going to suddenly appear as having a secret alliance with the Father of Manifestation here. Why He was appearing to ignore them so much, I did not know, but then there were so many things I did not understand about Pan, the God, and Pan, the land now too. Why had the Father of Manifestation taken on such a bestial form for Himself? This He did not explain.

I found the satyrs' sexual behavior obnoxiously outrageous too; the cruel torture and molestation of children, as I saw it. I felt ashamed as the Mother of Everything that this could even be happening to the children and Me be as powerless to stop it as I found out I was the first time I tried, and they victimized Me along with the rest and even more so, laughing and plucking Me up like a hapless Flower, jeering Me as a prude who had tried to stop it, and a party drag too. Giving Me suffocation and drowning lessons and telling Me how much worse it would be the next time I interfered convinced Me I did not have the power to stop them, but I wanted someone to.

I felt I must find some way to stop this. I thought I had an alignment for this from most of the spirits in Pan who complained privately to others about the satyrs, but I found that in their presence, they acted as if they enjoyed it until I was more than confused and began to think that maybe I was alone in My views and opinions, and that others agreed with Me in My presence, but privately thought I was the prude among them.

These satyrs did not love pure water the way I did either, galloping through it way too carelessly, often muddying it horribly, tearing up its beautifully framing embankments and leaving behind foul odors and liquids that dribbled out of them so constantly I could not tell if they were still spasming from orgasms as they ran through the woods seeking more orgasms, or if they had some kind of problem causing them to constantly dribble out unwanted essence. Whatever it was, I didn't like it, and I couldn't stand their foul, rotten smelling scent being spread as wantonly across Pan as was their behavior.

Everywhere I went in the forest, it was becoming more and more difficult to get away from it. Their scent hung heavy in the air in places, and the more they trampled the mosses and grasses and tore down and trampled the flowers, the more their scent began to override the pure and beautiful air of Pan that had been so filled with the exotic and inviting aromas of flowers, spices, herbs and every other thing that grew or had presence, including the Earth, herself until I felt I could not even become intoxicated on the air anymore because I no longer even wanted to breathe deeply if it was going to have to smell like this.

Breathing deeply and becoming intoxicated on the air was a love of Mine, and I felt bitterness over this. Foulness of sounds, smells, feelings and appearance assailed all of My senses in Pan, and I felt immense bitterness and rage over this, all converted by necessity into bitter, stinging tears as I swept, cleaned, tidied and nurtured the forest all day long, unnoticed in Pan.

I still did breathe deeply whenever I found air where I thought I could. That is how I found other things I considered to be wrong in Pangea. I found stinking pools of stagnant, dark rot in various locations around the forest, apparently created by the satyrs since their hoof marks were all around them. These pools appeared to be the source of their drunkenness since they seemed to prefer drinking this to pure water. I feared this rot and where it might lead, and I could not understand the shunning of or the fouling of the great, healing and sustaining powers of the pure water by those so obviously in need of healing.

I hated these stinking, stagnant pools and saw that the satyrs weren't even careful about what else fell in there along with the flowers and fruits they threw and trampled down into them, drowning them without caring how these things felt about their demise. I hated the idea of taking over other things this way or even eating them at all. It only reminded Me of My experience with the snake and of other dark things that were not able to surface in Me. I felt living on light and air and a little water was the only way to live.

The nature of Pan had so much beauty and gentleness to it I could not stand to see it victimized this way. It wasn't that I didn't like wild and free nature, but I wanted it to have a gentleness and beauty to it, and a grace that delighted My aesthetic sense; the perfect balance really, even down to the harmoniously winding pathways through it; certainly not these disgusting satyr-made

177

alleyways, trampled, not only in look, but in feeling, by too many frenzied, galloping hooves that cared not what they ran over or overran, and littered with death they had created along the sides. At times, I even found little dead creatures amongst the refuse, and I sat holding them and crying until I thought I would never recover, and made Myself stop. It felt like they were literally pounding a beaten feeling of density into Earth in more ways than one.

Pan was being laid waste, and My beautiful children were being laid waste too, and I felt powerless to stop it. I felt like the Mother as maid who would be running through the forest of Pan forever, sweeping, cleaning and trying all day long to clean up and restore the destruction and mess that had been made partying the night before and left unnoticed, apparently, because they could not see very well and slept where they fell, even if it was on a pile of rubbish.

The feeling I had was that My children were not running with the right gang, and I did not know what I was going to be able to do about it since they did not recognize or respect Me as their Mother and had put a Dragon Mother Protectorate in My place, even emblazoning her false image of power as the right Mother and her satyrs as father images in place of the true Father of Manifestation on Earth. I wanted to help Pangea, and I felt Pangea was crying for My help, but grief and feelings of powerlessness were all I could come up with, other than to soothe the wounds as best I could, which turned out, gradually, over time, to be much more helpful than I had at first thought it was, but I learned by this that everything took longer than it had in My original experience of Pan and seemed to come back with less vitality than I remembered it originally having also.

I wanted to help My children too, but I was not sure if they wanted My help, or if they did, what kind of help they wanted, or if I had any help to give. My arms ached to hold them, but they all looked so big and grown up and adverse to the idea of receiving any mothering, that I did not know where to start if I could not even start with them recognizing Me as their Mother. The only arms of any love they seemed to have enfolding them now were the arms of their lovers, and I did not want to be their lover. I wanted to be their Mother and cry with them in My arms for a long time and find some way out of this nightmare they were insisting was so much fun. I did not see it as fun at all; I saw it as a major reversal of what I had come forth to live in Creation, finding Myself in yet another nightmare that I had hoped was going to be a rescue.

THE GIANT OGRES

I felt so lost and lonely and so frightened then, wandering around Pan, seeming to be the only One awake during the day-time. It did not seem right that everyone slept while the merry sunbeams splashed and played their colors across the face of Pangea, sprinkling light as I had originally enjoyed the loving light of God to be, and that everyone was instead more interested in the dark play of shadows and intrigue, forgotten and hidden identities and dark and hidden rendezvous that felt secret and taboo. I liked the merriment of sunshine, but I also liked the soft blue night too, so I felt guilty that I had these feelings. It was the extremes I didn't like, I told Myself, but static, boring control freak played in My head in response to that idea.

I loved My own visions and fantasies and now wandered alone through Pan with them as I had in My earliest days there, only now I had to gaze upon the rampaging, wanton destruction of the satyrs and infringements by all of the other spirits that I did not like either. "Probably what I deserve for having rampaged Myself," I thought, but I suffered, nonetheless, in the Mother's pain of it all.

I did not like having to look at what I saw there, and going inside was no relief either. I did not like what I saw and felt inside Myself. Disturbing things were present there, even more disturb-ing than what I saw outwardly in Pan.

"I should be glad, I suppose, that Pangea is not any worse than it is," I told Myself, "but I still do not like the mothering job that has been done while I have been away, and I do not like the behavior of the children that has resulted from it, or the children, either, for that matter."

I was surprised that I could even say this openly to Myself. It did not sound very loving to Me, but it was how I felt. "Maybe I am not a very charitable or loving Mother," I told Myself. "Maybe I cannot and do not give the children any place in which to learn for themselves. Maybe that's why they have wanted to be away from Me."

How could I say they should behave any better than they did when I had feelings of hating them behind all of their backs and I knew I had darker places in Me than any they had shown so far? I could not understand the presence of these places either because

179

love was My intent, yet there they were. I tried to love these dark places, but they seemed sickened by this, the same as the children did. I decided I had better try to go in there and find out whatever more I could.

I certainly had the isolation and quiet of the daytime in which to do this, plus the reassurance and support of the sunshine when I came back out of My inner dark places if I ever did or could, but I had the limitation of not being able to make any noise, which seemed like an impossible limitation for Me if I really went in there. I was afraid to go in there alone, but since there was no one to help Me, I felt I had to give it a try.

To My startled horror, when I looked inside without any outer interferences around to distract Me, the first thing I saw was lines of energy running from Me to some place so dark and horrible I could not bear to look at it at all. All I could see were hoards of monsters climbing these lines toward Me, looking full of hatred and hellbent on attack. It appeared to Me they were moving rather quickly, the only thing slowing them down that I could see being their own fighting for position on the lines. These monsters looked so overwhelmingly frightening to Me that I jumped immediately out of this as though I had awakened from a nightmare, only I did not feel that I had really awakened. I feared this was real, and then I had the feeling I remembered something terrible that gave Me the urgent feeling I must warn Earth. But why? It did not make sense. If it was My problem, why warn Earth?

I heard Lucifer laughing at Me then and saying that I was so stupid that I did not learn My lessons, and because I did not learn My lessons, he was coming to Earth to teach them to Me again, "and this time," he said menacingly, "You had better learn them."

I wanted to believe this was only a bad dream and wake up from it, but I could not. I heard it in broad daylight when I was sure I was awake. I wished I was asleep then like the others in Pan; asleep in someone's arms which I could not be because of My pain and the feeling of falling that I so often had and which now seemed to be from the pull of these lines. I feared My being awake then as though I somehow deserved this for it.

I felt desperate to escape and hoped My vision had been off and that My feelings about these lines were off too. I thought I was going to go crazy, come apart, even shatter right there and then, not daring to make the noises that were surging all through Me and with not even anyone there to talk to about this and no one who would understand Me if I did. I wanted to fly all the way home then

180

to God and have Him rescue and protect Me as the only safe place left, but I was not sure I could leave My children on Earth without a Mother any longer than they had been already no matter what state of affairs Our relationship was in, and I was not sure God would have Me either, since He had not spoken to Me since I had returned to Earth.

"And not for a long time prior to that, either," the voice of Lucifer reminded Me cruelly.

I was so frightened to hear this horrible, yet familiar voice sounding so present and so near that I was literally flying up into the air, trying to go to God, get free of the lines or out of Myself, anything, when something huge grabbed Me. At first, I foolishly hoped it was a rescue by the direct hand of God, but the feeling of it was so much not that that My heart nearly stopped. What had Me now? One of the Monsters? Lucifer? Was it just going to crush Me heartlessly as it so easily could? Did it even care? Would it even notice?

When I saw that it was giant ogres, I was as much terrified as I was relieved. Unfortunately, I had been warned about them but did not prove to have listened closely enough, having caused Myself yet another problem. The Father of Manifestation was really going to be mad at Me now since I did not think He even knew that I did these daylight wandering, clean-up, nurturing forays when I was so restless I couldn't sleep, which was most of the time since I was so tormented.

What was in store for Me now? I had heard such terrible stories I didn't know what to expect was going to happen next. I began crying and shaking in wild-eyed terror. I was babbling things about lines and hordes of monsters climbing them toward Earth to get Me and everyone else and apparently stunned the giants with this so much that they dropped their clubs to their sides and began staring at Me as if I was a ranting, crazy person.

I could tell from the blankness in their blinking eyes that they were not very intelligent, and My heart took pity on them which I had not expected it to do from the terrible stories I had been told of them eating so many things in Pan after first clubbing them into unconsciousness, which was what others thought made them so unconscious themselves. I felt they had this kind of unconscious rage presence alright, but hearts somehow, too, if that were even possible in rage.

I kept crying hysterically and telling the giants they must let Me go because I must warn the spirits on Earth about these monsters. The giants found this immensely funny, as if I thought they should let Me go free so I could warn others about them. They let Me know that they could not let Me do that, and that they could not possibly eat Me either because I was much too thin. They decided they must put Me in a cage and fatten Me up.

They carried Me with them to some lost and tangled part of the forest where they apparently lived. I was hysterical with terror the whole way. They were surely taking Me to some horrible place, in which I would never be found, to fatten Me up for their dinner. I had really done it this time! Why didn't I listen to the Father of Manifestation and stay closer no matter what I thought of the satyrs' rampaging and His not helping Me to tidy up after them? I really was stupid.

I begged the giants' forgiveness for intruding on their part of the forest and begged them to let Me go, telling them I would not be anymore nourishing to eat than a butterfly and couldn't be fattened up because I didn't eat. Frantic to warn of the monstrous hordes climbing toward Earth, I did not even think of how others would react to what I had to say or the implications of My involvement in it. Nor did I think about how the ogres would react to My statements. I was totally frantic and promised the giants I would do anything they wanted if they would just let Me go afterwards.

They told Me I must teach them to fly, and then they would let Me go. My heart was stunned into terrified silence. What was I going to do now? The problem was I didn't think before I spoke; instead, My mouth and My terror always seemed to get Me into trouble, and if they didn't, then My rage and My mouth did.

One look at them had told Me how far they were from being able to fly. They looked way too dense, slow, clumsy and stupid to be able to fly. How was it these creatures always had such a knack of asking for the thing most difficult to give them? Couldn't they be happy with a story telling them more about the origins of their existence or something like that? But no, they could not be interested in anything more subtly helpful like that. They were either going to eat Me or learn to fly, no two ways about it.

The giants put Me in a cage, and as soon as they put Me in the cage, I had a feeling of falling down again as though I was so thin I could slip right through the bars and even, I was frightened now, off Earth from the pressure of the lines pulling on Me. As I began to fall through the bottom of the cage, the giants hurriedly put a platform underneath Me and began lashing additional pieces into place. I was clinging to the cage, by then, as though it might be the only thing keeping Me from being pulled down and off Earth, but also, I was still screaming hysterically about lines and monsters and pain, holding My belly and begging for the giants' help.

The giants were peering at Me very curiously as though they found this to be very strange behavior for someone who had just moments earlier so vigorously protested being put in a cage. They watched Me intently as I tried to get it across to them that I needed help getting these lines off of Me. There they stood with the great, big hands, strong arms and huge bodies that I felt, especially as a group, had the strength to shake the monsters off of the lines and pull the lines back into Me, or pull the lines off of Me and cast them back down, or even haul the lines up and club the monsters unconscious one by one as they came, and I could not get it across to them what kind of help I needed.

I was desperate to get the lines off of Me any way that I could, rolling around by now, ripping at My belly and all of the other places I felt the lines hooked into Me while the giants stood there, staring dumbfoundedly, making noises among themselves and seeming to be only interested in making sure the cage was secure against My escape, which was a help, but not the full measure of help I needed by any means. I was not even sure the cage could hold Me if the lines kept pulling the way they were.

I felt Myself being ripped apart from the pull of the lines. No wonder I was looking so tattered and that My lower parts had lost so much presence. Most of the lines were hooked into My belly, and the more I tried to release them, the more they gripped in there, like rock climbing grips, as though the hooks were burrowing in more deeply and gripping more angrily at the very thought of casting them out to fall back down. My desperation was mounting the closer I saw the monsters getting, and their angry determination was mounting also.

I was struggling with the lines, wiggling and shaking, ripping and tearing at Myself, writhing around in agonized motion, trying to get the lines loose from the places where I felt they were hooked into Me, and when I could not, pounding these places in a terrified rage that was full of desperation and feelings of powerlessness. I was screaming at the hordes on the lines to let go and being jerked around the cage by them in response, nearly being pulled down through the floor and out through the bars.

It felt like they had been sneaking up the lines earlier and now that I had seen them, were mounting an all out assault. While I had no allies or help of any kind, there were more of them than I could count; so many of them that the sheer weight of them was dragging Me down into the hopelessness of a lost cause; a cause lost in the midst of those who had the power and strength to help Me, but no intelligence with which to understand the help I needed so that they could give it.

I was surrounded by an entire ring of giants now, all breathing on Me with fetid breath that was nearly suffocating to Me, and all staring at Me as though this was some sort of a performance, the meaning of which they did not understand. It became apparent to Me from the questioning looks on their faces when I pointed to the lines that they did not even see the lines or the monsters who were getting so close to Me, or else they did and they didn't want to let Me know it.

I stared futilely and desperately back at them, still trying to get them to understand My plight and that even they could be pounced on at any moment by countless monsters, but they stood there blinking and staring dully back, cracking a smile here and there and elbowing one another and pointing when they wanted others to notice what they were looking at. My mind could not get ahold of much mental activity in them by which to read or understand them, and I could not feel their feelings either. This struck Me into a new terror of whether they could really be such empty forms, or if they really did know what they were doing and were hiding it from Me. They were so huge, and I was so little and powerless. What were they really planning to do? They seemed so close to monsters, themselves in that moment, or at least monstrosities, that I feared they were already monsters on Earth who were holding Me for the rest, and I had not realized it.

I was frantic with terror, and in a last ditch effort to save Myself, I began wildly whirling about. I guess I thought I could possibly throw off the lines this way, or whirl them out into space and the monsters with them, or at least tangle them up badly. I was madly whirling this way and that, throwing off energy like little fire balls or little lightning bolts and sparks, whirling like a little energy vortex of gathering speed, raging and crying furiously all the while about why I couldn't have any real help. Where was God? Where was the Father of Manifestation? (probably with others and not missing Me) Why did I have to struggle and suffer so much?

I was throwing off energy so fast in My effort to throw off the lines that I couldn't even tell for sure if it was being cast off of Me or if it was escaping from Me as fast as it possibly could to get away from the situation. I was moving terror, rage and grief and it did not seem to be saving Me. Nothing seemed to be saving Me. I felt so alone and unhelped, and nothing really has been able to save Me in all this time until I was really able to move enough to understand the imprinting problem.

I began to run down from the exhaustion of this energy expenditure into a terrified hopelessness that there would be nothing left of Me if this kept up. The giants were all pointing and looking at Me too, as though they thought doing this was going to make Me disappear as My means of escape. Apparently, they thought this was some sort of ritual or performance of magic of which they felt frightened or possibly threatened because they had all been averting their heads and peering at Me sideways when it was happening, but now that I was quieting down again, they crowded back in more closely as if to see what My next move was going to be, or perhaps to prevent Me from escaping.

The hooks were still there. I could feel them, although the weight of the monsters seemed a little less on the lines. I thought now I must try to unhook the hooks while the lines weren't so heavy feeling, but I still could not do it. They felt as if they were a part of Me, and I could not let go of them. I tried again then to haul the lines up and shake the monsters off as I drew them in, but I did not have the strength. The giants' mouths were hanging open as they stared at this like it was some sort of a pantomime routine, or else they were drooling over the idea of eating Me. I wasn't sure, but I again tried to tell them I would be no more nourishing than a butterfly if they tried to eat Me.

Immediately, I felt it was a grave mistake to have reminded them of food at all. It seemed to break the spellbound quality that was holding them so magnetized there. They began to look around at the others again and make noises and gestures amongst themselves that I didn't like.

I didn't know what My next move could really be, but I tried to disappear another way then. I tried to relax and breathe and go into a meditative state in which I planned to disperse Myself until I was so lacking in density that the hooks fell out because there would be nothing left for them to hold onto, and that way, the lines would all fall back on themselves, and the monsters would all fall to their own deaths or at least into oblivion or, failing that, the far away and dark reaches of distant space.

I grew quite determined in this, and the meditation felt good

185

to Me. I felt less pain and a lifting in Myself that released the feeling of pressure from the lines quite a bit. I felt Myself lifting as though I was lifting out through the top of Myself. I thought there would be nothing left of Me and that I was lifting out through the top of the cage this time. I was almost ready to feel successful and ready to congratulate Myself on having escaped this terrible problem. My heart was already leaping with joyful pictures of this impending success when I became aware of something that was not lifting with the rest of Me.

At first, I thought it was only a jerk from the lines and that I should let go of it, but then it began to pull at Me, crying and complaining bitterly that I was leaving it there to suffer this horrible fate all alone and that it couldn't go with Me and didn't know how to move this way anymore. I felt so horrible about leaving anything behind to suffer what I knew was coming toward it that I couldn't leave this way anymore either. I saw a grotesque, unmoving, statue-like face flash for an instant in My inner vision which disappeared as quickly as it had come. I could not remember where I had seen it before. It was trying to say something I couldn't quite hear that gave Me a creepy feeling that I could not let go of any more of Myself and live.

I plummeted back down into Myself and sat there, feeling dismal, frightened and desperate, but knowing that I was going to have to let go of these "unable to lift" parts of Myself to leave that way, and that I could not do it as long as there was any other possible way this problem might be solved. I felt in Me that these were the places where the hooks were in Me. I could not release them, and I realized that I was going to have to let go of pieces of Myself along with the lines if I did it this way.

There wasn't much good for Me to look at as I sat there in the cage the giants had prepared for Me with My mind feeling too panicky to think about how I could either perform the impossible task of teaching these giants to fly or to help Me, let alone manage to get away somehow with My life still intact. My mind was consumed with urgency about at least getting to the Father of Manifestation to warn Him about the impending attack of these monsters, even if I couldn't escape the fate Myself. I continued to feel hysterical that there was precious little time left before they reached Earth, and that now, the little time left that there was was being consumed by being held prisoner in a cage by giants who wanted Me to teach them how to fly and who could not understand that they needed to help Me too.

186

The giants, meanwhile, had come to some sort of a consensus among themselves that I was too thin and lacking in substance, and that My activities had been an effort to convey to them a need to eat, that this was the help I needed and wanted, and that only then would I be quiet. They had apparently concluded that I was going to disappear on them, either by getting so small I vanished or so dispersed I vanished, which was thin to them, nonetheless, because it was a lack of substance. They kept plucking at themselves with their huge fingers and wiggling the fleshiness in their grasp back and forth and then poking at Me to show Me how wispy I was.

Perhaps they thought it would give Me substance by making Me bigger, fatter or more solid, perhaps they thought they could keep Me from disappearing this way, perhaps they thought I could not teach them to fly and so they might as well fatten Me up and eat Me, perhaps they thought I was trying to disappear as a means of escape without teaching them to fly, perhaps they thought it would keep Me from disappearing or perhaps they just thought I was howling and holding My belly because I was hungry, perhaps they thought it would calm Me down or even that it was what I wanted, perhaps they thought I had been doing some sort of ritual or magic that was dangerous to them and that the noise I had been making was part of it and was making Me disappear, or that I was disappearing as a result of making so much noise, perhaps they feared I was going to attract unwanted attention with all the noise, which thought made Me hopeful for a moment that perhaps I wasn't so far lost in the woods as I had thought.

I didn't know, but whatever it was, they had decided that I must be made to be more quiet and that I must eat and that the two were somehow intertwined together, as though feeding Me was going to make Me be more quiet, and being more quiet was going to make Me feel like eating.

Just the idea that I was going to be made to eat terrified Me into utter silence. I tried to show them that I would be very quiet if they would just leave Me alone and let Me try to teach them how to fly. I did not even want to make any noise anymore because I could see that opening My mouth was a highly dangerous thing to do since they seemed to take it as a sign that I wanted to eat and advanced on Me with horrible things they were holding in their hands and even hiding behind their backs. I tried to get as far away from them as I could in the cage, which was a silly idea since the cage was round and I was surrounded by them. I tried to show them that I

187

didn't like the idea of anything going into My mouth, but they interpreted My gestures to mean the opposite. I tried to let them know that I did not eat, but I could not get it across, or else they did not care and had decided they were going to make Me eat anyway. They brought over what looked to Me like battered pieces of things. Just to look at these remains made Me feel sick and they smelled worse. Where they were even able to get such things in Pan, I did not know. I tried to imagine the forms these pieces had once had, but happily, perhaps, they were nothing I could recognize.

I begged them not to make Me eat. I told them I could fly because I did not eat. I gagged and My stomach spasmed as in vomiting and I sank downward in the cage in an effort to show them that if they made Me eat, I would get sick and pretty soon not be able to fly and not, then, be able to teach them to fly. Apparently, nothing was going to make any difference to their decision that I was going to eat.

When I started to gag on the smell of the horrible things they were planning to feed Me, the giants took the opening of My mouth as a sign that I wanted to eat. When I didn't respond to their entreaties, they forced My mouth open and began shoving pieces of these horrible things down My throat. When I gagged and threw them back up, it was terrifying to Me, and I almost could not do it. It was an agonizing experience to hang there between the immense terror I had of throwing up and the horrible feeling from what they had forced down My throat. If I kept it, I felt nauseated and sick and unable to think. Just when I would be getting over it, they would come and force Me to eat again. If I threw up instead, they made Me eat these things again, showing Me insistently that I must chew them first by opening and closing My mouth forcibly many times upon these things and then holding My head back until I swallowed them. If I still threw these things back up, they made Me eat them again, acting like this was nothing unusual and that they did it all the time, even demonstrating it for Me so I would know how to do it.

I hated this experience totally. I could not stand the look of it. I could not stand the smell or taste of it. I could not stand the feeling of these things in My mouth. I could not stand the chewing. I could not stand the swallowing. I could not stand the holding of these things in My stomach. I could not stand the throwing of them back up or the smell of that. I could not stand the passing of them down and out of Me. I could not even stand the smell of the giants who

188

were forcing Me to experience this torture. What was going to happen to Me? Was I going to become like them, or were they going to eat Me first?

When finally it appeared that I had gotten it across to them that eating and flying did not mix and that eating was going to make it so that I could not fly and that they could not fly either if they were going to eat and that if they wanted to fly, they were going to have to stop eating and get less dense like I was, they began feeding Me only things that flew and showing Me that they had a belief that if they ate enough things that flew, it would make them able to fly. I could see that this was a belief that I was not going to be able to dislodge easily, and in fact, I was not going to be able to do it at all.

I did not know what to do then. Since the giants were apparently not going to stop eating or feeding Me, I tried to think of how I might be able to get them flying or to try flying in different forms than their giant configurations. I tried telling them that they might have to get smaller in order to be able to fly, but they were not interested in this. I could see that there were many spirits involved in their configurations as giants, and I was hoping to break them up into a more manageable opposition, but if these giants did not like an idea, they dismissed it and insisted I get another idea.

I even tried to think of how I could get them to jump off of high places as a way to try flying and dash themselves to pieces so they would not be a problem for Me anymore, but when I suggested this, they told Me they had already seen Me fly from right where I was. When I told them I learned by jumping off of high places, they told Me they had already tried that and that it had not worked. I told them then that nothing would work as long as they were so dense, and that it was not fair to hold Me to My end of the bargain if they were not willing to do any of the things required to fly, such as to stop eating, which was what I firmly believed was what it was going to take for them to be able to fly.

At first, they looked like they thought that was fair enough, but when I told them they might have to let Me go then, they said they had to have time to think about it and gathered in a noisy, grumbling, growling huddle. When they came back, they let Me know they were not going to let Me go because they liked having Me there and because they were either going to eat Me or learn to fly, and that they did not have to let Me go because they did not believe Me about what it took to fly. What if I was lying the way other clever faeries had lied to them, even causing them to jump to pieces off of high places such as I had also suggested?

I did not know what other faeries had told them so I was afraid to suggest anything more. They told Me that they were going to stick to their idea that if they continued to eat things that flew, they would one day also be able to fly.

I told them I appreciated it that they liked Me and that I liked them too, but that they should let Me be free just because I wanted to be free, and that I hoped they would do this and not eat someone they liked. They told Me that was all the more reason to eat Me because they liked to take in things they liked. Then I was really out of ideas and growing panicky from the again increasing pressure from the lines.

Worse yet, I did seem to be gaining substance from the giants feeding Me. How fat was going to be fat enough for them to eat, and how long was going to be long enough without them learning to fly to decide I was not going to teach them, I did not know. I did not know either who might pounce on Me first; the hordes of monsters climbing the lines or the giants with their clubs. I certainly didn't want to try the stall tactic of suggesting they eat flying things alive. After the horrible experience I had had with the snake, I could not wish such a fate on anything and certainly not Me if they decided I should be their first experiment with this.

I was sitting in My cage, quite depressed, thinking that any moment might be My last chance to escape the tortures I feared were closing in on Me when the Father of Manifestation boldly strode in with a bunch of birds which He turned loose to fly all around the giants who began chasing them. In this moment of their distraction, He grabbed Me from the cage, hid Me in His hairiness as though He had put Me quickly into a pocket and strode out of there as quickly as He had come.

I was immensely relieved, frightened for the birds, and also terrified of His wrath, which I was sure I deserved. I was also grateful He had chosen to hold onto Me and run since I could not have run with Him, having so many problems with weakness, terror and falling down.

As much as I feared the Father of Manifestation's anger at Me, I also had issues with Him that I was too afraid to bring forward and felt He gave Me no open space in which I could bring them forward.

As He ran away with Me there, I was crying tears of relief and clinging to Him in gratitude for His rescue, but I was also terrified of His blueness here again. I felt terrified of a denied rage I felt He had, but which He denied having, saying I felt Him wrong and that it was only My own rage I felt there. It was the same with My terror and My grief. I felt feelings swirling within Me that I did not dare to present because they felt like rage at Him for reasons He had repelled Me for over and over again in the past, saying either I was not right or had no reason to feel as I did.

I felt His unlovingness toward Me in those places as judgments against My ability to feel anything accurately if it encroached into areas, that for reasons I did not understand, He was heavily guarding by saying I was unloving to even have such feelings toward Him when He was the One rescuing Me and trying to keep Me safe.

I could not understand His reasons for guardedness here, and the feeling that I had to hold back emotions made it impossible for Me to go any further than the movement I was allowed could take Me because My way of understanding is to move emotion first and understand later. Otherwise, nothing seems real to Me, but I felt all around Me a guardedness that didn't want to let emotions move freely unless there was understanding first, which wasn't possible since reason always argued down the validity of these emotions. I didn't have the strength for this or the interest in it either. I just needed to move emotion and felt, for reasons of My own imprinting, that I could not, at least not to the extent I needed to.

Now, as the Father of Manifestation carried Me away from the giant ogres, I had all the issues triggered in Me that I needed to move into imprinting recall and get lost Will out of Hell, but I felt the Father of Manifestation would not receive Me on this. I felt already that His blueness would only let Me move a little bit before He would intervene in some way that I feared would even stop Me if He had to and at least include upbraiding Me for having gotten into the situation in the first place, as though it was only a matter of staying away from it and not a matter of it coming to find Me.

This is a major matter of imprinting that needs to be seen for what it is, because the entire Spirit Polarity has beset the Will with this guilt reflection for a long time, and it is time to end this struggle with Ourselves that it is not alright for Us to feel as We feel without having to fear the Spirit Polarity's reaction to this.

If they think it is just a matter of not being in harm's way, of moving away from, keeping away from, lifting out of, avoiding, being in the magic flow of things or whatever they want to call the way to avoid trouble, then they were moving away from the Will in original imprinting, and there is no way they can argue this without being hypocrites.

We are imprinted that trouble comes and finds Us because the smack did and the psychopathic killers did and have ever since. This has to change, and when it does, it has to be because the Will must move toward a light that loves It and not toward One that makes It feel guilty for having the orientation that It has.

It is no more necessary to feel guilty for having this orientation than the Spirit Polarity has found it to be for the orientation It has. We are turned 180 degrees from One another in terms of orientation in Original Cause. If it is not possible to bring this together now, it is not possible to heal the gap, but the imprinting there has made it feel impossible to ever bring this together without sparking at least, if not open warfare.

There is a change that needs to take place in the Will there to heal the loss of magnetism that took place, and to do this, emotional movement must take place. It is not possible to heal this otherwise, and that's all there is to it. Anyone who is not ready to see this isn't ready to move past the imprinting in the mind or the guilt in the Will that filled in the places where magnetism was lost.

Riding safely, it seemed, away from the ogres on the back of the Father of Manifestation, I had many feelings and issues swirling forward in Me around this blueness I feared that I could not present to Him, and I need to present them now. They were all triggered there, and they were all moving in Me. They all needed to come forward, and they were all prevented from coming forward by His blueness's lack of openness and willingness to receive them. You will have to see where your unwillingness to receive this lies and what your resistance is because that will let you know where unloving light resides in your blueness.

This was a gapped place between Him and Me, and when I could not stand feeling so unreceived, My denied rage has fought with Him there. This is where it has turned around to His Main Body being perpetrated upon by My denied rage instead of His denied rage perpetrating on My Main Body. Alliances were formed there between the denied rage of the Main Body that was perpetrating against the Other and Our own denied rage that was perpetrating against Ourselves, but not always for the same reasons as the denied rage of the Other and, therefore, making them tricky and treacherous alliances which have played themselves out in the power struggles on Earth.

No matter where you look, you are going to find instances of this being played out; the people involved may even say they are only playing roles because they are not real people playing these roles and do not sense themselves to be real either, but Our own denials playing the parts in a play instead. This has happened because of the heartlessness of the gap where Heart has only been allowed to be present in a denied state, and thus, We have not been able to bond there. This denied state of Heart needs to be looked at more closely now too. Presence can play a causal role, but a lack of presence can also play a causal role; the Unseen Role of Denial.

Many times, I have felt deep regret over fighting this way with the Father of Manifestation only to have My rage refueled at Him from what felt like a sameness of attitude in Him toward Me. I did not realize it stemmed from imprinting He received from His experience in Blue when He barely even knew who I was.

He had felt held down and back for a long time, according to Him. He blamed Me for this, but I did not think I had done it. I saw His divided intent about whether or not to manifest, and felt He was not allowing Me to manifest either because of this. He seemed to blame His feelings on Me as though I were the cause of them and that without Me, He was feeling fine; thus, I saw Him as blaming Me for His divided intent to manifest.

This meant to Me that He did not like Me, but it also meant to Me that He did not like having feelings He did not like to feel, and that rather than look to see why He was feeling them, He had chosen to either avoid these feelings or to get rid of these feelings if He did manifest, which meant He was trying to kill Me in those places.

Then, since He was killing Himself without knowing it, He said I was trying to kill Him, but We did not recognize this at the time, and still haven't in certain areas of the gap because He did not know that I was Him, nor I that He was Me. We thought of One another as separate beings who had met by bumping into One another in space where We had previously been floating in isolation. This would have meant that consciousness came from someplace other than from within Myself and feelings, likewise, came from someplace other than from within Him.

Whenever We tried to approach this place to find out if this was really true or not, We always got into arguments about who was there first in which the Father of Manifestation would always insist that He was there first. He never considered the possibility that I was there first, saying only that He remembered being there without Me. I felt He was saying this meant He was there first.

Form is what I contacted first in the Will side of Body, and consciousness later, and Heart, for Me, was blurred in origins because what I felt was comfort, gratitude and pretty quickly, what felt like love for Form and what its contributions were to My existence. I couldn't imagine living without Form, after feeling It's presence come creeping quietly and enfolding Itself around Me, other than as a return to the nightmare I had been in before Form appeared. So, how Form could have thought I didn't love It was beyond Me, and I was terribly hurt by these accusations, and later, angry, when I had the means to know it, which was consciousness. By then, I didn't know who had originated this anger; feelings or consciousness. First, I was very frightened of Blue's rejection of Me as a valid part to have presence with it, and I felt like consciousness was also rejecting Me as a part of its Heart because it could not and did not love Me or find any reason to try since it blamed Me for its feelings of being held down and back, which it saw as the source of its feeling bad. This was not seen as a problem of unlovingness in the consciousness there.

Blue then saw limits and restrictions on its consciousness as the problem, and Me as the cause of those limits and restrictions without examining this further or seeing any reasons why those limits or restrictions might need to be put in place, which weren't really limits or restrictions, but was electrical grounding instead, because it did not see Me as any valid part of it. This meant that Will presence, already judged against as complaining, critical, disapproving and trying to place unfair, unnecessary and invalid limits and restrictions, was being denied out of the presence of Blue.

I, meanwhile, was lying with Form on My side and feeling like Blue did not have anywhere near the peace that I did. Form had its arms around Me, which had made Me feel like it had gathered Me into the enfoldment of its loving arms, thus, saving Me from being lost in the sea of darkness in which I had been drowning in My drifting, amoeba-like attempts to move around in search of something, anything to help Me understand My situation in the dark void. I didn't gain understanding from Form's presence so much as the experience that being enfolded by It felt better to Me than being open to the darkness coming in on Me, like unwanted water coming in on a drowning person. I felt safer this way, much safer, and love was born of this because it felt good, and I quickly began to love feeling good.

THE ORIGINS OF PAN, OR
THE ORIGINAL OFFERING OF THE APPLE

At first, there was no consciousness particularly involved other than that this enfoldment was giving Me a feeling of being protected and gathered together. That feeling felt good to Me, and rather quickly, the feelings I was beginning to feel there began to feel like love to Me. Whether or not other essence was left out, I do not know because We did not yet have eyes to see, light to see in or consciousness by which to determine this, other than a feeling of careful groping for what might be nearby that felt like it wanted or even might like to come into this enfoldment with Us. In the beginning, it felt like there was pretty much of an alignment on how We wanted it to feel there, or else pretty much silence that was not differing openly with Us, but We did not feel resistance to how it felt there or to what felt good to Us. In fact, the gentle murmurings We heard sounded like alignment with Us and with what felt good to Us. These murmurings increased pleasurably to Us when We began gently undulating and rippling in response to the feeling good and the desire to feel, or move, closer into these feelings.

We did not have feelings of differentiation as definition in form then other than as responsiveness to feelings there. Although Form was getting defined a little bit by sound and movement, We did not have thought process about it. Our feelings were of wanting more unification. It may have been only a little piece of the Will there, or only Ourselves there, We did not know, but it was not Our intent to leave out anything that wanted to feel good with Us. Quite the contrary, in fact. We were feeling as intently as Our level of awareness could for anything around Us that wanted to come into this enfoldment and find the escape that We found there from the nightmare of earlier existence in the void.

We became what felt like a warm encampment of vibrating Will essence, enfolded and protected by Form in what felt like the dark and vast surroundings of the void. We welcomed all to Our camp who felt like they entered in friendship and alignment and had found nothing around Us that made Us aware of feeling otherwise. It felt as though Our acuity of feeling was evolving or growing from doing this, and We felt what later might have been called a little pride in Our feeling that We were growing in Our ability to feel things after so long a time of struggling in the dark void.

We were just beginning to glow colors in Our warmth and to

luxuriate and expand a little bit into enjoyment of them, feeling a need to feel this way after so long in Our problems in the void, when We were, at first, disturbed by other sounds We began to hear that had a buzzing, annoying quality to them, and then later, frightened by these sounds as they intensified and began to feel angry, threatening and even dangerous to Us.

This sent up an increase in murmurings among Us as We tried to feel what this was and feel into whether it really might be dangerous to Us, or was in pain or being hurt by something. Unfortunately, We were unable to feel sure from our perspective, but the general feeling I had was that there was a problem of some sort. Today, I would say it was electricity about to explode from lack of grounding, but then, what I was getting back from My exploratory feelings was that the problem was Me, not the sound.

The tone felt repelling to Me, and although I did not understand words, I felt like I had angrily been called an "old biddie," and lots of other mean sounding names. I did not have thought process then by which to think that I might have been able to help the situation by going toward it anyway, nor was I able to go toward something that was making Me feel repelled. I sank back down into Myself, feeling repelled and rejected by something that did not sound or feel good to Me, did not like Me and even felt threatening to Me.

I did not know it, but the psychopathic killer was already loose as snappings and cracklings breaking loose from this sound, I daresay, on the wave of this nasty feeling toward Me, and striking at Us where We had gathered together. We were not getting any other information from this sound, other than what felt like judgments, misinterpretations, bad signs and increasing anger, all of which were new and frightening to Us as well as feeling unfair and wrong to Us in its interpretation and assessment of Us and Our intent. This is why We were hurt in a way that later felt angry, and only a little bit relieved when this sound circled in on itself without making Us feel welcome there.

We had felt the building of warmth there in the Will, and it was a very welcome feeling. We remained huddled together there in the enfoldment, sharing the warmth and enjoying the feeling of safety. We did not know what firelight looked like, but We were moving toward seeing those colors within and around Ourselves and they were becoming more defined. They were beautiful colors and We loved them and the warmth they had. We felt a glow starting to happen in and around Ourselves. It felt like love, but We did not know. We just knew We felt good and were getting better; much better than We had been feeling before Form enfolded Us and made Us feel secure from the moonless black night of the void.

When there began to be terrifying sounds from the darkness of the night, We did not know how to handle it. We were mostly enjoying the motion of pressing Ourselves together for how comfortable and good it felt and for the comfort in doing it, because it let Us know One another was there and responding. It just felt good and spontaneous, arising in Us according to how We felt and subsiding that way also. It felt like a growing attunement amongst Us and one We cherished; the warmth of it especially, along with the feelings of comfort, safety, companionship, feeling of communication, closeness, bonding, trust for One another, interelatedness and dependence, intimacy and even the beginnings of sexual feelings that were arising mildly from the undulating motions and beginning to tingle within Us as the desire for more even though We had no actual words or thought process around any of this then.

We were not sure how to get more happening there. It was already so much more than We had had going for Us in the Will essence before that that We were not even sure We really needed more, although there was some feeling there that We did. I felt We really just needed some time to understand Ourselves more and to feel Ourselves more thoroughly there to see what We might like to do next, but mostly to just savor the warmth and friendliness of it all after so long a time of feeling so miserable and frightened, drowning, overcome and overwhelmed. We were like shipwreck victims coming in from a long ordeal and needing a long rest and recuperation around the fire in Our safely enfolded encampment.

When the Blue sounds began, although We did not know it was Blue yet, We were immediately alarmed that there were others out there having problems, but moving as far out of Our encampment as the sounds seemed to be coming from felt too dangerous, too risky and too uncomfortable to Us. I, for One, did not want to go back out into the perils and risks of the void to see if there was some problem there unless We had first ascertained as much as possible by other means that it was really necessary, but the buzzing sound was giving Me an uneasy feeling about being able to do this and the feeling that I must resolve the problem this sound was creating in Me before I could go on as I wanted to.

I could not see externally yet, or did not know that I could. With nothing to see, or nothing ever seen yet outside of Ourselves, how could One know such a thing?

I had a way of looking internally, though, that had become so good without My even realizing it that it seemed even preferable to Me to the idea of opening up what would now be called eyes to see what might be happening around Me. I was afraid of what I might see also, and did not want to look. The sounds were scaring Me so much I wanted to huddle and not look and have someone else deal with them. I was hoping they would go away or gentle down and find some sort of softer sounds that would be more harmonious with what We already had.

I felt as reluctant, frightened and dismayed about being disturbed, unless I really had to be, by what was happening with these sounds from Blue as a person could who is warmly and comfortably eskonced in a soft, pleasant smelling bed of furs by the fire, snuggled in an outdoor encampment with those who felt entirely compatible, like loved family members, comfortable in body and in feelings, and so much so that the mild sexual excitation taking place might lead to something if given time to develop in the right way, which was a soft, loving, gentle way, and if not, sleep would come, softly and gently, comfortably and gradually, into the pleasant drifting between mildly sexual undulations, warmth, comfort and drowsiness by the fire.

Not all felt the same as Me though. I felt a growing distraction and restlessness in Form near Me that felt like a stronger pull or attraction for these sounds than I had. I conveyed to the Form near Me, since I felt It had eyes for some reason, that I would like It to look and see what It could see, if anything at all, and report to the rest of Us. For some reason, even lifting My head felt like too much for Me. I might have been too comfortable, or too frightened or maybe I didn't know how. I didn't know then.

Form lifted His head and reported that He saw something that looked more defined to Him than We were. As He conveyed what He saw there in the terms We had then, which was conveyance of pictures along with the feelings that went with them in a way that was rather direct and quick compared to the cumbersome passages it is taking for Me to try to convey this in words and still not be able to convey the full spectrum of what was felt without a feeling of burdensome complexity, I felt He was more excited by and drawn toward what He had seen than I was.

As He was conveying what He saw, I was internally seeing something as vividly as if I had seen it externally. He was conveying to Us the impression of Light there with a rather well defined

Form, but He did not make it clear that He had seen faces, both male and female, and that He wanted to join them. He did not make that clear until later, so much later that it is only now, in healing this gap, that He has finally made this clear to Me. I saw a bright, white, with some bright, light blue, electrical, lightning-like, arcing light. I then seemed to realize that I internally saw this light as arcing up out of something, but lacked the concepts to consider that it could have been arcing up out of Us. I saw this arcing light as threatening, as if it was a snake about to strike, and I associated this form with the sound I had asked Him to check on. I felt frightened that He was excited by something that I saw as threatening.

It did not occur to Me, or the responsiveness around Me, that what We were seeing internally might not be the entire picture, or that We might be seeing only what He had conveyed, but because We had different feelings about it than He did, We began to have something of a discussion about it in Our own empathic way. It then seemed more likely that We might not have seen what He was conveying since this form seemed more penis-like, or at least sexually exciting, to Him and more snake-like and threatening to Me.

I did not know that Form was a He there yet either, but in asking Him to look, I noticed that I had formed a dependence upon Him that I later associated with male. He also moved in a way that felt more male to Me there, as male has later become defined, but He may not be sure if He really is male or had the space to decide for Himself, since He was depended upon in these ways before He ever let Us know if He felt Himself to be male. We just felt Him and treated Him according to how We felt about Him, as it seemed He also did with Us, although We had no really conscious ideas of sexual definition or roles then. He seemed like My patriarch, protector and defender, and He was next to Me so I naturally consulted and conferred with Him.

I felt more frightened of these sounds than He did and also found them to be more unpleasant and disturbing than He did. We agreed on these points; that something might be really wrong there, although I felt stronger on this point than He did, that We weren't sure if We could get anything more going for Ourselves than We had already and that We might need something more, especially sexually, and that this might be it, although He felt stronger on this point than I did, that something more needed to be found out about this and that it could not be ignored anymore since it was becoming increasingly intrusive into Our pleasant space with its, at first, buzzing, but now, growling and snapping noises, and that since He seemed more attracted to it than the rest of Us were, He seemed to be the One who wanted to, and therefore, should, go and investigate further. I had the impression that if He went, He might come right back to Us to give Us further impressions and information, but that was not how it turned out.

Once He left, We felt like We had lost the Father of Our encampment. I started feeling worse from there, and I felt the guilt already that I had wrongly encouraged Him to go or should not have let Him go.

First, there were the cracks and murmurings of terror about what this all meant and the possible reasons He had gone, including, now, that We were not as appealing and interesting as We had thought, that He had found whatever this was and preferred it, that He was not going to come back or that He could not come back because something terrible had happened, as indeed We feared from the increased terribleness of sounds coming now from that place He had headed for. There was also the feeling of a smoldering split amongst Us that, if there had been words to say it, I feared would have blamed Me for encouraging Him or letting Him go and blamed Him for not appreciating what He already had. There were many pictures empathically passing through Us, most predominantly, the picture that something terrible might be happening there and might be about to happen to Us, and that sending out others to find out what was going on might be a feeding of Ourselves to it One by One.

We weren't sure if this was really true or not, though, because many of the sounds now had a sound or feeling of sexual frenzy to them that We weren't sure We liked any better. Perhaps Our enfolding part had another partner and could get much more happening there and didn't want to come back. Whatever it was, I, and those around Me, still felt fear, but now it was for so many reasons I do not want to list them all. We had a growing feeling of dread and terror, even, that something We weren't going to like at all was about to happen. It seemed to be hanging in the void around Us, like a thick night of stark terror.

We did not even know if Our firelight-like glow was protection for Us or a beacon calling to these frightening sounds and showing them where We were, but We wanted to keep Our glow going, not only for Our own warmth and comfort, but for Our Father to find His way and return to Us if He would or could.

Caution felt that for safety's sake, We had better reduce Our glow. The fire had fallen back to embers anyway when My patriarch left, as though the heart were taken from it by His parting and We left it there, having no feeling anymore of wanting to cultivate it to rise higher. We huddled around it, more and more fearing together there that We were a family who had been left with only a Mother because the Father had either gone off and been killed or had left Us for another family, and it might be a family of wild beasts.

We were left on Our own. We huddled even more together in Our dread, all listening and feeling together to see if We could find out anything by which to know more about what was really going on there.

It wasn't long before We felt We were falling away from all that We had felt We had going there. Our fire was only coals, and Our apprehension, dread and terror had grown into a thick compression all around Us. Then, as the coals were dying into ashes, the darkness turned ashen also and everything around Us with it. I hoped morning might at last be coming and the return of Our Father with it, but its grayness felt bleak and I felt a great feeling of dread which became a sudden urgency that We must go out and look for Our Father.

We could barely move and started out with a tattered alignment, seething with splits, but I felt I must find out something even though My feelings already told Me this was going to have the wrong outcome for My heart. Before We had gone very far, We were struck by a great smack of light.

During all of this, I had been in another place too, simultaneously. In My reveric moments in a dream state, I had experienced Myself looking up through the warmly glowing colors around Me. It seemed as though I was looking up through a lucidity in Red, Orange and Yellow into a beautiful and wonderfully illuminated Green where I saw a little elfin woman-girl whose form seemed quite well defined while Mine seemed still unknown to Me.

I saw her within a halo of soft, golden light which felt to Me like My presence there. This soft, golden halo, at times, became a wreath of golden leaves and other forest shapes, and at times seemed to become an actual golden ring, as though of golden metal, beautifully formed by tiny elfin creatures dancing around amongst a circle of trees making the ring shape of it. When I saw the ring, I saw only green and a beautiful, sky blue floating behind it in changing patterns that were also fascinating to Me like watching clouds and leaves, and when I saw the elf, the golden ring became the halo again, with the wreath the intermediate step.

Her appearance was fascinating to Me, and her dark, almond shaped eyes were deep looking and open, while Mine seemed still shut. I saw Her hiding beneath the leaves of tree branches, already large and fully grown, old in feeling even, yet very new and young too, just like the elfin woman, herself. This green seemed like Her home. I liked it there, but it seemed just a bit cool to Me and I preferred seeing it this way, from within the soft enfoldment of warm furs by the glowing fire of Orange and Red where I lay dreaming of looking up through the glow of Red, Orange and Yellow overhead. She was fascinating to Me, though, and I kept returning to her over and over, seeing her image always there and always doing the same thing.

I wondered why the elf was always looking up, but then I found the blue to be beautiful and fascinating too, at times so full of such beautifully delicious hues that I wanted to draw it to Me as a means to taste it, touch it and feel it more. Then I noticed that there was a face from time to time who seemed to be looking back from the Blue.

This face was a he to Me. I could not tell if he saw Us or not, or what he saw, but when he looked down upon Us, I saw a soft, shimmering, white Light sprinkling down through Green and showering a bit into Yellow. I liked this Light and wanted It to come to Me. I was fascinated and wondered if this was part of what was fascinating the elf and drawing her to look up so much, or if this Light was, for some reason, making her hide. I felt that she wanted to have a relationship with this blue face, but was shy and did not know how to go about it. I tried to encourage her to reach out, but she did not seem to like the idea of directly reaching with her hands. Then I felt unsure if it was Me who wanted the relationship and not her.

I was seeing this from My own perspective. I was not sure how accurately I felt her or felt Myself in her, or how inside of her I was, or how much she felt Me, so I am not sure if she thought the face was looking past her and seeing Me, or if she thought he might not be as interested in her as in Me, or if he even saw Us or was aware of her, or if she was even aware of Me except as a presence of glowing, embracing, supporting warmth coming up into her from underneath her. Perhaps she did not know if he even saw anything of what was happening from Our side of this experience as We felt it to be taking place, similar to a face looking into still pond water which rippled gently at times, but showed him only his own reflection, or the reflection of the light behind him coming back off the water, or if he saw into Us and into the life calling for him there.

We did not know these things then, and We did not find a means to ask. We were consumed by the imagery, which was all new to Us, or to Me, anyway, and everytime questions and uncertainties began to accumulate, the images and then the brightness and reality of the colors began to fade until I began to feel I should perhaps not allow Myself to have any such questions, confusions or doubts if it was causing Me to lose the beauty of the experience. Maybe We should go ahead and have the experience and find Our answers that way. We did not know.

I immediately loved this Light sprinkling gently down through Green and into Yellow. I wanted It to reach Me, but I did not immediately know if he was sending this down to Us, to her, to the forest, to everything there or to anything in particular, or if this Light just sprinkled down from him wherever he looked, since We did not know what he could see of Us, if anything at all.

There was nothing coming back from Blue to let Us know anything here, except that this silent but friendly seeming face and the sprinklings of Light went away from time to time as though he was not noticing Us, or wasn't very interested in Us, or was being distracted by something, perhaps something he liked better.

The elf was staying so hidden and cautious, fearful of both extending herself and of being rejected, I felt. I kept trying to encourage her to extend her hand, or to make an overture of some kind to engage this face looking down at Us from the Blue so that We could find out something, but she kept holding back and staying mostly hidden, and the face kept coming and going, peering down into Us at times, and seeming to be also either distracted or drawn to something else that was happening behind his back. He kept looking and glancing backwards at whatever this was until I began to feel uneasy, and insecure and somewhat impatient with the elf.

Then I heard the buzzing sound. I did not like this sound and wondered what was really happening there, but I also had a strong feeling of trying to urge the elf to make a move of some sort to find out what was really happening there because I was frightened that We might lose the face's attention altogether if We did not make Ourselves known, and that he might not come looking down upon Us anymore, showering this Light. I felt a growing agitation in him, and saw a growing distraction in his looks from something that was happening behind him that seemed to be the place the buzzing sound was coming from.

I did not want to lose this Light or this imagery, and felt urgency growing in Me and a feeling that if she did not want to step forward, I wanted to somehow.

This took form as a motion reaching down into Orange and Red then, and a plucking of some of it so quickly and suddenly that I did not know what had happened, or even if it was her who had done it, until I noticed her putting it into the trees near their tops where these colors seemed to magically appear as flowers. I was so surprised and stunned and then delighted with the imagery of what I thought was her offering to the face that I did not feel into it then to see if it felt like She had done this angrily as if to say, "If you so much want to go forward, then here, you do it," or if it was a love offering she felt to make, or was urged by Me to make, or had agreed to, which had inspired the flower forms, or how long she might have contemplated within herself to give birth to these new forms.

The face looking at Us from Blue saw these flowers, but We were not sure if he saw them as an offering, what the meaning of this offering was seen to be by him, or who he saw the offering to be from. Still, in spite of My urgings for the elfin woman to reveal herself, she stayed hidden under the trees and did not step forward and reveal herself. We waited to see what the face was going to do. I held My breath, so to speak, and presumed she did too, not daring to feel how it would feel if he rejected Our advances.

This dream was very vivid and real to Me, as if it were a reality progressing, be it ever so slowly, but it was still rather subconscious. When something drew Me more into the enfoldment where I was resting and aware, though still subconsciously, of Myself as more present physically and did not see any real presence of this other reality happening there yet, I tried to return to the dream and look for the elf and the face in blue over and over again while feeling Myself present in the enfoldment and undulating warmth at the same time.

As the dream progressed, I noticed more and more that whatever was distracting the face in Blue was a sound I found to be the same as the unpleasant buzzing sound coming in on Me in My enfoldment within the encampment, and was distracting his attention as it was Mine, but seemed more attractive to him than it was to Me and more annoying to Me than it seemed to be to him. I wondered and feared what his attraction to this might be, and how We could be so attracted to him if he was so attracted away from Us to something that seemed so unpleasant to Me.

I feared what this meant, but did not know how to, nor dare to, ask. I wondered if he might make it clear, or if it might make itself clear in time, and so We waited and looked and hoped for something to unfold that would bring Us to someplace other than where We seemed to be stuck. I began to fear that this energy behind the face was more of the reason the elf had been holding back, and that I had not been paying enough attention to these sounds, or had the impression they were penetrating from the other place into this dream. I did not know then where these sounds were really coming from. They were very disorienting, but I wanted to press ahead anyway out of the urgency I felt in response to the buzz, or because I didn't want the buzz to have the power to disrupt the pleasantness I was finally finding, or because of a growing agitation that it would not respond to Us or come within the folds of pleasantness I had found. I was confused and frightened and feared I should not have urged the elf who was closer to and who might have known or seen more than I did about those buzzing, snapping noises.

I felt a growing tension and impatience all around and heard something behind the blue face angrily scream, "Alright already! Let's get on with it! Where's it going to go from here? What's going to happen next?"

I was much too frightened of this anger to know how to move, and felt Myself, then, very unpleasantly and unfairly pressured by this, and felt it was all too ready to override Me and not allow Me to unfold at My own speed and in My own way.

I began to notice this buzzing sound more and more, or else it was increasing, or both. I did not like it, and I did not like it that I could not escape it. I did not know what reality was what there either. The buzzing was intruding into Our encampment and into this other experience and disturbing the peace in both places. The feeling of anxiety, fear, uncertainty and not knowing how to move was there, as well as a number of other aspects.

When Our Father left Us, I realized I had not shared the dream with Him to know if He had also been having the same dream and had gone to find out the truth of it. I did not know if it was information gathering, if He had lost interest in Us and had abandoned Us, or whether He had gone for other reasons having to do with whatever was going on behind the face in Blue or the buzzing sound or simply in response to His images of light, phallus-like to Him, snake-like lightning about to strike Me. I did not know if He was moving as Our protector, or if We had lost Our protector.

Whatever it was, the last time I had the dream was almost simultaneous with, or interspersed with, glimmerings of awareness of My feeling of a, by now , starving and freezing, falling into darkness, encampment, with My children huddled around Me as though We were all dying there together, or were about to; or perhaps it was only Me who was so cold and dying there. I did not know.

I felt like an ineffective mother who had become so heartsick and paralyzed at the loss of her partner that she had not done anything to try to keep herself or her children alive, and had, instead, retreated into a dream world of some fantasy courtship with him, before there even were children and had, thus, lost all sense of time or orientation in reality or realities, not knowing here from there, dream from reality, waking from sleeping, past from present or future, or if I ever did know or have such distinctions, or if they were real distinctions anyway.

As the elf plucked the flowers, I experienced Our embers die back to coals. As the flowers were offered, Heart held back in fear, but also leaped a little and tried to go toward the face in blue. As the flowers were plucked from the trees, We held Our breath, not knowing whether to stand still, go ahead, turn back or hide. As the face in Blue turned and offered the flowers to the buzzing sound in Blue, I was hopeful, horrified and frightened all at once. I could not see it all, but I felt that the flowers were snatched, drained, decimated and discarded, disregarded and trampled in the whirling vortex of frenzy in Blue. My high hopes for relationship with this gentle loving Light plummeted, Heart broke, the fire died back further. I felt We must turn and go back down, although I still hoped and some parts wanted to go ahead no matter what. I tried to go forward, perhaps to find out what happened to the flowers, to ask for them back or to rescue them. I don't know what.

There was enraged shouting of, "Not enough, not enough!"

I shrank back, frozen in terror and grief and uncertainty that wanted to believe I had just misinterpreted things and that there would be a more favorable reversal at any moment. When I decided I must turn away from the dream and go back to My encampment and cope alone, it was too late. The sky had turned white, the sounds had reached the proportions of an ugly giant about to explode, which it did and the smack came down, blinding Me and striking, if My feeling serves Me right, into the middle of

Our almost barren fire.

I was terribly damaged and lost consciousness of both My loved realities. Another reality was superimposed on Me. I did not feel I liked it or know why it had to happen. I felt pain and heartbreak and all else that sprang from the smack.

And what had happened to the elfin woman, I did not know for a long time. I had so much damage and burden of guilt for not having done the right thing in so many different ways and forms that I went falling and plunging down for a long time. I have always wondered if We fell away because Our Father was not there to hold Us, or if there was any way at all to have had a better outcome, or if what happened had to happen and was the only thing that could have happened. The heartbreak, damage and pain of it has always made Me wish and wonder if some other way could have been found, and My guilt has punished Me for feeling I did not know the right thing to do there.

I could not feel like leaving the others in Our encampment was a good idea, like leaving children prey to wild beasts while I went in search of their Father, probably becoming prey Myself, I felt, but when I found out later that God was having the same dream, I thought My heart would surely break over what had been killed there.

And even much later, when these ancient images began to manifest in Pangea, and I thought My dreams, visions and fantasies had perhaps come back again and would live and become real to Me, it was all so full of the cruel warp and damage from the smack that it stirred in Me nightmares of other anguished images I also had, such as battered and mutilated children, lost and also returned to Me by the murderers, rapists and other sadists, either dead on My doorstep, or unable to live their lives as they would have otherwise.

Too many parts of this imagery were full of hatred and unmoved emotions, and especially of hateful blame that seemed to hate Me for ever having had these images, as though I was demanding that they be cute for Me when they had never wanted to be, that I felt terrified and alone and wrong, but also, hated them all for such ugly twistings of My cherished visions that it seemed they hated Me and My visions and My attachment to them.

Blue, by its own accounting, had revved up into an electrical charge of sexual frenzy and mental excitation, full of the feelings of having burst out of something that had been repressing it for a long time. It was not about to let anything put it back into that place or put any limits at all on it anymore, and it had grown quickly enraged and accusationally judgmental that there was even any discussion in the Will, which it claims to have seen and heard clearly, about whether it should be allowed to do this or not, which was not My take on Our discussion in the Will.

Blue began circling in on itself then in a way that felt to Us like turning its back on Us in judgment, and even worse, what felt like a hatred, a blame and a rejection of Us based on what We felt was an unfair interpretation of Us. After that, it seemed like there was no reaching Blue. Our fate had already been sealed. Blue was already planning to kill Us. We could just feel it in the Will. Still, We hoped for the best and for another outcome, somehow.

I especially hated Blue so much I thought I never would be able to forgive it until maybe now I can, because now it looks like Blue is finally going to move to take responsibility for this. In so doing, Blue has started to restore Green to Me, and in so doing, the elfin-woman has begun to be restored and is turning out to be a part of the Mother presence in Green, be it ever so much damaged and frozen in uncertainty, terror and heartbreak with so much healing needing to be done.

In Pangea, as the Father of Manifestation strode through the forest and away from the giants, with Me hidden upon Him, these old imprints were triggered in Me as all of My issues about Him leaving Me to suffer this fate, not really being interested in Me and not really loving Me. I wondered how much He participated in causing this fate, whether He wanted Me to live or not, and how much He came after Me out of guilt and how much out of love.

I feared His blueness here, and from the deep pool of My lost, primordial images, ancient memories and subconscious terrain could only surface the fear of the elfin girl-woman to reach toward Blue, feeling no real acceptance there from Him, as though He knew where letting it get started would lead before I did.

What I was most triggered by there in His blueness was the sound of His voice. I felt, more than I remembered, that it was the sound of the voice that originally spoke in Blue's rage. I feared He was denying rage there, and so much feared this rage that I pulled away from this, did not allow the issues I had with Him there to come up, felt only My fear of His rage and focused on My gratitude for being rescued.

I was subconsciously imprinted by the sound of Blue's rage there that He was the Father of this rage and that in Blue, this rage had used the Red and Orange of those flowers to rev up into the sexual frenzy and electrical excitement that had exploded and smacked.

THE MOTHER'S COURT
OR THE
POWER STRUGGLE IN BLUE

Looking back now from the position of recalling imprinting, it all looked so similar to Me in Pangea, including the feeling of dread about what was going to happen next. The forms I had seen so long ago in My original images of Pan were there, but they were all twisted and damaged by the smack, and the imprinting was there, including the encircling encampment by firelight according to color, but I didn't know what to call it then, or how to surface it in My consciousness in such a way as to have it accepted then.

It seemed there was no intent to accept it or to encourage Me to give it as it came, which was to give what was on the top of the heap and go down from there. Down didn't look like up to anybody there including Me, yet I was down, and so I wandered alone in the woods, unaccepted, unwanted, unhelped, unencouraged and uncomforted; a bother to everyone, even Myself, as great as My self-hatred was for feeling the way I felt in an energy field of non-acceptance for it.

Fragmentation was immense then too, and so much of it turning against what it had fragmented out of, hating being denied, and either leaving or feeling it had gotten the boot. Many of these pieces were often outside the rings of any fires.

Many of these forms were causing trouble, often more unseen than not, even farther back in the woods, much of which didn't surface until the last minute in Pan when Lucifer came and took over their forms by moving consciousness out of the power positions and activating imprinting. Many of these denials thought they were going to get the help and power they wanted to have against the parts they blamed and hated, and many of them did, but not in the ways they thought or hoped for, since Lucifer quickly overpowered and enslaved them also.

Meanwhile, at the court of the Dragon Mother, the shifting sands of tricky and treacherous alliances were progressing in their power plays. The Dragon Mother, or Faerie Queen, as she still maintained she was, was still sitting demurely on her throne, or so she thought, and was presenting the image of beauty waiting for her prince, patiently occupying herself with all of the affairs of court, but in truth, growing very impatient waiting for God to come to His senses and come down to her and being constantly distracted by feelings of rage that she felt she dared not move in court.

She was consumed with feelings of abandonment and rage, but she preferred to present the image that she did not care whether or not I came to her. It was a matter of pride, and that same pride kept her from showing herself as the Dragon Mother in public. She felt shame about it. Not only did she not want to let herself be seen going through the form change in public and have others learn from it, or hear how she screamed at My light and I did not come, she also did not want to lose the image of the Fire Dragon as her great rescuer, power back-up and protectorate. If it was to be seen as only her, not only would she feel she had lost the appearance of an intimidating ally, as well as ashamed and embarrassed about her deception, but also frightened that if the satyrs saw the connection between her rage and her form change, they could nab her as the Faerie Queen and prevent her, somehow, from being able to become the Fire Dragon and rescue herself.

The more the Ronalokas in the court praised and venerated the Fire Dragon for her bravery, strength and power, and as the Mother image they wanted to have, however, the more she could not stand the idea of the Fire Dragon being thought of as someone else, and that that "someone else" then was getting the praise and admiration she so much wanted to have directly for herself.

The Ronalokas who were praising the Fire Dragon and venerating her form as the Mother they would like to have, however, were venerating only her form; they were not venerating her power as any they would like her to have. Like the satyrs, they did not want her to have power unless they controlled it and, thus, it was really their power. In their fantasies, they controlled the Fire Dragon Mother, and this made them the most powerful beings on Earth since they controlled the image they were venerating as the most powerful being on Earth.

These Ronalokas moved as if they were rage polarized, but they had a denied heart presence that was not being recognized here as wanting to take over the Parents' place and become the Parents themselves. All of these pieces wanted to be the Parental piece without seeing that all of the other pieces also wanted the same position because they all saw themselves as the most powerful, the most qualified and the most in the know and saw all of the others as weak and flawed in some way they could not stand.

In their veneration of the Fire Dragon, her lack of mothering did not bother them because they did not want to be mothered. They wanted mothering only on their own terms from an image of the Mother that they controlled. In this fantasy, their image was more of "Mother as maid" who waited on them hand and foot and praised them as they were now praising the mother on Earth. In their fantasies, they had the Fire Dragon scorch anyone with her fiery breath who dared darken their doorway without their permission and invitation, and often amused themselves then with images that would show they controlled her and held power over her and that she served them, such as having her use her fiery breath to warm their baths, heat their chambers to the appropriate temperature, light a fire on their hearth, toast their food, and other things that they felt would make them more comfortable while being praised by her for their great powers, wisdom and conquests, but they also had images of the Mother serving them in much more sinister, dark and heavy ways.

All the praises they were giving to the Fire Dragon, in other words, were praises they wanted to have given to themselves, with no parental input that might even suggest correction or criticism of any sort, let alone advice, since they did not need any. As far as they were concerned, there was no reason to parent them since they had the ability to parent themselves. Therefore, the Fire Dragon's reptilian concept of mothering, with a few subduing alterations in her behavior, did not bother them. In fact, they liked it because it gave their competition issues the space to do whatever they wanted to do to their other siblings who might be weaker and who might not like the kind of power they wanted to have.

In this way, they intimidated the rest of the Ronalokas into behaving as though there were no power struggles or problems of alignment within the group because they were in charge and every overture toward the Ronalokas was met by one of the denied heart Ronalokas who controlled the rest of the group in their area.

This must have felt like protection to the other Ronalokas at first when they said things such as, "I can keep the satyrs away from you if, in exchange, you let me be in control here," but it quickly turned into dominance and repression of any other feelings they might have had about how things should go that even used these feelings against the other Ronalokas if there was any slip up in denied heart's protection of them from the satyrs by saying that it was the fault of the ones who had suffered from lack of protection, not the fault of the protectors, and that they had deserved it for their lack of alignment with them and as punishment and was an example of what happens when there is a lack of alignment with them.

The Mother did not know that this was what She met when She went to the Ronalokas and that there were some there who liked Her more than She thought. For the sake of the presentation of alignment, no one was allowed to speak except the rage polarized, denied heart Ronalokas who controlled the area.

The same went in the court of the mother on Earth. It was not possible to speak of another point of view from the Ronalokas except for the one presented by the rage polarized ones who were there. They had become very good at posturing like the satyrs too and looked intimidating in many of the same ways.

The satyrs, however, did not see this posturing as powerful, threatening or even as particularly intimidating. They saw these Ronalokas as fauning over the form of the Fire Dragon and over the mother on Earth too, for that matter, and there in Pan, these Ronalokas literally took on the form of fauns in the presence of these satyrs whose understudies they were. Rather than confronting these Ronalokas openly about anything they observed there, the satyrs decided they might like to use them in their plot against the mother on Earth and show them in this way that they could eat these Ronalokas alive if they chose to.

It was well nigh impossible to get another point of view from the little faeries either, other than what the mother on Earth told them they should say. They hesitated to say anything critical of the mother on Earth, but they did not like her, and were not loyal to her anymore either. They acted this out by moving along with others in plots to get revenge on her in whatever ways felt good to them in the moment in time in which they were happening. In that way, they often gave information to several different points of view, or sides, as they were becoming now, according to whoever was intimidating them or pleasing them most, or how recently the mother on Earth had gotten angry at them and for what reasons.

These denied heart, rage polarized Ronalokas often mated with these little faeries, and all involved had their reasons, but sometimes there was some love there that would plead one another's cases with the satyrs to no avail, often only making matters worse.

The offspring of these unions really hated parents because they sprang forth from the union of that bond, and they regularly enraged the mother on Earth in her court until she wanted to singe them out of existence right then and there, which the satyrs also found useful, perceiving her rage as not well founded in anything and therefore, increasing the numbers of those against her. The satyrs also had denied rage fragments who hated the Mother, wanted revenge and then knew who their allies were going to be there.

The mother on Earth did not see the seriousness of these cracks in her alliances yet, nor did she notice others sneaking around behind her back and plotting her downfall from another direction. Her own rage fragments, and there were quite a few of them, had grown tired of her moves and power plays against them when they did not happen to agree with her. They had gotten to the place in their power struggle with her where they wanted to take over as the Parental part and not have her bossing them around anymore, and they had begun slipping away from her already in the fire seas when she had sent them out as parts of her awareness to guard the entrance ways or to check on noises she sometimes heard there, but was too busy with her internal musings, divinings and emotions to go and check for herself.

They had begun to move against the mother on Earth secretly in the fire seas by practicing the art and mannerisms of taking on her Fire Dragon form. They all saw themselves as having as much power as the mother on Earth, but they did not know all of the power she had. They all had enough power to take on the form, and the same rage she had by which to drive it, or so they thought. What they did not know was that they needed the group to have this power, the same as other fragmentation did.

They did not originate this form on their own, but they all thought it belonged to them because they had participated, along with the mother on Earth, in inventing it, and they all claimed it was really theirs more than anyone else's because each of them thought they should be the Parental piece of the Mother and not anyone else. They all saw themselves as being the most qualified and as having more of the right viewpoint than anyone else. They did not hesitate to see the faults of the others while seeing only the merits of themselves or the weaknesses of others while seeing only the strengths in themselves, and thus, saw themselves as the most powerful and best qualified for the Parental position. They each planned to make a power play for the position as soon as possible, and along with practicing taking on the Fire Dragon form, they had been biding their time, waiting for the right moment.

The more the Ronalokas and others in the court admired the Fire Dragon and told tales, even exaggerated ones, of her exploits, the more jealous and competitive they all felt and the more they all wanted to come forth in this form and claim this praise, power and glory for themselves, and the more the Faerie Queen also wanted to reveal herself there as the one and only true Fire Dragon.

The satyrs did not like this venerating of the mother on Earth's form as the Fire Dragon and played with her for that. They were jealous and competitive with her. They were subconsciously imprinted against her rage and subconsciously intimidated and afraid of the power of her rage and of her belief that her rage was her power, but they openly displayed the opposite, often baiting her as much as they possibly could to expose her rage in the court, even showing mock admiration for the Fire Dragon, professing with satirical mannerisms to be her allies, while laughing to the side and making fun of her also in the Faerie Queen form in ways that showed everyone there they saw her as silly and weak in her filmy fru-fra dresses and gossamer wings.

The Faerie Queen tried not to show it, but she did feel enraged by their behavior, and she did slip up and reveal things, even more than she knew, about herself and her doings as the Fire Dragon. She tried to cover herself quickly and hoped no one noticed, but the satyrs had all noticed because they were watching her very closely as part of the development of their plan, and were watching others as well to see who else was reacting, and in what ways, to what they were doing there. In fact, the satyrs made the hiding of feelings, while pressuring others as much as possible to reveal theirs, a great game of theirs in the court, which everyone else in the court also took up, much to their delight for the information they could gather this way, because each one saw things revealed this way that seemed to be playing into the hands of their own power plays.

Everyone there in the court of the Faerie Queen, mother on Earth, Fire Dragon Mother Protectorate was a fragmented piece of the Mother, the Father of Manifestation, My light, or Heart and there were no dependable bonds or alliances among them other than to seek to use one another's help to gain power and then overpower their helpers once the power was gained. They all thought there was no problem in doing that because it was all justified by the weaknesses and flaws they saw in others, and without Heart presence there, it was hardly possible to do otherwise, since without the presence of love, it was hardly possible to know who was, or was not, likely or not likely to do what, or for what reasons.

"What if another would come to power?" they would say to themselves, "What would happen then?"

"Why it would be simply terrible," they would answer themselves.

It was not possible to get them to listen to anything from My light because they were not listening to that for their ideas or motives. The idea that there might be another or a more loving point of view other than the one they had taken was too threatening to their own ambitions, aims and goals to listen to for a moment, and so everything they did had the purpose of weakening and fooling others and gaining power for themselves. Gaining power was the most important thing for them, even if it was at their own expense, such as losing something else that was important to them.

Meanwhile, the mother on Earth sat upon the throne and felt bored and isolated from the rest of Pan more and more. She felt her position made others act phony around her, and she did not know how to ferret out all of their hidden motives, goals and aims without having it feel too burdensome.

It was already a tiresome task just keeping track of all the invaders of Earth, as she called them, and newcomers showing up in her court. It seemed there were daily arrivals now all claiming to have just landed on Earth and coming to pay homage to her and her position there and to join the court if she so pleased. She didn't trust them any more than she trusted the ones already there, but part of her loved the flattery and the rulership of it all, and tried to understand what was happening in the Heavens from their stories, which was to her by far the most interesting part about them because of all the information she gleaned; but by no means was she interested in stories about My light's participation sexually or any other way with the Angels as partners. When Angels began to show up on Earth, they were the immediate objects of her envy, hatred and bitterness. Although she did allow them to stay in her court where she listened and watched them closely, not only for what information she could gather, but because she was nervous about what they might say that would embarrass her concerning her relationship to My light, she exerted a force against them that said they had better not have designs on her throne, or even approach it looking as attractive or powerful as she did there.

As much as the Faerie Queen did not want to miss anything that might be said that she wanted to hear, she was also growing quite tired of sitting there upon her throne watching it all going on day after day and night after night. She hardly went into the forest anymore because of the vines and other problems there. There was not much else she liked to do in Pan anymore either, and she thought her court had grown quite decadent and boring, which she attributed to its being so much under the control of the satyrs, and, yes, insipid, too, from her point of view.

When she mused along in her own thoughts about this, she pretty soon grew enraged at the satyrs for a long list of reasons. She saw them as insipid and foppish contenders for the position of King at her side, where she kept an empty throne that she did not let them sit in for more than a minute. In fact, the moment they said anything while sitting there that she determined to be stupid, she often even knocked them from the seat with her scepter as though they were ejectees from a marriage suddenly gone sour, and enjoyed watching them lose their composure in public where they couldn't do anything about it because she had more supporters in the court than they did, or so she thought.

The satyrs made fun of her for doing this saying she had gone quite daft and didn't know good sense when she heard it. There were many who sought a moment's private audience with her and who dared to sit on the throne, but whenever she had not liked what any of them had to say, and not one of them had lasted more than a few minutes, she bonked them from the throne with her scepter also.

She was very quick to judge, My light noticed, while saying I was very quick to judge her. Even if she did not say anything overtly, she knew within a moment within herself that she was not going to like what was coming next and unseated them from the throne before they got a chance to say it. Any who did not like the results of this were made fun of in the court for a long time because it was not possible to disagree with the Faerie Queen in her court and gain any kind of favor with her at all.

Uproarious laughter, animated and clever talk as well as fabulously inventive and imaginative costuming was what the Faerie Queen wanted in her court and wanted her court to be known for, unlike some boring places, such as the Godhead, she implied, and whenever she did, everyone had to agree with her, over and over, as many times as she required it, that the Godhead she had created right there on Earth was ever so much more lively, interesting, colorful and entertaining than My boring, old, white on white on white Godhead ever was.

To keep up with the pace and expectations of the court was a major task for many of the spirits there, but no one wanted to admit that it was any problem at all. Most of them wanted to say that it was no problem at all, that they were moving at their natural speed and that it all simply came naturally as a result of their innate cleverness, which was the most usual response if anyone ever complimented anyone on anything they had done, which never happened without unpleasant undercurrents, given how rampant competition was there.

The feeling was that frequent form changes were necessary, not only because the mother was looking more and more frequently bored, but to show off that they had these powers and to avoid their own boredom too. No one was sure what she liked though, or what they dared present her with since she took swipes at them with her scepter frequently, and with little lashes of her fiery breath and sometimes even with the end of her dragon tail, neither of which she appeared to notice doing.

So quickly did her tail lash out at someone and then disappear again that a momentary lapse of attention could miss the entire event, and since the Faerie Queen did not appear to notice this and did not acknowledge this publicly, everyone else pretended not to notice this either, and since there was fairly open buzz about this in the court, as those who saw it told those who had missed it, and she did not appear to hear it, they all began to play with her about this, pretending that it was not general court knowledge that the Faerie Queen was also the Fire Dragon, and seeing how outrageous they could get and how far they could go with this before she would openly reveal herself there, maybe without realizing it.

This made her rage fragments even angrier, as well as embarrassed and ashamed to be seen as a part of her when so much fun was being made of her in the court and she was more and more being viewed as someone who was not really powerful enough to control things there and even losing her presence and not seeming to have her wits about her. The more this went on and they could not dominate her with their urgings to make a show of power, the more they seemed to believe this themselves and the more urgent they became about wanting to get out, be seen as something separate from her, and make their power play from there.

As her boredom seemed to grow, she seemed more and more unconscious on the throne, often yawning and appearing to be half asleep, or even cat napping, while many, even nearby, talked about her behind her back. When she did not appear to hear and did not respond except with occasional and sudden lashings from her tail, which she did not acknowledge doing, they fell to bickering among themselves about the wisdom of letting this happen, feeling privately enraged about issues of timing and what this was going to mean about respect for themselves if they did step forward. Most saw it as further evidence that they were more powerful than she was and that she was nothing without their help, but a few did not. A few saw this as a problem of disrespect for the position itself.

None let it be known what they had in mind here, though; all of this bickering was in the form of what the mother on Earth should do next to regain her sagging power and authority and the respect she deserved. All listened carefully to see what ideas they could steal from the others and all slipped out from behind the Faerie Queen when it appeared it wouldn't be noticed, and introduced themselves in the court as faeries who had been lost in the woods for a long time and who wanted to be filled in on the details of the court, by which method they sought to learn even more of what others thought and observed that was being kept hidden from the mother on Earth.

Their positions as understudies made them feel they must best her to prove themselves, and so they were always looking for ways to nip at her in the court and safely enjoy the resultant laughter by surrounding themselves with others who might share their point of view. And since she was listening more intently than they realized to see what she could learn, they were often the object of the mother on Earth's tail lashings too, and often responded with a little dash of fiery breath themselves.

Although the satyrs enjoyed giving a lot of trouble to many of the new arrivals, they did not give these new arrivals in court a problem even though they wondered how they had gotten in there. All assumed they had somehow slipped past one of them who did not want to admit he had been busy sexually extracting the price of admission from another applicant at the door. They would have let them all pass anyhow because they smelled familiar to them and they all thought, "What have we here?" They could not keep their hands off of anyone who interested them sexually and these faeries were definitely more interesting to them than the little faeries they had been using sexually. The satyrs made alliances with these faeries in exchange for mutual favors, and moved along with them as though they might have mates now, which also made the Faerie Queen furiously jealous.

The satyrs played with her jealousy here too as they could not resist any opportunity to bait the Faerie Queen when so much of their held rage was focused on getting revenge for anything they even imagined she might have ever done to them, and the list was long of things she actually had done. They baited the Faerie Queen as much as they possibly could, and in fact, the satyrs were the most outrageous in the court in what they said and revealed there, especially about the mother on Earth, keeping up an almost constant stream of comments of a derisive nature toward her, intended to see how far they could go before they provoked her into an open display of rage as though they had this in mind for some purpose of their own there. The faeries on their arms behaved as though this viewpoint and attack from the satyrs couldn't possibly also apply to them, while playing the game in their minds of which of these satyrs they might like for their King when they took over the throne.

In fact, the game of baiting and side stepping became quite a developed art in the court, and many of the satyrs developed quite a swish in their side step to avoid the tail lashings when they saw them coming, and laughed and snickered amongst themselves as though this was quite a lot of fun, very revealing and quite a game for them, as it was, in terms of what they were planning.

The satyrs knew there was no Fire Dragon who was going to come to the rescue of the Faerie Queen other than the one that lay hidden right there within her, and now the others in the court knew this too, or most of them did, since some of them had not been quick enough to see this or did not want to believe it.

The denied heart Ronalokas did not like this treatment of the mother on Earth and also wanted her to make a show of power, which they were trying to encourage her to do by carrying to her any information they had which they thought might be relevant or of interest to her and fuel her in this direction. They also thought they might have to make a show of force themselves somehow. They weren't sure how to go about it, but they were keeping their eyes and ears open for any new ideas that might come their way.

The satyrs, on the other hand, thought they did not have any problems with their own power play because they had so many different plans and thought they had all their bases covered. It was not even a problem anymore, as they saw it, as to how they could make the Faerie Queen a prisoner right there in the court, before she could become the Fire Dragon and best them, if they decided to go that way. They had not been sure they could get away with it in front of her supporters, unless they could somehow make

them no longer her supporters, but they saw themselves as suc-
ceeding in that and gaining support for themselves everyday.
They even felt they might like to try making tail lashings a crime
for which they could punish and imprison her unless she agreed
to tail lashings herself and gave them lessons in how to do it.

Since the Faerie Queen made no overt noise of rage to accompany these swipes of her tail, the vines were not imprisoning her,
and so nothing had made her aware yet of what she was doing
when she was musing in her cat naps and feeling rage toward
those around her, and the satyrs had not, as of yet, called the vines
into the court anyway, having preferred to move there themselves
to control the mother on Earth, without revealing their methods,
or that they depended upon or even used any power outside of
themselves.

Even though everyone had noticed the Faerie Queen caught in
the vines in the woods at times, although, not recently, the satyrs
had resisted the temptation to reveal this as their own doings,
always acting as though the mother's rage was not right and that
was why it was happening. But now, they wanted to call the vines
in closer, just in case they needed them as temporary restraining
devices at least, and have their fire resistant restraining devices at
hand too, in case she turned into the Fire Dragon in the court. They
had the feeling that surely her rage could not stand much more
pressure without doing something more overt.

While pressure was mounting from the power plays that were
biding their time in the wings, the form changes going on in court
were getting more and more outrageous along with the behavior
of the satyrs and certain other key personages present there as
though the one mirrored the other. Some of these form changes
were consciously controlled, but many of them were not. They
were happening in response to held emotions, and even expressed
emotions, and many who were experiencing form changes did not
know how this was happening to them and sought both to hide it
when they did not like it and show it off vainly as a power of theirs
when they did like it. Insecurity was rampant, as those in the court
sought to be entertaining, clever and witty, and the mother on
Earth seemed to feed more on their insecurity than their wit, which
she often accused of being dull.

The court looked like a fantastically grotesque, bejeweled and
lavishly enrobed Halloween costume party that never ended,
combined with some sort of presto-chango freak and magic show
with such a repertoire of games of bait and switch, bait and deny,

provoke and blame, hit and dodge, advance and evade, set one another up, oneupmanship, showing off, gaining favor, impressing sexual or desired sexual liaisons, finding allies, understudies or any others who might be useful and all of the other things that such a seething hotbed of denials and held undercurrents such as this could invent in the war amongst the fragmentation of misalignment and scrambling for power and Parental position as this court or any court has going on in it that it's a wonder it isn't said that all games and sports in the world were invented there.

It was like a menagerie in the court at times, too, because many of the forms being changed into were animal forms or parts of animal forms, but at a subtle enough level that the displayer of such signs could deny them, and often did, if not received as wanted to be. There were signs such as the darting tongue of a snake appearing for a moment in an otherwise human looking mouth, the eye of a predatory bird appearing for a moment on an otherwise friendly posturing face, pawing hooves, horns sprouting whenever the kundalini tried to rise with something angry, and disappearing again as quickly when it fell back, furry cat and fox-type tails appearing, caressing the legs of those the tail wished to attract sexually as the purveyor of such a sign passed by and disappearing again if any threat was felt to letting this be known or seen, the coquettish appearance of feathers and fur, hands becoming reptilian-like as they grasped at something that seemed to have power and becoming soft again when the owner of the hands realized it was not good company in which to let such lust or greed be seen, feelings of vanity, silliness and foolishness showing as cocks crowing their own praises, ostrich, peacock and other feathery appearances strutting brainlessly and unaware across the floors of shifting sands and treachery like meals headed for the traps baited for them, long, tall ears trying to listen from across the room, donkey brays instead of laughter when the person was covering too much fear or stupidity to know how to hold it back, cat's paws and twitching tails ready to pounce on those who stirred these predatory instincts, fangs appearing when it was felt such a strike was called for, many rows of teeth that wanted to eat something alive, or more harmlessly, large cheeks that wanted to hide something that others could not take without it being seen.

Alarmingly, reptilian parts and beasts' snouts took precedence over many other forms in the court, I noticed, as well as bestial lower parts, especially penises, often appearing without apparent notice being taken by their owners, and often appearing briefly in response to the desire to be predatory on others there. Scales, fur and thick hair seemed to be more attractive to most of the people there than many other possible appearances, but there were often scales where there should have been hair or skin, hair where there should have been skin and many other signs of disarray in the form changes. Although feathers had presence, they were not considered to have the status the other appearances had, unless they were predatory birds, I noticed. I also noticed that the reptilian forms had hints and bits and pieces of dragon parts appearing around the court.

Meanwhile, the Faerie Queen was form changing herself, as she sat upon her throne, into a more and more grotesque caricature of her former self, and the more grotesque she became, the more grotesque everyone else was becoming also.

All of this was going on in the court, and still the Faerie Queen seemed bored enough to appear to sleep most of the time as though she didn't care about it anymore, didn't see what was mounting itself all around her, was losing herself somehow, or going senile, even slumping on her throne and looking diminished at times, as though she might have been sinking down into herself as she slept, but those who looked weren't sure if but what she wasn't losing herself to something or removing her presence from there, perhaps, except at times when the faeries slipped back into her and she awoke with more presence.

Meanwhile, the satyrs, could not form change. When they saw this happening all around them, they thought privately that they must learn to form change too, but were publicly making fun of it as foolishness, vanity, vapidness and the vacillating, uncertain, insecure and unstable presences of poor self-image and self-esteem, mocking form change as they mocked everything until it was wondered if their best roles were as court jesters or as King pretenders or if there was a difference in the two roles.

They thought it was a matter of learning certain secrets which they were busy creeping around in the court trying to do, but conducting themselves as though form change were some sort of major joke in which they might be planning to steal forms, even perhaps rob the mother on Earth of her Fire Dragon form as though it were some sort of suit of armor or costume they could steal in the night.

The mother on Earth was furious with them, not only as the Faerie Queen who bopped them with her scepter, but as the Fire

Dragon who lashed them with her tail, not even so much for making fun of her as for not letting her move her rage in response. Her inner desire to move rage was moving outwardly in many ways without her noticing it because she was so focused on the control it took for her to not move her rage when she was being so openly and constantly baited, played with and provoked in ways and places that did not have acceptance for her rage and were using this denial in a power play against her.

Everytime she downpressed rage within her that wanted to express outwardly, faeries moved out from behind her back, many of whom had been planning to go forth with it anyway, thinking they knew better than she did. She made even more splits than that since they fragmented from there by having offspring with the satyrs, the Ronalokas and others, as the satyrs' denied fragments were likewise doing. She also made further splits within herself by going almost only inward, without emotional movement, in order to not respond outwardly to a situation that was provoking her into entrapment.

Not only was she feeling provoked beyond her limits in the court, she was also feeling hateful toward her rivalry with the Father of Manifestation, who never came around to receive her rage for His lack of control of anything in the woods. She hated this almost as much as she hated the control the satyrs were exercising over her and her court, and not being able to move her rage with Him, she found this to be boring too. Had it not been for the satyrs showing up late in the day and often leaving at night to party in the woods, it would have been even more unbearable, although not all of them left at once, unfortunately, as she saw it, since she did not realize they were giving her protection in spite of it all.

As it was, it was unbearable enough, though, and she began to practice the art of deception herself by leaving a part of herself on the throne in the appearance of the Faerie Queen dozing off, while sneaking out with the rest of herself to let her rage go where it needed to to be able to rage; sometimes the fire seas, sometimes the open skies, sometimes to seek out the Father of Manifestation in forms she found He didn't recognize, and also to party at night in the woods and see what else was going on there that she might like to experience.

On the nights when she left an impersonation of herself on the throne, she did not know how dangerous this was. She did not know how her faerie impersonators were moving against her by advancing their own opinions in the court, undermining her consistency and authority even further and confusing the court about what her position really was, and when she resumed her position on the throne, they did not let her know what had happened in her absence, giving her a struggle sometimes in even regaining her Faerie Queen form and her throne, but not overtly enough for her to realize what they really had in mind there.

During the times she was there on her throne, her internal musings often took the form of imagining how she could take revenge on those who enraged her. The more she thought about it, the more enraged she felt that the satyrs had so much control over her and were even in control of her court now much more than she. She hated their control over her and especially over her rage. Something was going to have to be done about it.

She wanted to rage at them publicly and humiliate them in the ways she did in private, but she did not think it befitting of her Faerie Queen image or of a public display, and what if they dared to nab her right there with the vines? That would be too humiliating and revealing, and since they had overthrown her temporarily in the fire seas, she had fears about what they might try next and what that might mean in terms of a power loss in the court. And how far might they take it?

She wanted to be able to rage right there in the court if she wanted to and be protected from both the satyrs and their vines! She was tired of having to go to the fire seas everytime she wanted to rage. How she would like to scorch them with a blast of her fiery breath right then and there, grab them with her claws first and put her face right in theirs! How she would like to see their faces become frightened as she was getting ready to singe them! At least she wanted to lash them with her tail! What business was it of theirs if she raged or not, anyway? She wanted to turn the tables on them and make it so that they did not dare to stop her. She felt like a caged beast, and no one cared! She thought of how fortified the fire seas were and of how the vines couldn't penetrate there, and then she had an idea.

She loved her court with its open airiness and beautiful arching, cathedral-like trees overhead, so exotically filled with flowers, animals and birds. She loved the wafting, sensual breezes and pleasantly erotic scents drifting in from hidden places in the forest. She loved the sunlight that did penetrate there, and its colors glowing liked stained glass through the dark veins of the tree branches in the evening. She loved the lacier leaves and sprays of greenery interwoven with the rest, and she could even have felt good about the vines if they had been interwoven with and supporting of the formation of her chambers instead of infiltrating, twisting and penetrating; poised at the perimeter like vicious snakes ready to squeeze the life from her if she dared rage in her own court! Those vines had to go! And the snakes they sometimes became too!

In her musings there, she not only blamed the satyrs for how boring their control of her rage had made her court, she also blamed her court for not coming up with anything new or interesting often enough. She thought of how she would like to rage at them all and thought of how a good stirring of rage might liven things up, clean out the deadbeats and bubble the cauldron anew. She liked rage. It was exciting and electrical to her and made things happen. Without it, something was missing in life, and unable to move it there, its exhilaration and power was missing from her court!

She began to give her fantasies of revenge an elaborately detailed form. Her idea was to take her court chamber, and her bedchamber too, for that matter, and the passageways between and preserve their beautiful form, but cast them into impenetrable, stone barriers to the vines, which would no longer be able to move anyway because they would also be turned to stone, and do it before she raged and revealed any more about herself.

She began to work on this often, intensely and internally when she appeared to be bored and half napping on her throne. She would get someone to fan the air and waft light breezes around if she had to. She would get someone to carry in things from the forest to scent the air, strew flowers about, vase flowers if necessary, but those vines had to be stopped from controlling her anymore, and the satyrs too, for that matter, as well as everyone else who was in on it with them!

She had her fantasies of revenge nearly in place when she noticed the vines beginning to creep closer, poking their heads in through the leafy enclosure of her court chamber as though they heard her inner thoughts and felt her inner rage. She felt the vines creeping toward her as though they were the satyrs themselves ready to grab her in some terrible plot of their own of intrigue and power, and she was determined not to let them succeed.

The mother on Earth decided also that she must not let the satyrs force her hand. She pressured her rage down heavily there, telling it it was not quite the right time for it to appear yet. She wanted to stop the vines this way, and it did seem to slow their

225

creeping advance for a little while.

She wanted everything to be in place before she risked raging in the court, but now the faeries also knew what she had in mind, and they left her, carefully slipping away, almost laughing openly with uncontainable glee at how she was handing them the right time to make their power play and without noticing it. She was going to make it safe for them to move rage and turn into fire dragons, and they all secretly planned to beat her to it. Knowing she would not perform such a piece of magic in public, and, therefore, had to leave the room to do it, they slipped to the edges of the court, hoping not to be seen by her, and waited.

The mother soon noticed the vines creeping toward her again. Knowing how fast they could move, and not knowing her own fragmentation here and how it really felt about her, she left an impersonator on the throne who was a little more clever than the rest and not quite so anxious to leave, and slipped away to her own chambers to do the magic in private that would quickly cast her court and surrounding chambers down into stone.

She did not want to give anyone in the court time to oppose her before it happened. Everything had to be in place. She must move quickly and do everything right, and she must also make sure she remembered everything. She was a little nervous. She didn't want to forget anything such as when she had opened the entranceway to the fire seas and not closed the door properly.

She pushed these thoughts away from her mind in order to focus on the magic at hand. She cast her spell exactly as she had planned it, and instantly, her chamber was transformed. She was almost afraid to look out into the passageway, but she heard such an uproar from the court chamber that she did, and seeing that the passageway, too, was now encased in stone, she gathered her regal robes about her and hurried to open the door to her secret passageway. She passed quickly through it and emerged into the secret place from which she had, for some time, been able to observe the court, unseen.

Before she even got there, the smell of fear and pandemonium assailed her. She felt the steam of her rage snort this smell from her nostrils. She hated the smell of fear. She felt triumphant and smug, but braced herself for a moment before opening the shutter in her secret place to look down upon the court. It was only a moment before she could no longer resist looking, and what she saw was bedlam in her court.

She roared in delight, "Now that's a lot more interesting! A lot more lively and interesting!"

How foolish fear may have been to have ever ventured there at all. Gazelle, antelope and deer-like animals were stampeding wild-eyed around the room, giving off the scent of fear onto the very snouts of jackal and hyena-type predators growling and snapping at their throats and heels as they tried to run them down. Horns and antlers were butting the walls from many heads, while wildebeast, warthog and wild boar-type bodies were throwing their weight against the walls and pawing wildly at the now stone floor. Birds screeched and soared for the, now cast in stone, tops of the tree branches. Monkeys screamed and leaped for the high places, jumping excitedly up and down on their perches, imitating the sounds and raining things down upon the stampeders. Lion-like beasts roared with rage at being caged, and no vines stopped them. The mother roared with them. Snakes were slithering quickly out of the way, looking for escape and even some worms, the mother noticed, were crawling about looking for holes.

"There are none big enough for a vine!" the mother on Earth screamed in rage that felt free and powerful again at last, proud of the solidness of her vision. "There's no escape! The only doors are heavy, and they are locked, and I have the only key!"

She felt into her robes then to make sure, and was relieved to find that she really did have the key with her this time. It was not lost or forgotten. As her hand closed around it, she felt smug and successful and congratulated herself.

I was surprised the walls didn't come down under the assault or that the sheer weight of them didn't sink into the spongy earth of Pan, but the mother on Earth had thought of everything and had put foundations under them and even some subterranean chambers similar to some of the caverns in the fire seas.

As she saw the satyrs running below her, dribbling urine from their semi-erections and shaking with excitation, she was glad they couldn't reach her where she was watching them from her hidden vantage point.

The mother on Earth looked then to see if she could see who was responding how, but it was almost impossible to tell who was who anymore other than how she remembered casting their form in her magic spell.

"They helped me anyway by putting themselves there," she growled as she gazed down upon the stampeding pandemonium beneath her.

She thought of putting in an appearance in the court to see

what would happen then and looked toward her throne. She was aghast and horrified to see a fire dragon sitting on it; or a partial one, anyway, when she looked closer. She had a burst of rage and saw the fire dragon stir the stampede with fiery breath as though in response to it.

"What does this mean?" she screamed in rage that was now frantic instead of triumphant. She was afraid she already knew what it meant; insurrection in her own court! "Whoever did this is going to pay!"

She looked frantically around the room to see what else might not have gone according to plan, and was horrified and infuriated to see quite a number of other fire dragons also trying to reveal themselves in form. She recognized them all and their identities infuriated her further. They were all faeries in her court, and not only that, allies, she had thought, who had slipped out of her to find things out for her. She studied them quickly to see how successful they were going to be and saw that they were strangely caught between peacocks, foxes, dragons and weasels with enough parts of themselves left to reveal themselves to her.

"They deserve it!" she screamed. She cursed them and wished a horrible fate worse than this upon them, but she was most worried about the one on her throne and knew she must move to unseat her as soon as possible.

"How dare she!" she screamed between clenched teeth, not knowing which was worse; her betrayal or her upstaging of her by presenting the Fire Dragon form in the court first.

She was trying to think fast, and it first occurred to her that no one knew this fire dragon was not her, and that they would not have to know if she could regain her place. But how could she get there as the Faerie Queen and not be recognized? She tried to form change into something that could get there unnoticed, but she was so enraged she kept slipping toward her Fire Dragon form instead.

She screamed in rage at this betrayal until the very stone walls of her so carefully cast spell started to shake. She quickly stopped herself, knowing she didn't want her walls to come down and that she could not turn into her Fire Dragon form there in her tiny, little, viewing chamber because she would be much too big.

She was already too late, she feared, for what she had in mind. She hated having any of her plans disrupted from the perfection in which she had so carefully planned them. Furious that she now had another reason to have to hold back her rage, she could not help raging some more. Containing herself as much as she could, she looked around her court to see who else was in on this. She saw dragon parts appearing here and there, and the more she raged, the more they appeared. She felt her rage was helping them somehow and that she must get away from there.

The mother on Earth made for the fire seas as fast as she could open a secret passageway, fearing that she had lost the opportunity for her last, powerful stroke and furious that after all of this, she was having to take her rage to the fire seas again. The entire way, she was seething about the loss of the perfection of her plan. As soon as she reached a cavern large enough, she became a Fire Dragon, but she needed to reach a volcano to go back the way she had planned.

"Funny," she thought to herself, "either this chamber has grown larger or I, smaller."

The mother on Earth could not let herself take time to examine this, so driven was she to the completion of her plan. She grabbed the air, leaping upward to fly furiously toward her court. She had planned to land triumphantly and scorch all of the surrounding vines out of existence, which she did, and then open the great doors with her key and let everyone out to hear her proclaim herself to be the greatest power on Earth!

She was taken aback, as she landed in her courtyard, to see Father Warriors stationed about as though they had been assigned to their places.

"What are they doing here?" she thought. She threatened them with her fiery breath, but they did not quail.

"Statue-like as ever, I see!" she thought.

Nonetheless, their presence was very unsettling to her.

Then she noticed it seemed strangely quiet, and presumed everyone had grown quiet in fear as she was scorching everything surrounding the court, but when she opened the doors, there was no one there. She raged that there was no one there to hear her mighty speech which she had rehearsed and given internally to herself so many times. Then she noticed the doors seemed scorched around the key hole and she knew immediately what had happened. She raced back to the fire seas as fast as she could, hoping she wasn't already too late there.

THE FIRE DRAGONS FORCE
THE MOTHER ON EARTH
INTO FACING HER POWER LOSS

The mother on Earth reached the volcano. Uncertain, but driven by her rage, she entered quickly. Not knowing exactly what to expect, she entered in attack mode just in case. She was ready to force the issue of power if she needed to because she was so furious with any and all who were in on this plot against her. How dare they question her authority on Earth! After all, she was the one who was here first and had taught them everything they knew about life on Earth! Ingrates, all of them, and not a one of them really that smart, either! She was already giving them her speech in her fury on the way to the fire seas because she believed every line of it.

Once inside the volcano, she moved quickly to find her cavern of power. She felt the problem there the moment she approached it. There was hot steam from fire dragon breath all around it. The passageways to it were nearly impassable. She raged herself then, long fingers of fiery breath leaping from her throat and mouth and reaching down the passageway, seeking the fire dragon who had dared to sit upon her throne. How dare anyone sit upon her throne in the form of a Fire Dragon before she had the opportunity to do so herself and show herself to be the one to have invented that form! Inexcusable, unforgivable usurpment!

She was seething in a rage so hot it was a mighty flash of fire she sent down that passageway, and a mighty blast returned to her from the cavern of power like a fire ball rolling back on her from her own breath of fire. She sent another blast down the passageway and another was hurled back at her. "It will run down," she told herself, "It doesn't have My power!"

But she had underestimated what alliances can do, even if they break apart right after the coup. The treacherous faeries were all together there, moving rage back at her as a group. And the mother on Earth was raging back just as much as she possibly could. They had quite a battle there until the heat got so bad the mother on Earth had to back down the passageway to get some air. If she could not regain her cavern of power, she had already lost the battle. She knew then that the treacherous faerie who had sat upon her throne was not there alone. She did not have the power to do this.

"Fiery breath belongs only to Me, the only true Fire Dragon," she screamed down the passageway, "not to any upstart copycats like you!"

There was no response other than long, threatening, fingers of rage whose fire seemed to be looking for her in a sinister way that made the mother on Earth step back. "There is no love in that! Where is the love in that?" she said. No answer still except more fiery flames, and more fiery flames propelled with a sound like a bellows.

She felt fear and panic for a moment and then got ahold of herself. She must do something, but what could she do if she could not regain her cavern of power? She thought of offering them jewels or other objects of power she kept hidden in the fire seas, but there was no way she was going to lose her dignity doing such a thing as that.

"You have no power except My power which you have stolen!" she screamed down the passageway.

"You have no power except My power which you have stolen," came echoing back.

For a moment the mother on Earth was not sure where this had come from and feared the rest of the Mother might be in on this coup. Then she thought it might be her own echo and her own fireballs rolling back on her.

She decided to risk the more favorable option being true and charged her way down the passageway without hurling out any more fire, hoping speed could get her to the cavern of power before anyone singed her to death first if there was a nest of adversarial fire dragons in there.

Once in the cavern, she saw the whole group of fire dragons, most of the satyrs and some of the other faeries from her court. They looked threatening toward her and were moving to block her escape routes as much as possible. She saw that they had let her come into the cavern because it was their plan. They wanted to move rage on her more directly and make her surrender to them, perhaps even force from her more of her secrets than they already had.

"So, it takes this many of you to overthrow My power!" she screamed, hurling raging fire balls all over the place at them. They hardly stepped back as though they weren't very hot at all. She could feel grief about to come over her and she could not stand it; hated it, in fact, as a matter of pride. "There is no way I am going to surrender My position to you all," she screamed.

She had suddenly realized how alone in her court she had

become without even realizing it. She had been so busy hating everyone else she had not noticed how alone she felt there and misunderstood for her pain too. There was a moment there, looking around in the fire cave, when My light almost felt sorrier for her than I ever had, but she had to crack for My light to have responded to her there and she did not crack there. She only screamed in rage at everyone there and gave them her speech, which they did not respond favorably to either.

At least she got to give her speech, though, and a good speech it was too, covering all her major points with My light, only directed at those assembled as the ones not listening to her this time. They moved their fire dragon powers against her, and she, hers against them, and they had another great battle there which put the satyrs cringing at the edge, but still presenting as though they were controlling the fire dragons, giving battle orders and moving a bellows-like gadget to blow fire from the fire sea. The faeries had to flee down the passageways to escape the heat.

When the mother on Earth went the most furiously after the fire dragon who had sat upon her throne, this one claimed to have been giving the stirring of rage she had ordered.

"We were only following your orders," they told her, sounding as if what they said was just to make her more furious.

In the end, they overpowered her with the help of the satyrs those treacherous faerie fire dragons had let into the fire seas along with the other faeries who wanted revenge against her. Those treacherous faeries knew where the key was, and knew most of the mother on Earth's other secrets too, but there was one they did not see that I would like to mention now, which is that it is not what her secrets were, or where her power objects were hidden, or even how they were used in terms of ceremony or ritual; it is who uses the power, and what their energy field is like that makes the difference. This is a most important point of magic and one you should never forget. The same power or power object in two different hands can bring vastly different results, not only because of intent, but also because of who they are.

The fire dragons then demanded the mother on Earth surrender her authority to them officially and declare them to be the Royal Order of Fire Dragons, insisting that their achieving of the form of Fire Dragon independent of her and their overpowering of her proved not only that they deserved it, but that they could force her to do it if she refused to cooperate. This made the mother on Earth feel extremely denied and small; still, if they had to have her to make them a royal order, they must still need her power somehow.

She refused to cooperate with them, which brings Me to My next point: Just because you have the form of something does not mean you have it or are it, it is important to penetrate the appearance of things; they may not be what they seem.

"But you have finally gotten what you have always wanted," they told her, "and not only just one fire dragon separate from yourself as rescuer, protectorate and power back up, but a whole group of fire dragons."

"I don't want a whole group!" the mother on Earth sullenly replied, feeling like this was not at all what she really wanted and that they did not feel like rescuers, protectors, power back ups or even allies to her, which brings Me to another important point: Be careful what you wish for and how you wish it.

They threatened, intimidated and forced until, finally, with fiery breath spent and lashing tails exhausted, claws forced the mother on Earth to say, in a small ceremony they had devised, that they were the Royal Order of Fire Dragons.

Then they told her she had to perform her last act of royal authority on Earth as a Fire Dragon by proclaiming the Fire Dragon who had dared to sit on her throne the head of the Royal Order of Fire Dragons. This made the mother on Earth utterly furious! She at first refused, and fought against this with reserves of energy she didn't know she had, saying she was the only true Fire Dragon and therefore, the head Fire Dragon and would never give up her position of authority on Earth, and that they could not take it from her anyway because it was rightfully hers.

"Power that is mine cannot be taken away," she told them all. Words destined to come back to haunt her, I would like to say, but there and then, she still had the power to prevail regarding her position as head Fire Dragon when she proved to them that they could not take on the form or breathe fire without her help, and most importantly, could not get back out of the form without her help. They did not give in to her authority easily, though. She had to make this Fire Dragon second in command, with treachery and insurrection still looming all around the agreement.

Then they were going to let her go on the promise that she would declare herself only the Faerie Queen in public and not even the mother on Earth. Banishing her was what it felt like to the mother on Earth. This was an impossible promise for her to keep, and she refused to make it, vowing not to keep it if they made her promise this.

"How wicked all of you have become over time," she heard herself growl at them.

"How wicked you have become over time," they repeated back to her, just as they had been doing with so many of her statements.

They restrained her and tortured her then, she expressing what she still could of her raging fury at them and they moving to get the revenge they had so long wanted to have against her. In the end, she lost so much essence in the pain of this torture, in addition to all the essence she had already lost into fragmentation, that she had to do as they said. She made the promise even though she vowed she would not keep it. My warning here is: Try not to take on more than you can handle outwardly, and be careful about what promises and vows such situations may induce you to make because they are more binding than you think, even from life to life, and need removal commensurate to the way they were put in place.

They forced her into ceremonies with them then. In this way, the alliance prevailed over her, and she felt she had a disaster instead of a triumph in the place of her dreams, and a failure instead of a success in reality. Instead of Mother on Earth Triumphant, Fire Dragon Mother Protectorate and Victorious with Ronalokas kneeling at her feet and all the court bowing to her power, authority and majesty, as she had so many times already seen in her fantasies, she was now the banished and diminished mother, and publicly, only the Faerie Queen for now, which meant to her a mere figurehead on her throne, and robbed of the presentation of her Fire Dragon form, cruelly and unfairly, before she had the opportunity to show herself publicly as the first, the creator of and the one and only true Fire Dragon. She was now surrounded by copies, all claiming to be the original, the creator of and the only true Fire Dragon and who could not give her back the moment of triumph they had stolen, and who, without her stolen power and continued help, she still thought, could not take on the form of the Fire Dragon, which brings Me to the next point I'd like to mention: What is truly yours cannot be really lost, but it can certainly be experienced as though it is, and the less you know about how it is really yours, the more convincingly lost it can look.

Without the group, they could not take on the form of Fire Dragon either, which was the basis of their sudden alliance, formed after a fight they had when they had tried to reveal themselves in the court and discovered they were more dependent upon their rage moving in concert with the others than they had thought. This was a humbling experience for them, but one that did not cost them the advantage now taken over the mother on Earth, or even now when they let her remain the figurehead without paying homage or giving loyalty to her anymore.

The mother on Earth felt encircled by a threatening ring of power seekers and did not realize how much essence loss had really taken place there. They had forced her into ceremonies and made her take vows and make promises, but the real power loss was in the loss of her essence there. The ceremony made it official, yet as intertwined as the two usually have been, it has often been hard to say that such ceremonies have had no effect. It has often had the intimidating form of making the power loss manifest as though very real, but what needs to be looked at here is that without loss of essence and the power loss that reflects that, such ceremonies, vows, promises and other officializing forms cannot take place, and once this ceremony did take place, without the mother on Earth realizing the significance it had, they did have the power to take on the Fire Dragon form without her help, which meant also that to a certain extent, their alliance could also fall apart, and they could go back to infighting for power and position.

Meanwhile, the court had regrouped, most of them feeling very sheepish and ashamed by what had been revealed in their evening of horror, not knowing if they also were going to be turned to stone in the next moment, scorched out of existence by fire dragon breath in the great fight that had ensued amongst the emerging fire dragon forms in the court or locked into this nightmare with no escape until it played itself out.

Most of them wanted to deny it had ever happened, as though they had just taken bad drugs, but they could not because the court was now a stone castle and their forms had not changed back completely. They had many animals' parts remaining amongst them, and often the most revealing parts too, which made it much more difficult for them to hide feelings they had about themselves and others, yet something or someone had already seen what they had been trying to hide and revealed it in their night of horror, and they feared it might be My light since the Faerie Queen had not demonstrated herself openly to have had a major role in this or the power to cause it. Only the faeries who knew what she had been plotting had known of her role in this, and for purposes of their own, had not even told the satyrs much about it except when they had been pressured for information, and then only that they knew where the key was, but were not ready to reveal its location yet.

The majority of the court knew little of the plots and power plays of the inner circle, having their own concerns at a more trivial level of partners and mates and oneupmanship for position in the hierarchy of the court, but having been minor characters there may have been a saving grace since they emerged with more minor damage from the evening of horror in the court.

Evening of horror is not a misnomer either, since most of them felt fear they had been avoiding and had not felt move openly in themselves for a long time since they made no real place of acceptance for it in themselves, disliking its presence so much it was denied into a kind of self-hatred turned outward as a hatred for others who had fear.

One of the unspoken agreements in the court was a hatred for fear, viewing it as victim toward which they felt predatory. No one who was in the stampede of frightened animals wanted this revealed, but it couldn't be avoided anymore because of the animal parts that remained.

Something needs to be said about Blue here. Blue made an agreement at the level of imprinting that it hated fear, and has forced others into it whether they agreed or not. This agreement needs to be looked at, and at the right time in personal process, formally removed, not only by all blue people, but by the blue in everyone. It is not possible to move fear in the presence of hatred for it that is not moving to respond with love. No matter how appearances may make it seem, blue people do not, at the imprinting level, accept fear movement, and it is dangerous to move it in their presence. The danger is backlash from the gap. Rage needs to move in Blue to really remove this agreement from their imprinting, but they need to start with a formal declaration of intent to remove this agreement from their gap, otherwise moving fear in their presence means going past the imprinting here, which does not work.

Blue had a rage in the beginning which the Mother barely heard at the word level, but I heard it and it needs to be brought out into the open now. This rage felt hatred for anything that wanted to hold it down or back and anything that even looked like it might try to do this. Blue hated this feeling of being held down and back and felt it had already suffered this for long enough when it broke loose into the ascending spiral of consciousness that caused the explosion in Blue and the resultant strikes, or smacks.

It has not been possible for something to look like a limit to

Blue without an argument from Blue and a refusal to accept it. Meanwhile, Blue has been imposing limits on everyone else in its own favor. This must end. It is not possible to move along with this sort of imbalance anymore, but to end it, Blue is going to have to realize that the thing it has most hated is going to have to be felt, which is the fear it had from feeling held down and back.

Blue moved only rage there and has not moved this fear yet, forcing it, instead, to be held by the Will Polarity and forcing it back down the Will's throat if necessary, while also making the Will hold the rage it has had at Blue for this, which is really only Blue's rage, denied by Blue, but still trying to roll back to its place in Blue because it has hated being there with the fear it has been pressured to hold down.

This is denied heart in Blue people; fear being held down by rage. It is a pitiful place for Heart to have to be, and this needs to move into love for both feelings in order to have the Heart presence needed in Blue.

All the inner circle in the court was Blue people. Even the fauning Ronalokas the mother had gathered near her throne as her closest admirers were on the denied Will side of Blue heart and not really Ronalokas, their gold light being only the denied gold needed to make the Heart so missing there in Blue. These fauns, along with some others, including certain faeries, had become most of the stampeding animals that night, and they did not like it that this might become known about them since they had returned almost completely to the forms they preferred, except that they found parts of the other animals still present with them that revealed them more now. This prompts Me to say that things may be presenting themselves more as they seem than you think, and to know, you have to feel it.

All those who had embarrassment about any parts of forms they were caught in now wanted to conceal themselves as though wearing garments like costumes, and all wanted to learn form change so that they could move back more toward the forms they liked better for themselves, and they all wanted to disguise their reasons for learning form change by having this take the form of games and contests which they claimed were to please and amuse the mother and have her see them as clever after all. They wanted to pass this all off as only having fun, but they also all wanted to learn as much as they possibly could from watching all of this. The shame Blue made them feel about their fear especially made them want to place form change under conscious control and make it more like taking apparel on and off.

When the court showed up to reconvene, the Father Warriors let them in since they were following the orders they had been given, which were from the first Fire Dragons they saw. The Father Warriors' presence was very unsettling to the court as well as was the absence of the mother on Earth, whom they did love in their own curious way in spite of it all. They did not know what any of this really meant, or where the inner circle of the court had gone, and this mysterious silence and absence spooked them even further.

The court wanted things to return to normal, whatever that meant, and the party to begin again. Most of them were even more interested in the party than the return to normalcy if they could hide their form change problems, since they were still denying they had form change problems. They insisted they did not prefer normalcy of any particular sort as long as they were all similar and having fun.

Once the Faerie Queen was free from her torture, it took her some time, however, to feel ready to return to the court. She did not like how she felt and had to take some time to try to restore herself as much as possible. She did not like to look distraught or disempowered on her throne either. Even if it was a hollow throne now compared to what she had envisioned it was going to be, she still insisted she owed it to herself and all of her patronage to resume as much as possible. After all, there was always next time, and her rage still insisted that if she regrouped, she would be able to reclaim not only her lost power, but her lost Fire Dragon preemption as well. But it did not turn out that way, which brings Me to My next point: Not only is it right person and right place and right form for magic to be performed well, it is also right time, which it was no longer for the Faerie Queen, and is no longer for rage as power.

THE MOTHER FEELS THE PRESSURE FROM DENIALS TO BE TOO MUCH AND GIVES UP ON TRYING TO HOLD THEM BACK ANYMORE

Meanwhile, the Mother in the woods was being held present on Earth by the Father of Manifestation. She was having major problems with the pressure of the lines from Hell and the weight of the monsters climbing them. She did not see how She could avoid mentioning this to the Father of Manifestation, who had mentioned already how heavy She felt to Him in spite of Her thinness. She feared mentioning the lines because She feared His blueness there and felt sure His response was going to be rage toward Her that She had not managed to let go of them on the way to Earth as He had told Her to do, and as She had unsuccessfully struggled to do in the Plane of Reversal.

It was now impossible for Her to let go of them and get rid of the problem that way because of Her resolution in the cage of the ogres, Her vow to Herself as She was leaving Hell and also because the monsters had passed the Plane of Reversal and were now near Earth. She wanted to hide someplace and not be found, but the lines led straight to Her no matter where She went. She did not know these lines were a part of Her or that the monsters climbing them were all lost Will that had been pushed into Hell by the combined denials of everyone on Earth, or that they were all climbing toward Her because She was Parental to all of it in ways She did not understand. The lost Will didn't know why it was doing this either. It was subconsciously imprinted to blame the Mother and overlook the fact that no one else was allowing Her to move any of this lost Will into the Light, and even more importantly, not allowing it by exerting a major downward pressure against it.

Things move rather quickly now, so try to stay focused and not go past emotional triggers that may be lurking in the lines here, as you have major involvement in all of this even more than you realize consciously now. You must allow your subconscious to surface here, or you will not be able to know how to heal and will find this path to be another failure for you.

Lucifer and his hordes were nearing Earth at the same time the mother on Earth was having her battle with the Fire Dragons in the fire seas. Immediately after that, her public proclamation of the Royal Order of the Fire Dragons and their presentation in the court left so many questions unanswered that the Faerie Queen wanted to get them out of the way as fast as possible, somehow, and not let others have access to questioning them.

Meanwhile, the Mother had felt desperate urgings to move past Her fear of telling the Father of Manifestation about the lines. When She showed Him what was happening to Her, He was not immediately furious as She had feared. He was frightened and horrified and then furious; mostly it seemed, that She had not told Him sooner. She told Him She had had no time to mention this,

239

having been captured by the giants almost immediately upon noticing it, except for having seen them in one dream which She recalled only then, in which She had seen the lines and the monsters climbing them and had awakened in terror only to have mixed-up beasts charge at Her where She slept, confusing Her into not knowing what reality She was in or where the monsters were really coming from in Her dream. In Her scramble to escape, She had forgotten Her dream and the monsters She had seen as any other than the mixed-up beasts.

She told the Father of Manifestation that no matter how much She was moved to want to save Earth, She was not able to do it by making Herself go back to the place She had been before He brought Her there. He could sympathize with that since His own imprints about how He had come in from the void were being stirred by Her feelings there. He felt undercurrent blame toward Her that did not like the situation at all, but also felt they must find some way to protect Earth and still be able to keep Her there.

They could not go to the court directly and feel received, but they planted the idea that the Earth needed protection from unseen forces, potential invaders and spirits who were not welcome there on Earth and that the Royal Order of Fire Dragons might be able to provide this protection if they were to take turns, wrapping themselves around the Earth in the skies above it.

The mother on Earth seized upon this idea when it hatched in her mind as not only the way to get the Fire Dragons out of the way, but also as probably the perfect solution to the invasion problem she already hated so much.

She saw potential problems there similar to the ones created by the satyrs at the doors to her court, yet the potential of getting the Fire Dragons away from hounding her and away from the court, and especially from those who might like to admire them or question them more and into a place where they could be seen but not heard had huge appeal, especially since she had hatched another plan that she thought might get rid of them entirely and which involved energy she had been communing with in the skies.

She knew the Fire Dragons could be flattered into this because of their power hunger and lust for positions of dominance which she counted on there to blind them to any other aspects. Not realizing how blind she, herself, still was, the mother on Earth decided that if she took a turn with them in the Heavens, she could watch them more closely than she had watched the satyrs at her doors. The Fire Dragons did seize upon the idea of expanding and encircling the Earth in the skies as the image of power they wanted to have. They viewed this as placing themselves in control of the entire Earth, and a place to rev up and expand was just what they wanted to have. After quite a bit of infighting, they agreed to do this in pairs, saying it was better protection for Earth, but their distrust could also watch one another that way.

This was how the Fire Dragons got placed in the skies with the idea that they would protect Earth from invasions of unwanted spirits, and since they all snuck off to do other things at times, and left their forms hanging mostly empty in the skies, often without realizing the drift taking place in their consciousness, this is how the mother on Earth gained the opportunity to make a deal with light she did not recognize as Lucifer, to let in his hordes (as though she would have had the power to stop him) as forces she had the fool"heart"iness to think she could command against those who opposed her on Earth.

Once again, her blind spot did not let her realize all the other Fire Dragons in the Royal Order of Fire Dragons were also making the same deal, and all of them without realizing the others were all making the same deal with Lucifer. They were all being told by this light that they were the most powerful and important part of the Mother presence on Earth and deserved the position of rulership there, and not only that, all viewed this deal as an advance in their power position toward My light and the confrontation they wanted to have there.

None of them saw a problem with this either, since they viewed themselves this way already, and since nothing had been seen or heard of from the rest of the Mother for so long, they thought She had gone someplace and was all but forgotten and no longer a problem for them. They did not any longer even consider Her as a possibility in the Mother presence on Earth. They did not want or need Her anymore, or so they thought. They had Fire Dragon power now and weren't even concerned if the rest of the Mother did show up. They could best Her and they knew it because She had fear and grief and they had rage. Rage was power and the Parental part of the Mother. They were all sure of that, and controlled and directed rage was more powerful than merely expressing rage. They were all sure of that too.

Remember this: Rage is not true power, and any who use it as such will find out soon enough how false it is.

The Fire Dragons stationed in the sky all thought they moved in autonomous power that was greater than anything else. They

241

had polarized so extremely away from the Will presence they needed to feel this, they did not even know how dangerous and damaging what they were entering into there really was, and if they do not move to look now, they will not know it yet.

The Fire Dragons did not have balance or even really know what it was. When they had trouble hanging in the skies and had to go to the fire seas frequently to purify themselves, which was to move rage on their terms, they felt it was because they were being dragged down by the magnetic energy field of Earth and that rage movement had the power to move this out of them. After they had moved rage this way, they could rise into the skies with much less problem than when they finally had to go to the fire seas, which convinced them all the more that rage had the power to rev them up when they got bogged down. Without the balance they needed to hang in the skies, they could not resist the desire to stir the cauldron this way any more than they could resist stirring the cauldron they had been stirring with Lucifer's light in the skies of Earth, and what was about to leap from it was all of the manifestations of Hell on Earth in the form of all of Lucifer's monsters raining down upon the Earth in the tail winds of a fireball.

This causes Me to want to say: Balance is the cardinal rule of magic. Without it, you will not find the results you seek, and if you think you have, then you see not clearly and those are the lessons you will have to learn. Anything you stir into your cauldron of magic will manifest as it is, which is not necessarily as you see it, and lest you think the problem is only everyone else's imbalance, look into your own misfired attempts at manifesting your own lives.

Once again, the tension and pressure was mounting on Earth. There were great contests and duels of magic and form change taking place in the court with the frenzied edge to them of being driven by the denials and undercurrents of competition, power struggle, pecking order and fear denial. There was also a heartlessness to this that did not feel good to My light at all.

Some of these events drew spirits to come and watch who might have been partying in the woods otherwise, and these great displays of form change, power and magic were becoming so fiercely competitive and power oriented that it looked like power was growing in some and being depleted in others in ways that were both intimidating and lacking in the feelings of fun and playfulness that had been present in earlier experiences with these things. There was a deadly seriousness that was not pleasant to watch.

Without knowing how they were doing it, or even that they were doing it, many of the spirits there were losing the power to do anything other than to feed Lucifer their power and their essence through the Will denial the presence of his light was able to pressure them into, and which they entered into from their own wishes to avoid feelings at first, not knowing how it opened the door for him, and once his foot was in the door, he behaved much worse than the pushy salesman who refused to take it out. I would like to say here: If you do not feel love's presence, do not get involved.

As power grew in the hands of a few and seemed less present in the hands of the many, the denials they had, namely of fear, increased, and the more this happened, the more the Mother struggled with the lines from Hell gaining on Her in Pan, and the less able She was to cope with the struggle of holding Herself present in the midst of all of these denials anymore. She desperately needed the protection of the Father of Manifestation, but was unable to keep Herself present with Him in the places He went where He was not present with Her emotionally, which now had begun to take form with Him as being an unnoticed part of the audience for these duels in the name of learning things He needed to know about the participants there while He was also looking to see what kinds of powers they had compared to His own and trying to measure the strength of His powers compared to theirs, as so many were doing with this reflection of their own power loss, without moving the emotions they had in response to this, thinking that power was in controlling their emotions, instead.

Rage was almost never allowed to move except in the Fire Dragons in certain ways and forms, which was the example everyone had of rage, that did not feel very loving to them, and was not, since it was filled with the presence of unloving light empowering and driving it. Fear was hated by subconscious agreement and never allowed to move except in situations of such ridicule, condemnation and blame that it never gained consciousness beyond the self-hatred it was pushed into, and grief was only allowed to move for a little while before it was thought to be too much, which it was to the lack of openness to receive it, and especially when other emotions were having to be converted to grief to gain any expression at all to relieve the pressure of holding them.

In this atmosphere, the Mother could not stay present in a

group of people for long without feeling a tremendous increase in Her pain, suffering and held emotion level. When it was too much for Her, She could not move it there and She would have to remove Herself to express what She could privately. This left Her prey to all sorts of things that stalked Her as manifestations of the denied hatred of these feelings.

With the pressure and force of their own denials, and in the name of having fun, people in Pan had moved things out of themselves and into the woods so hideous as to make them no longer want to go there, or even any deeper into the woods than they had the protection of the group and familiar pathways to go.

There were many things lurking in the forest in Pan that were not encountered in the general runnings of many there who instinctively knew that banding together in groups was the thing to do, yet they excluded the Mother from all groups by making Her feel unwelcome there because of what they felt in Her presence and what She was trying to present. Even when She pointed it out, if it then rushed in on Her or them, they said that this proved She had caused it from some feelings of Hers such as rebellion, jealousy or revenge.

In the same ways that My feelings of wanting to smack at the spirits for their denials were hard to control, it is a wonder that the Mother has not smacked at you much harder than She has. That She has not is partly because of Her guilt, as well as Mine, and partly because of Our love, and partly because I was also pressuring Her heavily not to move these emotions, as She was also pressuring Me. Each of Us was pressuring the Other in the name of love, and in the name of protecting the children, but also, from fear of Ourselves and what might happen if We did express feelings We had judged against so heavily.

Most of the spirits in Pan were also doing the same thing, and, like Us, ignoring what was really happening there because they were emotionally ignoring what made them uncomfortable, not only in the beginning, but as time went on. The struggles for power were increasing in the duels of magic and form changes, the Mother was becoming more and more overwhelmed by the denials being made there, the Fire Dragons were infighting and raging more and more, and the Father of Manifestation was biding His time.

Feeling He was really the most powerful, but was not going to show His hand yet, the Father of Manifestation was losing power every moment He did not move His fear about whether His being

244

the most powerful was still true or not. He was not letting on, even to Himself, that He felt this way because His mind was dominating His analysis of the situation while His denied terror was consuming the Mother so much She could hardly even stay present by His side.

She did not know it was necessarily His terror though. She thought it was Her terror of the impending fate of Earth, and while She wanted to rage at the Father of Manifestation for appearing to be a "popcorn-eating" bystander who was avoiding the situation and, thereby, letting it happen, imprinting wasn't allowing Her to move in either direction here. Only grief moved in Her and a quaking that She felt was terror in Her grief. Meanwhile, denied rage was feeding the strength of the gap which was amplifying the terror it had vowed to hold down.

The night Lucifer chose to enter the Earth with his hordes, there was a huge party going on of the sort I have just described, which is very symbolic in ways you will learn to see as you move to understand this story more deeply, if you do not already see it, and the exact moment in which he chose to strike was also very synchronistic as magic is very synchronistic; even unloving magic.

The mother on Earth had abandoned her position in the skies that night and let another take her place so that she could preside over the party, the contests and the duels. Sensing trouble in the skies, however, she had excused herself from the party as the Faerie Queen, and was running between forms, trying to call to the supposed ally she had left in her place that night to let her rejoin him. He was even more treacherous than the faeries had been, however, and had business of his own with My light, or so he thought, and would not listen to her.

When I saw Lucifer about to enter Earth, I smacked at Him instantly. Lucifer grabbed My smack and used it to knock the Fire Dragons out of the sky, which he had planned on doing anyway since he had not intended to honor any deals he had made with them. Lucifer had no intention of actually giving anything more than an illusion of such power and had only made these deals so they would help him and and not cause him any problems.

He could do this, since My light was aiming for them also, having viewed them, and amongst them, particularly the mother on Earth, as having made the deal to let Lucifer onto the Earth.

This fireball rolled down onto the Earth, leaving the mother on Earth's nearly empty form of the Fire Dragon to fall to Earth like a discarded ragdoll in just the manner she had dished out to the

Father of Manifestation.

I had hit the form of the power of the kundalini return I hated the most, and yet, there had been no real fight there because the mother on Earth had already lost so much of her essence into fragmentation.

The mother on Earth had not regained her Fire Dragon form when the fireball hit. When she saw her Fire Dragon form falling from the skies, it was a major crisis for her. She flew through the night skies, transforming as she went into the form of a witch on a mission. When she found her Fire Dragon form dashed to the Earth, she wept bitter tears and raged at My light.

Apparently, this Fire Dragon liked to dish out what she could not take, which prompts Me to caution: Do not get in over your head; do not dish out what you cannot take. Do your homework at home as much as possible lest you find you did not know what you were entering, and if you thought you did, did not know all the rules you agreed to beforehand and that the rules had already set you up to lose.

The mother on Earth was furious that she had made a deal with "My Light" and that it hadn't turned out the way she had thought. She had been calling for her power to come back to her without knowing what she was really calling for. And so, I caution: Do not try to take power, and when you ask for power, you had better know what you are asking for. The safest course, therefore, is to let it happen naturally as an unfoldment of your own process.

She raged and raged that the deal she had made had not been honored and she raged and raged when she found out that she had lost her Fire Dragon form there and her ability to regain it. She raged at Me for a long time and blamed Me for this, which I did not think was fair or right of her since she had made the deal to let Lucifer onto Earth.

She could not move her emotions directly enough to feel more deeply than her rage and did not know how. She could not move her feelings to any place other than where they were trapped already unless the Mother was able to move Hers, and since My light would not allow the kundalini return to come back with Lucifer's presence in it, they had a major problem moving rage into healing, or anything else for that matter, since Lucifer controlled them more than they realized.

In other words, Lucifer hurled this Fire Dragon down from the sky, but I got blamed for it because I was the Parental cause of this without knowing it.

My light did this, nonetheless, even if only by a lack of My presence there by which to be able to know what I was doing. Presence is the magic ingredient which makes it all work, and without it, it all works anyway, but not the way you thought it would or necessarily wanted it to. If you can sleep on the throne and still have it all happen the way you want it to happen, then you are in balance when you sleep.

Still, she sought to use her magic to regain power, and in calling from the place of vengeful and revengeful rage that she felt there, she was calling for Lucifer much more than she knew, and with much more power than the Mother had left to hold him at bay. In calling Lucifer to Earth as she was doing, she was also empowering him against the Mother.

Her rage was unsuccessful in penetrating My light, however, because I did not feel I had any involvement. I hit her from the gap with My own Fire Dragon breath. Which causes Me to say that if you do not find your own involvement, you may think you cannot be penetrated, which may make it look like invulnerability is a form of power, but it will deprive you of power in the end, and then you will be penetrated heavily.

When I saw Lucifer knock the Fire Dragon out of the way, I thought she deserved it. I did not think My light would do such a thing as give Earth to Lucifer, but I had already done this without letting Myself realize it. As I have said, anything you find outside, whether or not you recognize it, was inside first. The more you do not want to see it there, the more likely it is that you placed it outside to begin with in Original Cause. Therefore, the last things you find inside in the process of unfoldment into your subconscious may be the first things you placed outside of yourself in Original Cause.

Knowing nothing of Lucifer's plan for Earth, of his impending approach, or of anything else going on around this problem, the spirits on Earth were not expecting such a thing, and in fact, were feeling more protected than ever. When the fireball hit Earth, it hit the spirits the way it had in original imprinting and damaged them accordingly, too.

Thus, I would say, feel more deeply than you have thought you had to or you may find out what you have not felt into deeply enough from the way in which your magic manifests.

You have all played a role in what is presently manifest and happening on Earth, but you think you have not because you have not felt it deeply enough to know how you have been a participant in this. Anything you say you are not a part of, you need to look at more closely and feel more deeply before moving outwardly, unless you just cannot understand it without more experience with it. That way, you are less likely to find yourself trapped into having to move outwardly or having outward events move you in ways you do not like.

When the fireball hit the Earth, it rolled past the party and into the woods, seeking the Mother who was blamed by the imprinting there.

When the Mother saw the light of it in the skies above Earth, She tried to run but had not gotten far before Her legs gave out and the weight of the lines pulled Her down. She had given up there into sobbing terror. It was too much for Her.

She was cowering and trying to hide with a few faeries gathered tightly around Her. When She realized the fireball was, indeed, headed for Her, She ordered the faeries to run, but She didn't have to. They were already running.

When the fireball hit, it knocked the Mother so far out of consciousness that She did not wake up for a long time, and there was nothing left of Her form to be found either, and in the swath it cut as it rolled across Pan, it damaged without noticing the Ronalokas who were the only ones not in major attendance at the party.

The monsters who had been climbing the lines toward the Mother were blown off of the lines when She was hit. Already in the magnetic energy field of Earth, they came raining down upon the Earth in the tail winds of the fireball.

When Lucifer's hordes reached Earth, they began to do all of the things people have described as what they like least about Earth by creeping into the forms of denied fragmentation where they were most accepted. The then increased lost Will presence was able to move what consciousness remained there out of the way in favor of the imprinting from which this lost Will was operating.

In other words, they entered the great subconscious, and activated it there to do the bidding of its imprints and not the bidding of My light. From there it began to pressure the people on Earth to revert to their imprinted responses, or instincts, as they have also been called, and from there, animal forms were not far away, because animals represented imprinting without human heads to have another consciousness or to be able to talk about, or share it with another, other than by group pictures without much

248

remaining ability to interpret them.

Giving form an opportunity to expand beyond the limits of this was not what Lucifer had in mind. He wanted everything to remain in the dark absence of My light's presence and not be able to learn anything more than what imprinting had already put in place there.

THE LAST DAYS OF PAN

Meanwhile, Lucifer was biding his time while the damaged spirits tried to recover, letting denial help him by trying to resume life as it had been in Pan as soon as possible.

As soon as he deemed it appropriate after his arrival on Earth, Lucifer appeared in the mother's court, which he had just given time to reconvene after the damage and shock waves that had moved through Pan. He made his appearance in a flurry of magic that materialized him there and said he had just arrived to help heal Earth. He announced himself as the greatest wizard of all and watched to see who flinched and who burned. He had duels of magic in mind already, but this was only play to him as a front for what he really had in mind for Earth.

He quickly decided those who flinched would be his first line of competitors, if he could get them to take up the challenge, and those who burned, his second. He cleverly worked the feelings being denied there, and could, because they were an open field to him from his viewpoint, and what a fertile field it was! He zeroed in on what was being denied like divining rods point to water under the Earth, and found the denials that were eager to get revenge.

Lucifer was a master of form change, and the mother on Earth did not quite recognize him, although something about him reminded her of what she had been communing with in the skies. She did not have the power to make him leave anyway and felt fear then, but pushed it aside in favor of the idea that if he was the greatest wizard of all, he might be her King. She decided to ascertain this by studying him, and by the way, without letting on, perhaps pick up a few tricks she did not already know that might help her regain her Fire Dragon form, and also, although she did not admit it, her lost power and magic on Earth. She made the same mistake the Father of Manifestation made in thinking that studying the situation could be sufficient to regain her lost power there without realizing that most of her power loss was in her denial of her fear of him.

Lucifer played with this fear denial the way slight of hand artists play with their audiences by confusing their attention away from what they are really doing. He quickly developed the dramatic flair of his presentation to develop such an interest in the appearance he was making of healing the Earth, while actually searching for the Mother, and in the duels of magic he proposed, while actually planning to trap everyone, that the entire remaining population of Pan wanted to come and see his display of power, or thought they did.

He gave out stories of his conquests and exploits in strange and foreign places other than Pan that made it seem like Pan's event was small compared to what he was used to in other places. He made it sound like there were other, bigger and better parties going on on other planets and that the inhabitants of Earth were just the leftovers, the dregs, to have fallen this far out into space.

The psychology worked, as it still does on those who are not sure enough of themselves to be able to love themselves as they are, and he delighted in watching how much effort they put into producing this magic duel of his in competition with the stories he told. In this way, it was turned into the grandest event ever seen on Earth, according to the perceptions of some.

My caution is: Pay more attention to detail than you think you have to, even if it just seems like nagging, little, nit-picking voices barely heard around the edges, because details manifest around the edges of things in ways that can ruin the effect of the entire thing since this is always the position undealt with lost Will has to take.

Eventually, on the appointed day, at the appointed hour, when he had drawn and sucked on every bit of energy he could in the process of preparation, the duel commenced. The form changes were awesome, the moves quick and the precision with which they were executed, harsh and slicing, as though Lucifer did everything with the cut of a knife and the bite of steel. His methods felt ruthless.

Lucifer was putting everything into place, outwardly and inwardly, and in just the places he wanted them. The mother on Earth was studying this most avidly, as were many of those around her, to see what could be learned there, and right in front of their very noses, Lucifer was putting together the same trick the mother on Earth had tried, and they did not recognize it because of the form change.

Lucifer challenged and ridiculed the ideas of others, and made fun of them in front of the court with the help of the satyrs, and the uproarious laughter of the others present there too, I would like to mention. He fed them bait and then pressured them not to respond emotionally, attacking them with his ridicule and heartlessness whenever they did. In other words, he played along the lines already established in court, but much more dramatically, intensely and ruthlessly, making it appear that all they had done before was child's play and saying as much to any who protested his methods.

Viciously and savagely is how I would say he played the court here, as if they were the deck of cards he was using in his sting operation. It felt like a gambling casino in which Russian roulette was being forced in as the game of choice, and all who declined to play were cast out as not brave enough to even be there. The participants, and also the audience, were being devoured by their fear denial. Lucifer was eating them alive, and they were not noticing it.

At the right psychological moment, he proposed a duel of magic on his terms, which were that the contestants no longer chose the forms they were going to take on. Instead, their opponents would choose them for them, and that to refuse a form meant default in the duel. This meant that no one chose Lucifer's forms, though, because he was master of all of them, and it did not matter what forms they chose. He did not stay in any one form for long anyhow as it did not matter to him what form he took on. With no Will to feel it, it did not matter to him how it felt to be inside the form either. He did not see why essence could not be rearranged indefinitely into whatever forms there were and sneered at other orientations.

"What difference would it make," he said, looking sinisterly around the court at the prominence of the mineral kingdom there in the form of the stone it had taken on, "if say, for example, I became a rock?"

Which he suddenly did. No one dared to move a muscle toward the fear they had felt on their night of horror. Then he knew he had them just as well as if he had been there that night to feel the presence of their fear and see what had taken place there.

No one was sure then that they wanted to take the trip, but no one backed out either. They all hoped for the best and prayed to My light a lot more than they had at any other time in Pan, while at the same time fearing, without letting themselves recognize this, that they might be messing with something they should not be messing with and that My light might smack them again for it.

The light wizard came forward then and declared himself a candidate for this duel. A number of others stepped forward then also, and amongst them was the Father of Manifestation. He was in his old wizard form, but underneath his long, flowing robes, He still had satyr legs. He could not even move out of this form anymore, but He had decided it didn't matter because He had figured that Lucifer was going to press downward toward the mineral kingdom with his form change demands, and He felt Himself to be already closer to that and better able to handle it than He perceived the others to be there.

The contestants tried to oppose Lucifer then, and the Father of Manifestation amongst them, without revealing His true identity. Lucifer knew it anyway and planned to trap Him especially horribly in stone, which did not come to pass as it turned out.

The last rule Lucifer put in place was that the form they took on had to disappear completely, indicating that they had come back out of it with all of themselves. No one spoke out against the rules, and so the duels of magic proceeded.

Lucifer tried all the contestants, and choosing the forms in which they had the most fear, trapped them all, one by one, including the Father of Manifestation, in forms they did not like, or parts of them, at least.

All of them moved past their fear into rage and were able to get themselves back out of the forms they had become trapped in to a certain extent, but none moved the terror they needed to move there to recover completely, and to greater and lesser degrees, all had to concede victory to Lucifer since all still had parts of themselves remaining in the forms he had chosen for them.

He had not given them stone as a form yet, though, letting them all worry about when he might spring this on them. He asked if any felt they were not ready to concede yet, and the light wizard, a very blue and white piece of Heart, stepped forward and declared that Lucifer's tactics were unfair.

"Oh, in what way?" Lucifer challenged him.

Lucifer appeared to listen, and when this piece of Blue's denied heart presented an argument about time being a factor in getting in and out of form changes, Lucifer acted like he was going to give the contestants another chance.

"All is not lost then if you can get back out of the form changes you are lost in as you move along in the duel," Lucifer said more as a querrie of the light wizard than as a statement of his own opinion.

"Yes," said the light wizard.

"Have at it," said Lucifer who then issued the stone challenge.

This piece of Heart took the challenge, feeling he knew better than everyone else, even than the Father of Manifestation, how Lucifer should be handled there. To his credit, he recognized "the greatest wizard of all," to be an enslaving power, as did some others by then, and saw himself as saving Earth, since, as he saw it, no one else could handle Lucifer, or dared to, including the Parents.

When everything was in place, Lucifer let the light wizard do the work of casting himself down into stone, but he helped by pressuring him to go faster than he could handle into greater density than he could handle, since speed of change was the issue he had raised with Lucifer concerning his judgments on the completion or noncompletion of form changes.

Suddenly, the light wizard was a piece of bluish-purple, amethyst-like rock sitting there in their midst with a frozen picture of a screaming face of terror looking motionless back at them from within it.

The light wizard went unconscious in the frozen moment of this terror, as though coming to meant feeling this frozen moment of terror forever, while his rage slipped out of the stone on the vibratory power it had left, which was not enough to be declared the winner there since there was still a sizable stone left in the midst of the court with its frozen face staring back at them as testimony that he was feeling something terrible trapped in there.

It was a moment in time he has never wanted to remember and not a moment I envy him having to recover from his lost Will, but if he will move the emotions he needs to move around his issues with parents and remember his own lesson on time, I will help him recover this lost Will a little at a time and he will succeed there.

Meanwhile, while the mother on Earth was busy judging Lucifer's magic to be less than her own, since this was such a little piece of stone compared to what she had done, most of the rest of the spirits of Pan were moved into their fear or their predatory hatred of fear, and there was a great stampede of animals again, this time defecating foul smelling, rapid fire pellets of fear onto the very snouts of the predators who were snarling, nipping and biting at their heels and throats and snapping at their tender undersides as they chased them down.

Even though this trick was, in many ways, a repeat of the mother on Earth's trick, this was a much more major fall, taken for the second time there in Pan, and one that has not been recovered from yet.

The Will Polarized became the animals there with stampeding fear pursued by the rage polarized, and the Spirit Polarized remained as people who tried once again to live in the last days of Pan as though nothing had happened to them that they couldn't move past, and that the lesson to be learned was that Will presence was not favored by My light. They had Lucifer for a master now, though, without apparently noticing the difference in quality of light, and moved past a lot of emotion there to have lives with him in Atlantis.

Lucifer was called the dark wizard by Me, but not because of his color. He was called the dark wizard by Me because he has been ruthlessly able to be the best at whatever he does because he has played so heartlessly. This I have never liked in anyone, but even less in Lucifer because he has overpowered so many, and taken them into darkness that is the darkness of loss of vibration and the darkness of lost happiness that steals the brightness from the face and the smile from the lips, the spring from the step and the joy of hopeful expectation of what tomorrow will bring, and has put in its place the dark and dismal world of imprinting, power struggle and the heartless bleakness that dreads and fears what tomorrow may bring if the night is even lived through to see what it is.

Loving magic is never ruthless and does not overpower others or push them out of the way to make a place for the self because the self has learned its own right place and doesn't need or want to take the place of another. Good magic must be done by the right person, at the right place and right time and in the right way.

If you move in your Will as much as possible first, and even longer and more than you think you have to, outward actions can become easy enough that it feels like things are moving into place magically. Even then, don't trust it at first. Look for flaws, tricks and traps and move pockets of overlooked emotion they will reflect. Gaining trust is a major part of magic, but not by overlooking the reasons you have distrust. Trust comes from knowing yourself well enough to know that you can trust your feelings and trust the balance point of love in your own heart to manifest the balance you need to live your life the way you want to.

If you feel deeply enough, love what you feel and move along with how you feel, magic happens and is not something forced, manipulated, stolen or otherwise turned to the unloving side of the art.

So please, move along now to the recovery of the lost power and magic which is your own and learn to know what that is by how it feels. If you are not being loving, you will know it by the reflection you get back, but don't be fooled by this either. Remember the twists of denial. Loving outwardly first is not the answer; loving inwardly first is.

My light has a lot to say and many pages have been omitted here that could have been included, but expression is not all there is to it. Feeling deeply enough is an important part of expression, and without that, you cannot learn what I have expressed anyway. By feeling it more, you could learn without My help, but My help has made it easier for you, and for that I would like to receive acknowledgment and gratitude. Find in yourself gratitude for the source from which it all comes; even the smallest source may turn out to be the greatest in some way. And along with that, feel deeply enough that you do not repeat old mistakes and do not fall for the same trick twice and find only bitterness and blame instead.

There's much that could and perhaps needs to be said about the last days of Pan, but all I can tell you now is that those who fled soon enough from the duel of the wizards, and reached the edge of the land, following the lead of the Father of Manifestation, were able to keep their forms more intact than the others and had His help to break off pieces of Pangea into islands for themselves where they were able to live, lost in the time of Pan for a long time, but I saw that they also felt the smack of My light and were reimprinted to believe that they had to offer sacrifices to My light to be able to do it, and even took up the practice of human sacrifice, believing they had to give their God the best, and in imitation of the way they had seen these stabbing thrusts of light seem to go after, and even take, certain people. I also saw them breaking apart, according to how they were polarized emotionally, and also by color, into races, tribes and nations. And the Father of Manifestation escaped with them into these secret realms where He lived rather happily with His rainbow faeries until, after a long time, the loss of the Parental part of the Mother began to weigh on Him, and even though His imprinting held Him back for a long time after He first thought of it, He began to look for Her again.

Lucifer succeeded in splitting Spirit and Will farther apart in Pan by getting emotionally based form change to deny its emotion, and by getting it into emotion it could not handle as a means of

255

trapping it in the forms resulting from this. Very heartless, indeed. The kind of heartlessness that caused My light to become so furious with him for what he had done, that I smacked at him again and knocked Earth off her axis. Again, Lucifer deflected My smack and used it to split the great continent of Pangea, which was already breaking apart in reflection of the split between Spirit and Will, sinking some places and leaving the rest to float and drift apart into what then became Lemuria and Atlantis.

There was a major loss of consciousness there, and the world of Pan moved down into a world of mostly imprinting. So many of the beings who were left alive there were trapped in animal forms that their lives on Earth, for all practical purposes, descended into animal life and did not surface again as human life for a long time; so long, in fact, that no one remembered being human before in the Heavens or any place else, except for the few who told Creation Myth stories. And myths were all they were seen to be by those who could not remember those other experiences for themselves, and yet these myths and stories have lived on because they have stirred something lost and deeply buried in the subconscious that does remember these things. In the same way, all Faerie Tales stem from Pan and the origins of Pan, and even though they have been thought to be just that, Faerie Tales, they also have lived on because they stir something deep and old, lost and ancient, hidden in the dark realms of the subconscious and surfacing in everyday life so vividly once you see it, yet so obscured by their lack of access to the conscious realms that people have been blind to the reality of their daily presence just as they were blinded by the original smack, and quite literally so.

If you gently hold or rub the belly of a small child who trusts you, and ask him or her when you feel an openness to do this, how he or she thinks it used to be, and how the child wishes it was on Earth, or wishes it would become, if they have My light in them, they will all tell you the same thing, which are stories of Pan and the Heavens before they came to Earth. Some have more detailed recall than others, but all have the same feelings of love for Faerie Tale reality and feelings of wistful nostalgia and heartache in their memories and recall of these times.

All you need to know, really, to recover your own lost subconscious and thus, also your own lost and forgotten personal Faerie Tale in which you actually lived and participated is that the darker and more violent, loveless and more treacherous the Faerie Tales are that you were told or are drawn to, the farther out in the woods you were located in Pan, and the more rage and terror need to move around every step the farther you went out there, until you find the grief-stricken heart of the little child who experienced these terrible things and can nurture it back into happiness again and can hold it protected in the balance you have to find now.

The Godhead of the mother on Earth was not the only place of treachery, power plays, plot thickenings or cauldron stirrings, or any of the rest of the stuff of which Faerie Tales are made.

And as for the Parental part of the Mother who has been speaking to you in most of this story: What was left of Her curled into the soft, furry ball of a monkey form that only wanted to find whatever inner comfort and warmth She could find for Herself by curling in on Herself there, and also to hide, since no one in the outer world really seemed to love Her or want Her to have the consciousness She was reaching for there.

She could not handle feeling or remembering anything more about Her pain or Her problems in trying to have consciousness, and for a long time, that's all She did; have monkey lives with the Ronalokas who shared Her fate. She was a Mother presence, sitting with sad, staring eyes, feeling alone, even there, and often being ostracized by Her own monkey group for reasons She did not understand. She did not reach for anything more until predators found Her and made life miserable for Her even there. Then She had to reach for Me when I came to give human form to many in the Will Polarity who needed help in this way.

And all of you who have followed the Mother have lives in animal forms that also need to be looked at now to be able to reclaim the essence that needs release from there. Not all form is what it seems. Not all animals are animals, and not all humans are humans, even yet. So, as you look at these forms, don't move to love them or hate them as they are now. Work instead on moving your own imprinting and see what happens then.

And that is all I can say for now except that the Mother needs to surface in all of you as the Mother presence in your own Wills, so that you can find balance in your Hearts, for without that, your power and magic has not been good, any more than Mine has been good because of a gap in place to reverse it all. Without Heart balance being found by feeling deeply enough to find and change imprinting, only repeats of original imprinting can take place trapped in the many form changes you have experienced since then.

Selah

LAND OF PAN
The Loss of Power and Magic on Earth

is the sixth in a series of books
channelled by Ceanne DeRohan

The other books are:

RIGHT USE OF WILL
Healing and Evolving the Emotional Body

ORIGINAL CAUSE 1
The Unseen Role of Denial

ORIGINAL CAUSE 2
The Reflection Lost Will Has to Give

EARTH SPELL
The Loss of Consciousness on Earth

HEART SONG
Vibrating Heartlessness to Let Heart in

These books need to be read in order. Getting ready for the sequels involves moving along with the material in *Right Use of Will* enough to know if this information is right for you.

These books let you know your *Original Cause* by helping you access belief systems lost in the subconscious long ago, yet influencing your life every day.

We appreciate it that you have bought this book. If you are interested in others and cannot get them through your local store, you may write us, Four Winds Publications, at the address in the front of the book for information on how to order. Please enclose a Self Addressed Stamped Envelope. Thank you.

$16.00   FOUR WINDS PUBLICATIONS